PRENTICE HALL

Pre-AP*
Resource Book

Marcia L. Wilbur

Janice Hendrie

Fran Pettigrew

*Advanced Placement, Advanced Placement Program, and AP are registered trademarks of The College Board, which was not involved in the production or, and does not endorse, this product.

PEARSON

Prentice
Hall

Boston, Massachusetts
Upper Saddle River, New Jersey

Pearson Prentice Hall™ is a trademark of Pearson Education, Inc.
Pearson® is a registered trademark of Pearson plc.
Prentice Hall® is a registered trademark of Pearson Education, Inc.

ISBN-13: 978-0-13-320205-2
ISBN-10: 0-13-320205-4

3 4 5 6 7 8 9 10   V001   16 15 14 13

Table of Contents

Preparing for the Advanced Placement* Spanish Language and Culture Exam with *REALIDADES*

The integration of language, communication, culture, and critical thinking throughout all levels of *REALIDADES* provides a strong foundation for building the skills needed for success on the Advanced Placement* Language Examination. Teachers will find a wide range of activities and strategies within the Student Editions, Teacher's Editions, and program ancillaries (print and technology) to support pre-AP* skills development.

The sequence of instruction within each thematic chapter in the Student Edition is specifically designed to build language skills and communicative proficiency. The first section, *Vocabulario en contexto* provides comprehensible input through listening and reading with language presented in a cultural context. The second section, *Gramática y vocabulario en uso*, gives students a wide range of activities that progress from concrete to transitional to open-ended. This careful progression of activities is key to developing AP* language proficiency while building vocabulary and grammar mastery. Many of the activities practice the integration of language skills that students will find on the AP* Examination. In addition, many integrate culture through the use of articles, surveys, advertisements, art, photographs, and *realia*. The third section, *¡Adelante!* applies the different language skills and expands cultural understanding. The last section, *Repaso del capítulo* summarizes what students have learned in the chapter (vocabulary and grammar) and prepares students for the proficiency tasks found on the chapter test.

The Teacher's Edition provides extensive support and strategies that focus on building pre-AP* skills. The teaching support for each activity is conveniently contained within a "tab" in the side-margin wrap. The "Extension" ideas within this tab will be useful for teachers looking to expand and integrate more skills after completion of the initial activity. Across the bottom of the page, the section labeled "Differentiated Instruction" has teaching suggestions for diverse learners and the teacher looking for pre-AP* activities will want to focus on the ideas for Multiple Intelligences, Advanced Learners, and Heritage Language Learners. In addition, the different print and technology components found in the program are referenced at point-of-use and many support building AP* skills.

Using *REALIDADES* to Prepare for Cultural Understanding and Comparisons

An inherent expectation of the AP* Spanish Language and Culture Examination is an understanding of cultural products, perspectives and practices. *REALIDADES* offers multiple opportunities throughout the chapter for students to consider cultural aspects of the Hispanic world that will prepare them to understand linguistic inferences and a wide variety of cultural viewpoints. For each theme in *REALIDADES* A,B, 1 and 2 the *Videocultura* offers insight into an aspect of culture related to the theme. Each chapter has a cultural backdrop that holds the chapter together, seen first in the opening pages of the chapter where a work of fine art introduces the theme in a section called *Arte y cultura*. The Fine Art Transparencies with activities for students at the novice, intermediate, and advanced levels that accompany *REALIDADES* provide teachers a way to make this culture come alive to students while integrating ways for students to practice with and produce Spanish. Throughout each chapter you will find, and be able to use daily, appropriate cultural notes with standards-based questions (*Fondo cultural*) and activities that integrate culture into language practice. In addition, each chapter includes cultural projects and readings that help students understand the products, practices, and perspectives of the cultures of the Spanish-speaking

*Advanced Placement, Advanced Placement Program, and AP are registered trademarks of The College Board, which was not involved in the production or, and does not endorse, this product.

world (*Perspectivas del mundo hispano* and *La cultura en vivo*). On the chapter test, students are asked a specific question that focuses on a cultural comparison developed in the chapter.

Preparing for the Themes and Recommended Contexts

REALIDADES 1-4 builds the foundation for success on the AP* Spanish Language and Culture Examination by introducing students to the Themes and Recommended Contexts in the Curriculum Framework for the exam. The following charts shows how students begin to work with the Themes and Recommended Contexts through the different levels of *REALIDADES*.

Contextos	REALIDADES A/B/1 Chapter	REALIDADES 2 Chapter	REALIDADES 3 Chapter	REALIDADES 4 Chapter
Tema: Los desafíos mundiales				
Los temas económicos	7A, 7B	2B	10	7, 10
Los temas del medio ambiente	8A	9B	9	2
El pensamiento filosófico y la religión		5A	10	3, 7
La población y la demografía	6B, 8A	5A	9	2, 7
El bienestar social	8B	5B	5	2, 7
La conciencia social	8B	9B	5	2, 7
Tema: La ciencia y la tecnología				
El acceso a la tecnología	9B	—	6	2, 5, 12
Los efectos de la tecnología en el individuo y en la sociedad	9B	—	6	2, 5, 12
El cuidado de la salud y la medicina	3B	5B	3	2, 4, 8, 9
Las innovaciones tecnológicas	9B		6	2, 5, 7,12
Los fenómenos naturales	—	5A	7	12
La ciencia y la ética	—	—	6	2, 7, 12
Tema: La vida contemporánea				
La educación y las carreras profesionales	2A, 2B	9A	5, 6	10
El entretenimiento y la diversión	9A	6A, 6B	2	6
Los viajes y el ocio	1A, 4A, 8A	1B, 7B, 8A, 8B	1,8,7	6, 11
Los estilos de vida	5B, 6B, 7B	2A, 4A	9	1, 4, 9, 10
Las relaciones personales	1A, 1B, 4B	4A, 4B	4	3, 5
Las tradiciones y los valores sociales	5A	4B	4	3, 5
El trabajo voluntario	8B	9B	5	3

*Advanced Placement, Advanced Placement Program, and AP are registered trademarks of The College Board, which was not involved in the production or, and does not endorse, this product.

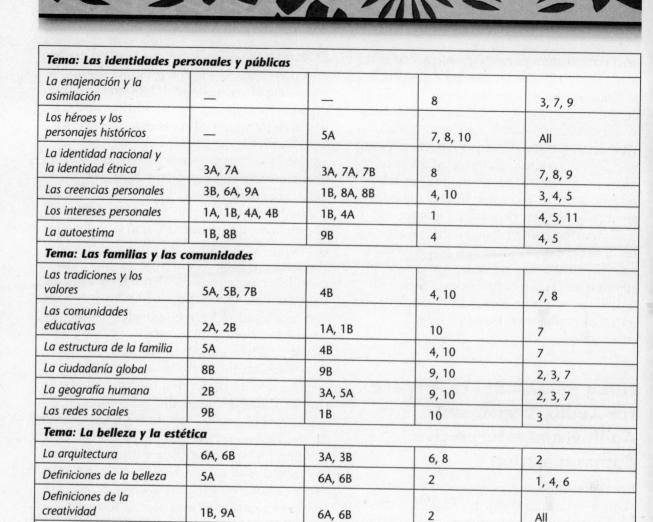

Tema: Las identidades personales y públicas				
La enajenación y la asimilación	—	—	8	3, 7, 9
Los héroes y los personajes históricos	—	5A	7, 8, 10	All
La identidad nacional y la identidad étnica	3A, 7A	3A, 7A, 7B	8	7, 8, 9
Las creencias personales	3B, 6A, 9A	1B, 8A, 8B	4, 10	3, 4, 5
Los intereses personales	1A, 1B, 4A, 4B	1B, 4A	1	4, 5, 11
La autoestima	1B, 8B	9B	4	4, 5
Tema: Las familias y las comunidades				
Las tradiciones y los valores	5A, 5B, 7B	4B	4, 10	7, 8
Las comunidades educativas	2A, 2B	1A, 1B	10	7
La estructura de la familia	5A	4B	4, 10	7
La ciudadanía global	8B	9B	9, 10	2, 3, 7
La geografía humana	2B	3A, 5A	9, 10	2, 3, 7
Las redes sociales	9B	1B	10	3
Tema: La belleza y la estética				
La arquitectura	6A, 6B	3A, 3B	6, 8	2
Definiciones de la belleza	5A	6A, 6B	2	1, 4, 6
Definiciones de la creatividad	1B, 9A	6A, 6B	2	All
La moda y el diseño	7A	2B	—	1
El lenguaje y la literatura	—	—	4, 6, 7	All
Las artes visuales y escénicas	All	All	All	All

Using *REALIDADES* to Prepare for Spoken Interpersonal Communication

Verbal interaction is the key to success in this interpersonal arena. Students need both the ability to speak and to understand what is said to them so that an appropriate response can be formulated. Activities in *REALIDADES* always progress from a mechanical level, in which students produce a word or phrase, to paired activities to open-ended language. *REALIDADES* gives students many opportunities to communicate, and partner or paired work is the easiest way to achieve this sort of practice. Interpersonal speaking tasks are labeled *Hablar* and contain a two-person or group icon. In addition to the text activities, additional Communicative Activities and Situation Cards are found in the Teacher's Resource Book.

Using *REALIDADES* to Prepare for Written Interpersonal Communication

Throughout *Gramática y vocabulario en uso*, a plethora of opportunities exist for students to write individual words and phrases, sentences,

*Advanced Placement, Advanced Placement Program, and AP are registered trademarks of The College Board, which was not involved in the production or, and does not endorse, this product.

brief notes, letters, personal opinions, and reactions. These activities are labeled as *Escribir*. In addition, components of the *REALIDADES* program—the Leveled Vocabulary and Grammar Workbook: Core Practice; the Communication Workbook, *REALIDADES para hispanohablantes*, the eText, the realidades.com activities, and many more—offer students writing practice outside the text. The *Escribir* sections of the assessment program provide excellent examples of opportunities to write in an informal way. Encourage students to provide rich responses, going beyond a standard, bare-bones vocabulary, and expanding on their basic ideas. The tone of these writing pieces can be personal and interactive rather than based on formal conventions.

Using *REALIDADES* to Prepare for Audio, Visual, and Audiovisual Interpretive Communication

Interpersonal and Presentational speaking skills are developed through-out each chapter. Each chapter has multiple activities that provide listening practice. These activities can be found in the Student Edition and the Communication Workbook. Students can access audio files and listening activities through realidades.com and through the eText. The *Videohistoria* (found in *REALIDADES* A, B, 1 & 2) and the *Videomisterio* (found in *REALIDADES* B, 1 & 2) give extended contextualized listening opportunities with comprehension checks.

Using *REALIDADES* to Prepare for Written and Print Interpretive Communication

Read, read, read. Then read more. With the traditionally valued emphasis on interpersonal speaking skills, teachers often forget that printed texts provide rich sources of comprehensible input that can lead to acquisition.

REALIDADES offers level-appropriate reading selections throughout the program. From the beginning of each chapter through the practice activities, the *¡Adelante!* section, and the test preparation, reading is emphasized. In the *Vocabulario en contexto* section, students are led to understand new words and phrases in context in paragraphs and dialogues. In many *Gramática y vocabulario en uso* activities, students are called upon to not only practice vocabulary and grammar but also to read for meaning. For instance, activities that require students to choose words from a word bank to complete a paragraph or that have them pick between two verbs before completing the correct grammatical form emphasize reading comprehension. Many *Gramática y vocabulario en uso* activities are based on *realia* that not only bring culture into the activities but also require reading. Extended readings throughout *REALIDADES*, like the *Videohistoria* text pages and *¡Adelante! Lectura* readings, provide strategy boxes on the student page. The teacher's wrap-around notes on these pages combined with the strategies presented in the Student Edition, when used consistently, equip students with a variety of tools for decoding texts. Pre-AP* teachers should consider lesson planning that allows for ample time to engage in the pre-reading activities that *REALIDADES* suggests, to complete the reading process, and to do the comprehension activities that cause students to engage in higher-order thinking like inference and interpretation. For heritage speakers of Spanish, who often need to be challenged to improve their reading skills, additional reading materials are provided in the *REALIDADES para hispanohablantes* Workbooks.

Using *REALIDADES* to Prepare for Spoken Presentational Communication

Interpersonal speaking is developed throughout each chapter. These frequent opportunities enable students to perform successfully on the formal speaking tasks that are found at

*Advanced Placement, Advanced Placement Program, and AP are registered trademarks of The College Board, which was not involved in the production or, and does not endorse, this product.

the end of the chapter in *¡Adelante!* section. The *Presentación oral* provides students a step-by-step performance-based task. Students are given strategies for planning and preparing their ideas and then are expected to perform a formal speaking task without the help of notes or a script. In addition, any activity in *REALIDADES* designed to be a formal writing exercise, poster presentation, and other such activities can serve as the basis for making formal speaking presentations. Students should have multiple opportunities to make formal speaking presentations on topics that focus on comparing cultural features of their community to those of a community in the Spanish-speaking world. Whenever possible, it is important to move students from a heavy reliance on written notes with lengthy preparation time to allowing just enough preparation time to outline the main and supporting ideas followed by an opportunity for spontaneous speech.

Using *REALIDADES* for Written Presentational Communication

Across the levels of *REALIDADES*, there are multiple opportunities for writing formal compositions. Each *Presentación escrita* and *Taller* task offers a process for planning, preparing for, executing, and evaluating the writing task. In order to provide thorough AP* preparation, students should be encouraged to engage in these formal writing situations as developed in *REALIDADES* A, B, 1, 2, 3 and 4. Across the lessons, there are many strategies given for pre-writing exercises as well as ideas for making revisions. Pay attention to these and again, remind students to use the suggested tools to improve writing. The writing process is evident in all of the formal writing tasks set forth in *REALIDADES* and culminates in the writing experiences in *REALIDADES* 4. A key element in that process is the revision phase—creating opportunities for students to improve upon their work both by expanding on ideas and correcting potential errors.

Using Rubrics and Scoring Guidelines with *REALIDADES*

Because nearly 50% of the AP* Spanish Language and Culture Exam is scored with scoring guidelines or rubrics, teachers should take advantage of the many sets of rubrics designed to evaluate specific writing and speaking activities found in the textbook. Each Theme Project (found in the Teacher's Edition interleaf pages), *Presentación oral*, and *Presentación escrita* has an accompanying rubric. Speaking and writing tasks in the assessment program also have accompanying rubrics. It is always important to provide students with these rubrics as they prepare for the performance-based tasks so that they know what is expected of them from the beginning. Time used in class to allow students to critique each others' work in groups using scoring guidelines is time well spent. Once students are familiar with this sort of evaluation, the teacher can assign and collect a task for formal grading, using the same types of scoring guidelines. For level 3 and 4 students, teachers might consider using the scoring guidelines used for the various sections of the Free Response section of the AP* Spanish Language and Culture Exam found at apcentral.collegeboard.com/spanlang. Familiarizing students with AP*-level expectations in levels 3 and 4 serves to build the rigor necessary for success on the AP* Exam.

Using *REALIDADES* to Develop Vocabulary

For students to be successful on the AP* Spanish Language and Culture Examination, they need a rich and varied vocabulary. *REALIDADES* does an excellent job developing vocabulary through its thematic, contextualized, and visualized approach to vocabulary in the *Vocabulario en contexto* section. Comprehensible input is used to present vocabulary which is reinforced with visuals, reading, hands-on activities with clip art and gestures, TPR Storytelling, and video. The vocabulary presented in each chapter is tightly connected

*Advanced Placement, Advanced Placement Program, and AP are registered trademarks of The College Board, which was not involved in the production or, and does not endorse, this product.

to the theme and presented in manageable amounts. The presentation is followed by the systematic build-up of mechanical to paired to open-ended activities using new and recycled vocabulary. Students are given a number of practice opportunities to learn and retain vocabulary in the Leveled Vocabulary and Grammar Workbook: Core Practice and Guided Practice, realidades.com activities, and the electronic flash cards in the eText.

REALIDADES has included a section called *Exploración del lenguaje* and *Ampliación del lenguaje*. The section exposes students to language patterns like cognates, prefixes, root words, suffixes, and word families. Students learn the connections between English and Spanish as well as Latin, Greek, and Arabic. In *REALIDADES* 4 a section called ¡Cuidado! focuses on vocabulary that is frequently used incorrectly. *REALIDADES* uniquely gives students the tools to learn about language, to make informed guesses about words, and ultimately, to empower students with strategies when they encounter unknown words on the AP* Language and Culture Examination or other standardized tests.

Using *REALIDADES* to Develop Grammatical Accuracy

Throughout the speaking and writing sections of the AP* Spanish Language and Culture Exam, a strong command of grammar is essential, in addition to the message conveyed. While the focus of the classroom activities in *REALIDADES* is on communication, helping students use language in syntactically appropriate ways can make communication clearer. In *REALIDADES*, students are provided grammatical input models in *Vocabulario en contexto*. This input is followed by clear explanations in *Gramática y vocabulario en uso*. Since most students are not motivated by grammar study, each grammar point of *REALIDADES* A, B, 1 and 2 has an

AP* Spanish Language and Culture Exam Format

Section I: Multiple Choice Approx. 95 minutes				
	Item Type	Number of Questions	Percent of Final Score	Time
Part A	Interpretive Communication: Print Texts	30 questions	50%	Approx. 40 minutes
Part B	Interpretive Communication: Print and Audio Texts (combined)	35 questions		Approx. 55 minutes
	Interpretive Communication: Audio Texts			
Section II: Free Response Approx. 85 minutes				
	Item Type	Number of Prompts	Percent of Final Score	Time
	Interpersonal Writing: E-mail reply	1 prompt	50%	15 minutes
	Presentational Writing: Persuasive Essay	1 prompt		Approx. 55 minutes
	Interpersonal Speaking: Conversation	5 prompts		20 seconds for each response
	Presentational Speaking: Cultural Comparison	1 prompt		2 minutes to respond

*Advanced Placement, Advanced Placement Program, and AP are registered trademarks of The College Board, which was not involved in the production or, and does not endorse, this product.

accompanying engaging *GramActiva* video segment available for classroom use and in the eText. As mentioned earlier, the sequence of activities in *REALIDADES* always leads students to move from mechanical grammar activities to paired and open-ended activities in which students create language, applying accurate grammatical concepts. Grammar Study Guides help students to "see" the entire Spanish grammar system come together. Correct structural usages can be practiced and built by drawing students' attention to the practice activities in the Student Edition and eText. Activities outside the text in the Leveled Vocabulary and Grammar Workbook: Core Practice and Guided Practice, and *REALIDADES para hispanohablantes* workbook plus the realidades.com activities give students additional grammatical practice. *REALIDADES* 1–4 gives students many opportunities to use grammar as a tool for authentic and meaningful communication, thereby helping them develop increasing accuracy with grammar.

The AP[*] Spanish Language and Culture Exam is designed to measure students' proficiency in the Interpersonal, Interpretive, and Presentational modes of communication, as defined in the *Standards for Foreign Language Learning in the 21st Century*. Students are expected to communicate orally and in writing in informal situations, to acquire information from written and spoken sources, to use the acquired information in a persuasive essay, and to make an oral presentation on a cultural topic that integrates cultural comparisons.

An Introduction to Pre-AP[*] Strategies for Spanish

The College Board's Equity and Access Statement[1] seeks to make Advanced Placement[*] programs available to students everywhere. A goal of the Statement is for the enrollment in any given school's AP[*] program to reflect the demographics of the entire school population. This is best achieved in a Spanish AP[*] program by targeting two critical objectives. First, the district's Spanish program must be aligned between levels to include integrated AP[*] skill building over the duration of the program. Second, teachers should identify a broad range of potential AP[*] students early in their academic careers and provide them with opportunities to enhance their proficiency.

The preparation for the AP[*] program ought to begin as soon as students embark upon the first level of formal language study, which can be as early as the middle school. Often, the designated AP[*] Spanish teacher is the only person in the department who is familiar with the rigorous demands of the AP[*] Exam. Other teachers, especially those who teach the very beginning levels of Spanish, may not realize the important role that they play in the process. For this reason, we have developed the *REALIDADES* Pre-AP[*] Resource Book with all secondary Spanish teachers in mind. Furthermore, since the AP[*] Spanish Language and Culture Exam is a measure of students' overall proficiency, strategies that are used to prepare students for the exam are also helpful in building proficiency at all levels.

In my experience, teachers and students are often intimidated by the concept of Advanced Placement[*]. Some assume that the challenge will be too difficult for even the most dedicated or gifted students. In order to dispel the notion that the exam is too difficult, the Pre-AP[*] program focuses on strategies that will not only help students prepare for the exam, but that will also help them build proficiency at every level.

As a Pre-AP[*] strategies program evolves from beginning levels on up, teachers will enjoy a sharing of ideas and reflective practice as part of a greater AP[*] teaching community. Students will benefit from their teachers' combined efforts to collaborate and establish effective strategies that are reinforced at each level. Because the AP[*] Spanish Language and Culture Exam is proficiency-based, adopting the Pre-AP[*] preparation

[1] http://apcentral.collegeboard.com/article/ 0,3045,150-157-0-2200,00.html

*Advanced Placement, Advanced Placement Program, and AP are registered trademarks of The College Board, which was not involved in the production or, and does not endorse, this product.

continuum is appropriate in any Spanish program where proficiency is the goal.

Pre-AP* is not intended to be a separate course for gifted students only. Instead, the Pre-AP* concept is intended to represent instructional strategies designed to help all students achieve success. As you use the *REALIDADES* series, you will see how it aims for overall proficiency, and how it is an ideal resource for teachers who want to build their students' skills while keeping AP* goals in mind. The *REALIDADES* Pre-AP* Resource Book aims to:

• acquaint all levels of teachers with the sorts of tasks required on the AP* Spanish Language and Culture Examination.

• demonstrate very simple and direct ways that teachers can incorporate strategies and activities from all four levels of the *REALIDADES* series into their instruction, in order to prepare students for the AP* Spanish Language and Culture Exam.

Based on college comparability studies, the AP* Spanish Language Course and Exam are equivalent to a fifth- or sixth-semester college Spanish course. As of May 2014, the AP* Spanish Language and Culture Exam aligns itself more closely with 21st century instruction and assessment practices and with the *Standards for Foreign Language Learning in the 21st Century*[2]. As a departure from its long-term format of testing the four skills in isolation (listening, reading, writing, speaking), the 2014 revisions to the exam format reflect an integration of skills that is more reflective of real-life language use. The exam prompts are from authentic sources (radio broadcasts and interviews, magazine and newspaper articles, etc.). In 2014 and beyond, students are expected to:

• Answer multiple-choice questions in Spanish related to authentic reading selections. The questions are often of a higher-order thinking skills type, requiring inference,

interpretation, and synthesis. The questions reach beyond mere factual recall of the passage.

• Answer multiple-choice questions in Spanish based on an auditory selection and a reading selection from authentic sources.

• Answer multiple-choice questions in Spanish based on auditory selections from authentic sources. The selections may include news broadcasts, interviews, advertisements, conversations, podcasts, announcements and presentations.

• Engage in interpersonal writing by responding to an e-mail message.

• Write a formal essay based on a given topic statement. Students must read passages and listen to an audio prompt, which present different viewpoints on the topic. Then they are required to synthesize the information from the sources, present their own viewpoint, defend it thoroughly and cite all 3 sources in their essay.

• Engage in interpersonal speaking by participating in a simulated conversation. Students' answers are recorded on an audiotape or CD.

• Prepare and deliver a formal, two-minute presentation on a topic that includes a cultural comparison. Students' answers are recorded.

The AP* Spanish Language and Culture Exam format is intended to serve as an instrument for measuring the extent to which students are capable of communicating accurately and fluently in the interpersonal, interpretive, and presentational modes; understanding and being understood by a variety of speakers and in different settings; and acquiring information from authentic sources, remaining aware of cultural perspectives.

What students need to know and be able to do for the AP* Spanish Language and Culture Exam goes well beyond mere language acquisition. Teachers will want to provide language-use opportunities in Spanish that require their students to engage in higher-order thinking skills, reaching to the upper levels of

[2] American Council on the Teaching of Foreign Languages. (1999). *Standards for foreign language learning in the 21st century.* Lawrence, KS: Allen Press, Inc.

*Advanced Placement, Advanced Placement Program, and AP are registered trademarks of The College Board, which was not involved in the production or, and does not endorse, this product.

Bloom's Taxonomy. Not only must students have the ability to comprehend the information presented to them in Spanish, but they also need the ability to synthesize and analyze what they have learned. The tasks on the AP[*] Spanish Language and Culture Exam are designed to reflect those higher levels of capability.

By examining the skills needed to successfully complete the AP[*] Exam, departments can use backwards planning to determine how much time is required to prepare students to be ready for the challenge. Many schools offer the AP[*] Spanish Language and Culture Exam as the fifth year of the program. Others are able to accomplish this in the fourth year. Since each school is unique, teachers and administrators must determine the amount of time that they have to prepare students. Regardless of the skills that are designated as goals for a particular level of Spanish, it remains essential that teachers ensure that the students have an in-depth understanding of the concepts covered. Developing students' long-term retention of materials is key. It can be frustrating for both you and your students when a concept was covered in a previous level, but was never quite learned. Thus, the manner in which the material is taught is just as important as the amount of material covered. If the right strategies are taught, the students will grasp and retain key information with ease. By making sure that students are equipped from the beginning with strong learning skills, you can help them maximize their learning and ensure their proficiency.

Though proficiency is the primary goal of the *REALIDADES* program, written and spoken accuracy is also important to a student who is learning Spanish. However, the direct instruction of grammar often fuels methodological debates. While it should not become the focal point or the goal of instruction, brief explanations can speed acquisition and lead to more accurate usage.[3] Since syntactic control is a key component of the AP[*] Spanish scoring guidelines, providing students with concise grammatical patterns and formulas can serve as valuable tools.[4] As you help students achieve greater accuracy, however, it is essential that you keep in mind that the first objective of instruction should be communication.

Students must be aware of the expectations that you have of them. They should also understand what is expected of them on the AP[*] exam. An excellent way to clarify expectations is to review scoring guidelines from previous exams with students. For your convenience, the *REALIDADES* Pre-AP[*] Resource Book includes a variety of suggested rubrics that have been simplified, yet remain similar to the rubrics that students will encounter on the AP[*] Exam. Review these rubrics with students and make sure that they understand what is expected of them. Ask them to identify their strengths and weaknesses on the rubrics, and help them focus on improvement. By acquainting students with the "rules of the game" early on, you can help your students to be winners.

Pre-AP[*] Strategies for Spanish is about building students' proficiency by providing them with the tools to comprehend and produce the target language. When students have effective strategies and clear expectations, they can all be successful. When students achieve success, they gain confidence and further motivation. Your instruction and the resources available in the *REALIDADES* series can combine to achieve student success on the AP[*] exam and help your students become confident and proficient Spanish speakers outside of the classroom.

MARCIA WILBUR

[3] Ellis, R. (1997). *Second Language Acquisition.* Oxford: Oxford University Press.

[4] Bransford, J. D., Brown, A. L., Cocking, R. R., & Educational Resources Information Center (U.S.). (1999). *How People Learn: Brain, Mind, Experience and School.* Washington, D.C.: National Academy Press.

*Advanced Placement, Advanced Placement Program, and AP are registered trademarks of The College Board, which was not involved in the production or, and does not endorse, this product.

Interpretive: Listening

On the AP* Exam, students listen to a variety of authentic audio selections, which may include interviews, podcasts, public service announcements, and brief presentations. Some audio selections may be accompanied by a reading selection. The selections are followed by multiple-choice questions. Students can skim the questions and answers before hearing the selection. In order to prepare students at the Pre-AP* level for listening success, you must prepare them to be skillful listeners. Teaching strategies such as sound-symbol recognition and listening for the gist of a passage or a dialogue at the earlier levels will provide a strong foundation for overall comprehension. As students become more skilled, encourage them to listen for details and extract meaning from longer passages. Listening strategies such as these will prepare your students to be strong AP* students.

Preparing Students for Listening to Interpersonal Audio Selections

Teaching Tips

Make the input comprehensible

Use as much Spanish as possible in the classroom at the earliest levels. It is important that the level of language used be salient to the learner. Non-comprehensible input does not have positive effects on students' listening abilities. You can make the language more meaningful by simplifying it as appropriate for the level of study. Gestures, pictures, and props also help to convey meaning. Students have access to comprehensible input in the *Vocabulario en vontexto* section of each chapter. The *Escuchar* activities found on the second page of each *Vocabulario en uso* section can help you to assess students' comprehension of the new language. You also will find many useful suggestions on how to deliver language effectively by using the input scripts in the *Teacher's Resource Book*. In addition, the vocabulary and

grammar transparencies and clip art in the *Teacher's Resource Book* can be used as resources around which you can design supplemental listening activities. *TPR Stories* also provides suggestions for delivering language input that students can comprehend.

Recycle Listening Activities

It is important that students do not shut down when given a listening task. You may want to "recycle" listening activities from year to year. Occasionally allow students who are using *REALIDADES* 3 to listen to activities from *REALIDADES* 1 and 2 that talk about the same topics as your current chapter. You may want to do these reviews as a quick warm-up activity at the beginning of class. Students will gain more confidence listening when they have the opportunity to succeed.

Try to simulate the exam activities when possible

It is important that students be familiar with the exam format as well as with the content. Multiple-choice questions are commonly found throughout the AP* Exam. Use activities from *REALIDADES* such as the questions in the *¿Eres tú, María? Video Workbook* or in the Communication Workbook to help students practice answering multiple-choice questions. You can supplement activities found in *REALIDADES* textbooks and workbooks with quick comprehension checks that are in a multiple-choice format. Develop two or three questions to put on an overhead projector and have students copy the answers in their notebooks. Review the answers and have students describe their strategies for getting certain answers. Help students to use the process of elimination and educated guessing when doing such activities. You may want to simply give some multiple-choice questions in order to further the listening activity.

Sample Activities

Dialogue input from classmates

Encourage active listening to dialogues. Dialogues presented to the class are an integral part of early levels of language learning. While one pair or group of students is in front of the class presenting their dialogue, have all other

students write a question that they could pose to the speakers when they finish. Then choose volunteers to ask their questions. This activity holds the audience accountable for listening participation and also allows for continued communication after the dialogue is complete.

True / False comprehension

Ask students to write true / false sentences about the content of a dialogue presented. Then, have volunteers read their true / false sentences to the class, who will respond accordingly.

Listening and Speaking

Have pairs of students record their own dialogues about a topic in your current *REALIDADES* chapter. (See the section on Speaking, p. 44 for suggestions on how to record.) Then, ask those students to listen to their dialogues again and create 5 multiple-choice questions to accompany what they say. Collect tapes and dialogues, and redistribute them to other pairs. Have each pair of students listen to the dialogues and answer the questions.

Graphic organizers

Using the example below, have students prepare a T-chart on a blank piece of paper. Have the whole class decide on the most important topics that students should be listening for in a given dialogue, and ask them to list those topics in the first column. Then, have students take notes on what each group is saying about each topic in the appropriate spot in the second column. You might want to ask students to extend their charts if more than one pair of students is presenting a dialogue.

Temas importantes	Lo que dicen_____ *(nombres de los participantes)*

Identify the situation

On index cards (so they can be reused) or on slips of paper, write a description in Spanish of a situation that is appropriate to the chapter topic. Make as many cards as necessary so that there can be one situation for each pair of students in the class. The *REALIDADES* Situation Cards, as well as other speaking prompts in the series, are good sources for ideas. Have each pair of students randomly draw one scenario from the cards. Allow the pairs enough time to prepare a dialogue appropriate to their situation. Provide a handout or prepare an overhead that lists a one-line description of each situation on the cards. Have students present the dialogues to the class without explaining the situation beforehand. As the students listen to each dialogue, have them correctly match the situation on the sheet with the dialogue they hear.

Sample Activity

Sample situations: *REALIDADES* 2–Capítulo 3B
1. Explícale a un nuevo estudiante cómo llegar a tu casa desde la escuela.
2. Visitas una ciudad que no conoces. Pregúntale a un(a) policía dónde estás y cómo llegar a la casa de tu tía que vive en la Calle del Cristo. (See Activity 10.)
3. Estás en el coche con un(a) amigo(a) nervioso(a) quien acaba de recibir su permiso de manejar. Ayúdale con las señales de tráfico mientras te lleva a casa después de la escuela.
4. Estás manejando el coche con tu papá. Pregúntale si puedes manejar al centro comercial y explícale por qué.
5. Eres un(a) estudiante que está aprendiendo a manejar. Estás poniendo nervioso(a) a tu instructor(a) porque estás mirando a la gente y no estás mirando la calle.

6. Explícale a tu papá o mamá por qué saliste mal en tu examen de manejar.

Teléfono

This activity can be done at all levels. Write sentences that are appropriate to the current unit of study on slips of paper. Divide the class into teams of four or five. Each team sits in a row, facing away from the board, one behind the next. Distribute the same sentence to the last person in each row. On cue, the person farthest from the board turns to face the board and speaks the sentence to the person seated directly in front of him or her. That person says the sentence to the next person in the row, etc. The person seated closest to the board must correctly write the sentence on the board in the space assigned to that team. (Students should be encouraged to whisper so as not to help the other teams.) The person who started the *teléfono* is responsible for noticing any errors in the sentence written on the board and must pass the necessary corrections up the telephone wire! The first team to correctly write the sentence on the board scores a point. After each sentence, have students rotate and give the new person a different sentence. The team with the most points after five rounds wins the game.

Teaching Tips

Point out the importance of listening to (not just viewing) videos

Encourage active listening when using videos. Videos are important for communicating cultural values and developing listening skills. Normally, students tend to focus on the visual, not the auditory, aspect of a video. To emphasize the importance of listening, bring in a video (ideally one that students have not seen yet) in which two people are simply seated at a table, having a conversation. Play the segment with the sound down. Ask students what the scene is about. After students have tried to guess, play the video again, pointing out the value of understanding what is seen *and* heard.

Maintain variety when using videos

Showing video segments in class is an excellent way to supplement your lesson and to build listening skills. However, a video may do more harm than good, depending on its length. It's important to remember that a student's attention span is generally about half as long as his/her age. In other words, a fourteen year old has an attention span of about seven minutes. In order for instruction to be effective, you must remember to change what the student *does* every seven to ten minutes. The change should be more significant than merely changing from activity 4 to activity 5 in the textbook. It is best to change the sensory modality that the student is using. For this reason, care should be taken when considering the use of a lengthier video. Students are not likely to be actively engaged in the viewing (or listening) for a long period of time. Show video clips and follow them up with short discussions or quick written comprehension checks. Longer videos might be more effectively implemented if spread out over several days.

Pre-listening suggestions

When using videos from the *REALIDADES* series, be sure to review ideas, listening strategies, and photos that accompany the *Videohistorias, Videomisterios,* or *VideoRed* in the student texts. As students review the information, encourage them to talk about things that they might be listening for as they watch the video. Refer also to the notes in the Teacher's Edition that can help you maximize students' comprehension of the video. The comprehension activities in the student text and the Communication Workbook provide you with ways to check what students understand.

Sample Activities

Pre-listening predictions

Show the video the first time with the sound off. Have students talk about what is happening and what the people might be saying. Then play the video and see how their predictions match what they hear.

The second time around

When using the *Videohistoria* videos, play the second segment (which has no words on the screen) a few days after seeing the first segment. Pause the video periodically and ask students informal questions about what is being said. They will be amazed at how their

comprehension has developed and how they no longer depend upon the written words to understand the story.

Video true / false

Ask students to write three true and three false statements about the main events in the video. Encourage them to avoid statements that could be answered by only seeing the video. In other words, have them write statements about what is being *said* in the video. Have students read the statements to a classmate after showing them the video again. The classmate will answer according to what he or she understood from the video.

Video plot summary

On a transparency, create a random list of quotes from characters in the video. Make sure that the quotations you choose are relevant to the plot. After showing students the video, have them number the quotes in the order that they were said. Students can do this activity alone or with a partner. This activity serves as a reading comprehension exercise also.

Can't see the TV!

Turn the television around (or ask students to turn their chairs to face away from it). Allow students to listen to the video segment. Pause the video periodically and ask students to speculate about what is happening. Turn the television back around and have students determine how accurate they were by watching the video. If you choose to do this activity with the *Videohistoria* videos, you might want to make photocopies of the eight panels that that are found in the *Vocabulario en contexto* section in the textbook. As students listen without watching the television, have them point to the panel that corresponds with what they hear.

Video cloze activity

Type a short portion of the script of a *Videomisterio* episode and create a cloze activity. Leave blanks for certain key words that students must listen for and write.

Teaching Tips

Using dictation exercises

Dictation practices and quizzes are helpful during the early levels of Spanish instruction to ensure that students are making correct sound-symbol correlations. In the *REALIDADES* series, you will notice activities entitled *Escucha y escribe*. These are meaningful dictations that help students to practice writing the vocabulary and grammar structures for the given unit of study.

When doing dictation activities, be sure to read the script three times. First, read the selection naturally. Have students listen, but not write. During the second reading, students should write. Read the passage in short segments, linking the words within a segment, but pausing in between segments so that students have time to write. Encourage students to leave a blank space if they miss a word, but remind them not to interrupt the dictation in progress to ask for a repetition. For the third reading, read naturally, but just a bit more slowly than the first time so that students can proofread their work and fill in any missing words. Remind students to check for spelling and correct accentuation. To assess dictations, make each correct word worth a point. Give students half credit if the word has only one incorrect letter or an incorrect accent mark.

Sample Activities

Textbook selections

Choose a reasonable amount (about two pages) of text from your current *REALIDADES* chapter. The day before the dictation, ask students to read the pages carefully as a homework assignment. Remind them to pay special attention to any word that might cause spelling challenges. Encourage them to read the text aloud at home as a preparation strategy. Recommending that students write out difficult words can also be helpful. In class the next day, read only a portion of the assigned pages (not the entire selection) as the dictation. One paragraph generally should be enough. Have students write what they hear. It is helpful for students to check their own work. After they finish writing, point out the paragraph you read in the book, and have students use a different colored pencil or pen to correct their answers.

Student-created dictations

Have students work in pairs and have each student write a six-line dialogue. Then, have them take turns reading their dialogues to

their partners. Encourage them to follow the dictation pattern of reading the text three times. While the one partner reads, the other partner should write down what is being said. After the third reading, students should check for errors. Students can then switch roles and repeat the activity.

Dictation as a final evaluation

As part of a chapter evaluation, you might consider creating sentences using vocabulary and structures from the current *REALIDADES* chapter, and dictating them one at a time. Or, you can create small paragraphs or use scripts from audio activities listed in the *REALIDADES Teacher Resource Book* for dictations. It is helpful to review scoring guidelines with students before beginning the evaluation.

Turn songs into cloze passages

The *REALIDADES* series is accompanied by a varied selection of songs in Spanish. In *REALIDADES* A/B/1-3 *Canciones de hip hop* can be found on **realidades.com** along with cloze activities to use with students. In *REALIDADES* 4 the songs and lyrics in *Ritmos* can be used to create a cloze activity. Distribute a handout of the lyrics with key words left out. You may choose to leave blanks for certain types of words such as adjectives, nouns, and pronouns, to reinforce a particular structure being discussed in class. Allow students two or three opportunities to listen to the song and to correctly fill in as many of the missing words as possible. After students have completed the activity, put a list of all of the correct words on an overhead transparency, and play the song again, so that students can recognize any words that they may have missed.

Strategy for Students

Remind students that when doing listening and drawing activities, they should focus on the listening. Many students are too busy trying to be artists to be effective listeners. Have them listen once to the entire passage, and draw a rough sketch. Then, on the second time around, they can begin to add details. By the third reading, students should have detailed drawings that they can share with classmates for future activities or discussions.

Listen and draw

Look for two illustrations that can be reproduced in your current *REALIDADES* chapter. Choose from any *REALIDADES* text, workbook, or ancillary. Illustrations can also be found by searching on the Internet. Be sure to select drawings for which students will generally possess the vocabulary needed to describe the picture. The drawings need to be simple enough for students to easily describe them, yet complex enough to create rich descriptions. (See sample drawings on p. 37 of the *REALIDADES Level 1 Teacher's Resource Book, Para Empezar*–Tema 4 and p. 131 of the *REALIDADES Level 2 Communication Workbook*.) Be sure each student has a blank piece of paper and a pencil. Have students work in pairs. One student describes the chosen drawing to his or her partner while the other student tries to recreate the drawing based on the description he or she hears. Discourage students who are describing the drawing from showing their partners the drawing or helping them in any way. Once the new drawing is complete, ask students to compare their efforts to the original. Have students switch roles, using the second drawing.

Preparing Students for Listening to Presentational Audio Selections

Teaching Tips

Using *REALIDADES* resources for presentational audio selections

You can help students be better prepared to listen to these selections on the AP* Exam by using the resources available to you in the *REALIDADES* series. For example, at the end of each chapter of *REALIDADES* 3 there is an *Integración* page which has a listening section. This listening section is a part of the chapter review, which prepares students for the chapter test and, ultimately, for the AP* Language test. These activities mirror the listening portions of the AP* Exam. In REALIDADES 4 students work with a variety of audio passages that enhance the development of their listening skills. Additionally, the activities in the *Communication Workbook with Test Preparation*

are easily adaptable at the intermediate level as practice for listening tasks on the AP* Spanish Language and Culture Exam. You may wish to read the passages to your students. To give them a more authentic practice activity, have a native speaker record a passage (or record it yourself) before you do the activity. Provide questions that accompany each passage. Let students scan the questions before they respond, and then read the passage or play the recording. When students are finished listening to the narration and answering the questions, give them a printed copy of the segment and have them listen again as they read along. See the *Communication Workbook with Test Preparation* for samples of this activity.

Sample Student Activities

Dictogloss activity

The Dictogloss activity is highly effective in helping to prepare students to be able to extract meaning from longer listening selections. In this activity, the focus is on what students *do* understand. Students should not be expected to comprehend each and every nuance of the selected piece. With practice, students will become adept at performing this type of task. This activity can and should be practiced at all levels of study. Follow these five steps for optimal results.

1. Choose any reading passage from your current chapter of *REALIDADES*. The length may vary depending on the students' level of study. One half to one page is sufficient in length. It is not necessary to use an entire reading.

2. Have students close their books as you read the selected passage aloud, at a natural rate of speech. Ask them to listen and concentrate on trying to extract the most essential points.

3. Read the passage aloud to students a second time at the same rate of speech and ask them to jot down, in Spanish, the main ideas and most important details of the reading. Students should not try to capture every word as in a dictation exercise.

4. Ask students to combine their efforts with a partner and write a one-paragraph summary of what they heard.

5. Once students have finished, you can choose any of the activities below as an effective follow-up:

   a. Have two or three sets of partners share their summaries aloud for the class. Have other students share any details that they did not hear during the presentations.

   b. Ask each pair to share one main idea from their summary. List the main ideas on the board or overhead. Continue to ask pairs until all of the main ideas of the reading have been listed.

   c. Ask each pair to use their summaries to prepare two questions about the reading. Collect the questions and ask some of them to the class. Encourage students to be creative when giving answers that cannot be taken directly from the passage.

   d. Prepare a short list of questions to ask students about the main ideas of the story. You may want to ask students in a whole-class setting, or walk around to each pair as students finish their summaries. Have students use their writing to support their answers.

   e. You may want to continue reading the entire text containing the passage that you are working on, thus using the Dictogloss as a pre-reading activity. After students summarize and share details of the passage, allow them to open their texts and read the selected passage aloud with a partner. By already participating in an in-depth discussion about a portion of the reading, students will be more familiar with it as they read for meaning.

Strategy for Students

Students must be prepared to answer multiple-choice questions that accompany the listening section of the AP* Exam. When preparing them, encourage students to scan the questions that accompany a listening activity before they listen. By reading the questions, they know what to listen for. When students have multiple-choice questions that accompany a listening activity, ask them to use common sense to eliminate any illogical answers right away.

Creating questions

Choose two different segments of one reading from a *REALIDADES* student textbook to record or read aloud to the class. Divide the class in half and give each group a different reading. Have them create multiple-choice questions for the segment they were given. Then, collect the questions and redistribute them to the opposite group of students. Ask students to take a few moments to read the questions that they received. Next, read aloud or play a tape of each segment (one at a time). The students with the multiple-choice questions listen for the correct answers, while the students who wrote the questions follow along with the passage as it is being read.

Listening and memory

The *REALIDADES* Communication Workbook has many activities that require students to correlate the events from a story or a series of descriptions to a drawing. (For examples, see p. 102 of the Level 2 Communication Workbook and p. 96 of the Level 3 Communication Workbook.) To develop students' capacity for listening to longer selections, you might consider reading all of the prompts related to the pictures for the activity while students have their workbooks closed. After reading the script, direct students to open their workbooks and complete as many of the identifications as possible from memory and/or any notes that they might have taken. If students have difficulties, repeat the script a second time and allow them to have their workbooks open as they listen.

Listening for details

A second step that requires students to listen for additional details can be added to some of the activities in the Communication Workbook. Have students do the activity as indicated in the Communication Workbook. Then, replay the audio DVD and ask students to write details that support the answers they gave. This scaffolding approach to listening allows students to focus on the main idea first, and then the supporting details.

Preparing for Audio, Visual, and Audiovisual Interpretive Communication

There are many different activities in the *REALIDADES* Student Editions and program components that develop the listening interpretive skill.

Student Edition

• Various audio activities: *REALIDADES* A/B/1-4
• *Preparación para el examen: REALIDADES* A/B/1-3

Communication Workbook with Test Preparation

• Audio Activities: *REALIDADES* A/B/1-3
• Integrated Performance Assessments: *REALIDADES* A/B/1-3

Vocabulary, Grammar, and Communication Workbook

• Audio Activities: *REALIDADES* 4

TPR Stories

Various activities: *REALIDADES* A/B/1-2

Assessment Program

• Listening tasks: *REALIDADES* A/B/1-4

Video Programs

• *Videohistoria: REALIDADES* A/B/1-3
• *Videocultura: REALIDADES* A/B/1-2 (Spanish version)
• *¿Eres tú, María?: REALIDADES* B/1
• *En busca de la verdad: REALIDADES* 2
• *¡Adelante!: REALIDADES* 3
• *¡Pura vida!: REALIDADES* 3
• *VideoRed: REALIDADES* 4

Interpretive: Reading

Teaching students to read in Spanish presents a unique challenge. For many students, reading is a difficult exercise in decoding and translating. It is important to teach students to read for overall meaning from the very beginning, and to avoid trying to translate every word. Do not develop or use activities that require them to extract every minute detail from the reading. Instead, point out to them that a global understanding is sufficient at first. As their reading fluency develops, they become better prepared to take on a passage for a deeper understanding. Once they are equipped with the right strategies to master texts at their reading level, they will want to read for enjoyment or information. Practice will result in fluency, which will help students advance their reading level. For success on the interpretive reading section of the AP* Exam, students must be able to know the content and vocabulary, but they must also have strong strategies to apply to material that may be above their reading level. Therefore, your two main goals as a teacher should be to instill useful strategies in students' reading practices and to promote fluency to make reading Spanish less intimidating for them.

The Role of Pre-reading

Teaching Tips

Pre-reading at all levels

Regardless of the reading level of the assigned text or the students' abilities, it is always important to prepare them for what they will be reading. Use visuals around a text and the title of the passage to provide indications to students about the content of the passage.

Also, remind students to notice what type of text they are going to be working with, and encourage them to handle it appropriately. For example, students would not approach a short story with the same reading skills as they would an informational text. In one, they are focusing on a developing plot and characters, while in the other they are looking to gain factual information. Students may have already been taught about various texts in their Language Arts classes, and may already be aware of how to treat each type of text. Remind them to use these practices in Spanish, too.

A third important factor in gauging how much students will comprehend from a given text is their background knowledge. When presenting students with a text (fiction or non-fiction), try to access the information that they already know. If you find that they are limited in background knowledge for a particular text, be sure to provide them with comprehensible information that they can use to better understand the text.

Finally, it is recommended that you carefully examine a reading selection prior to presenting it to the class. This way, you can choose to focus on a selected set of vocabulary and/or structures that are present in the reading. Make sure that students are familiar with the vocabulary and grammar in the reading. By using the vocabulary from the chosen text in other activities prior to doing the reading, students will feel less intimidated. The same is true for syntax. If a reading is particularly heavy with a certain type of structure, extract some samples of the structure from the reading and use them to practice the structure before doing the actual reading.

Activities

Student Strategy

Encourage students to scan the last paragraph or sentence of a passage before they begin reading. By doing this, students can form expectations for the content of the text, which will help them focus more on the content when they do go back and read it.

Two possibilities

Have students read the last sentence or paragraph of any text you may assign to them. Based on what they read in that segment, have students conjecture two possible details about the body of the text. Ask them to write these

guesses down on a piece of paper to share with a partner. As students share their work, have them determine which two possibilities are the most probable. It will be helpful for reading comprehension if students not only make predictions, but also discuss them with someone else. When students read the text, have them check their predictions for accuracy.

Dictation and the Dictogloss activity

Before reading, have students write out a dictation of a segment of the text. (See p. 13 of the Listening section for a complete description of this activity.) This will help to familiarize them with the content and type of text you are using. Or, have students do a Dictogloss activity, which is a listening activity that provides a thorough introduction to the gist of a longer passage. (See p. 15 of the Listening section for a complete description of this activity.) If students understand the basic gist of the passage before beginning, they will have an easier time when it comes to reading.

Teaching Beginning Reading

Teaching Tips

Promoting thoughtful responses

Often, students are assigned to read a passage in their textbook and answer the associated questions. They become quite adept at copying a corresponding phrase from the reading without ever truly reading the selection itself or understanding it. Even at the most basic levels, it is essential that they try to read for understanding, and not just write the answers. Vary activities that accompany a text in a way that promotes open responses and discussions about what students thought of the content of the reading. Supplement the activities in the *REALIDADES* reading sections with some of the suggested activities to help build reading comprehension and, consequently, reading enjoyment. Students will fare much better on the AP* Exam if they read for meaning and not just for answers.

Graphic Organizers

Graphic organizers are one way for students to obtain information and show comprehension of a text. The type of organizer you use depends on the type of text students are being asked to read. For example, when reading short pieces of fiction, you may wish to have students use a flowchart to show main events of the story. Graphic organizers can be found in the *REALIDADES* Teacher's Resource Book and on PresentationExpress Premium. There are also many graphic organizers available on the Internet. Explain how to use the organizer before beginning the reading, and then have students fill in information after they have read the passage, or during a second read.

Strategy sharing

Don't forget to point out all of the strategy boxes that accompany each reading in the *REALIDADES* series. It is also helpful to ask students to share their own strategies for obtaining information from a text. Have students explain how they got a particular answer, or ask them to back their opinions up with passages from the text.

Reading aloud

Encourage beginning readers to read aloud at home. Often, the sound of a word will trigger comprehension, and this provides good speaking practice. However, try to avoid having students read aloud in a round-robin fashion in class. Students will only focus on their segment of the text and will not gain meaning from the entire passage. Of course, it is often the case where students are eager to read aloud in class. In this case, instead of calling on students to read, you should model the pronunciation of the passage first, and then have volunteers repeat what you say. In this way, students will be modeling your correct pronunciation and intonation as well as reinforcing the content of the text by re-reading.

Cognates

Remind students that cognates can be helpful in understanding the meaning of a word that has not yet been formally introduced to them. However, advise them to be aware that false cognates, such as *asistir* and *realizar*, can throw off their understanding. When they are not sure if a word is truly a cognate, suggest that they try to read the entire sentence and determine its meaning through the context.

Activities

Paired Reading

Choose a variety of texts from the *REALIDADES* series, as well as from outside sources. Assign the readings to pairs of students. Separate the students in your classroom so that they will be able to read the passages aloud in a low voice without disturbing other pairs. Give students three minutes to discuss what they read and list the main ideas. Then, have two sets of partners join together to share the information that they read.

True / false

Have each student or pair of students write one true sentence and one false sentence about the reading. Tell students that the sentences should be in their own words, rather than taken directly from the text. Have students share their sentences aloud with classmates, or you may prefer to compile a list of their statements on an overhead projector to review with students. Have students turn false statements into true statements using information from the reading.

Plot summary

This activity is best completed with a narrative. Have each student or pair of students write one sentence on the board that summarizes the main events of a reading. Monitor students' choices to ensure that no events are repeated. When students are finished writing their statements on the board, label each sentence with a letter. Students must put the sentences in the order that best reflects the events from the reading.

> ### Student Strategy
> Have students read, read again, and then re-read! Reading a passage the first time gives the general sense or gist of what it is about. The second time, students should use decoding skills for the difficult vocabulary and structures. A third time allows students to synthesize the passage and complete any comprehension activities.

Random answers

After students have completing a reading, allow them to choose from questions that cor-

respond to the text, instead of requiring them to answer all of the questions. It's okay if students tend to focus on the easier questions in the early levels. It builds confidence when they focus on what they *do* understand. As students become more confident, you may decide to ask your advanced students to choose from the more difficult questions. When students finish answering the questions, ask volunteers to read their answers, without revealing the corresponding question. Have the class listen to the answer and determine the correct question. As a variation, you may want to create and read the answers yourself.

Be an Artist

Choose 3 or 4 different reading selections. Then, organize groups of 3-4 students. Give each group a reading selection and be sure to give the same selection to at least 2 groups. Give each group a sheet of newsprint and a set of markers; tell the students to divide the newsprint in 4 quadrants. Have each group read its selection, discuss it, and create 4 large illustrations (1 in each quadrant) that depict important points or events in the article. Each member of the group is responsible for one of the illustrations. Students may use no words or a maximum of 2 words in each illustration; the words must be in Spanish. It is important that the students understand that they are not creating a cartoon strip. Give the students a limited amount of time to complete the task. When the time has elapsed, ask each group to present its illustration to the class. The group should explain how the illustrations represent key points or events from the reading selection. It is a good idea to have groups that read the same selection follow each other so that the class can see how different groups illustrated the same selection.

Teaching Intermediate and Advanced Reading

Teaching Tips

Building skilled readers

At the intermediate and advanced stages, students should have a fair amount of fluency. The goal at this point is to continually advance students' reading levels. Raise the bar for students, and promote independent reading with open discussions. (However, do not forget to reinforce strategies that students have been using as beginning readers.) Have students discuss their reflections and opinions as they read passages. To increase student interest in reading, be sure to provide a wide variety of reading materials. You may wish to develop a classroom library of short story collections, novels, Internet articles, and magazines in Spanish. Make sure you have plenty of authentic texts (those written for a native speaker) in your classroom. Use these varied resources to create your own reading comprehension activities. Student comprehension is attained with greater ease when the topic that they are reading about is of high interest to them.

Reading as vocabulary building

As a culmination to reading selections in intermediate and advanced courses, have students keep a "vocabulary journal" of new words that have been learned through readings. This could simply be a small pocket notebook that they keep in their backpacks. The vocabulary they note could be representative of a particular topic of interest or a list of high frequency vocabulary that the students have not yet mastered. By making their own lists, students are associating meaning to words, and by revisiting the list from time to time and creating meaningful usage situations with the list, students can enrich their working vocabularies.

Additional reading strategies

It is important that students be able to use their reading strategies to make sense of a passage, even if it is above their reading level. Intermediate and advanced readers may be interested in reading authentic texts that are too difficult for them. However, they can still get the gist of the passage by applying effective reading methods. In addition to the strategies already mentioned, remind students to use strategies that they have learned from reading in their own language. For example, point out to students the importance of context to determine meaning. A second strategy is having students identify the part of speech of a word that they do not recognize. Often, they have an easier time determining the meaning when they know the function of the word. A third option is to have them remove prefixes and endings from unknown words to get at a word root which may help to reveal its meaning. By teaching and reinforcing these strategies, you are helping students to be more independent readers and to develop greater comprehension of challenging texts.

Using *REALIDADES* resources to prepare for the AP* Exam

The *REALIDADES* series offers a wide variety of resources to help you advance your students' reading capabilities and prepare them for the AP* Exam. Use the readings from the book and create activities that simulate the AP* Exam. For example, you may want to create multiple-choice questions to accompany a reading in the *Lectura* section of the student textbooks. Be sure to include some questions that require the students to make inferences about the reading. In addition to the readings in the book, the Communication Workbook with Test Preparation ancillary has a selection of intermediate-level readings accompanied by multiple-choice questions.

An additional option for reading comprehension activities is to use the listening scripts for each chapter of the *REALIDADES* series. You can reproduce these scripts and the listening activities that accompany them, and turn them into reading comprehension exercises. Promote fluency by having the students read along as you play the recording.

Activities

Show what you know

Give students a reading that is likely to be above their reading level. Be sure each student has highlighters of two different colors. Have them work with a partner. Ask students to scan the text and highlight each and every word in the passage that they *do* understand in one color. Then, using decoding skills, have students use a different color to highlight all of the words that they are able to understand using good decoding skills (such as saying the word aloud, breaking it down into roots

and affixes, or using the context of the text). Then, ask both students to read the passage aloud in small sections. Have them pause intermittently to discuss what the selection means. After they have read it together the first time, ask them to write down the main ideas. Then, have a group discussion on the reading and on the process that the students used.

Be an Artist

A variation of this activity described on page 21 works well with intermediate and advanced students. Select a short story, preferably with a twist that students may not understand. Divide the story into 3-5 sections, depending on its length. Label the first section "1', the second section "2", until all sections have been labeled. Divide the class into groups of 3-4 and give each group a section of the story. Give the section with the twist or a particularly difficult section to more than one group. Have the students read their section and discuss it within the group until everyone understands its content. Then have each group prepare 1 large illustration showing as many details of their section as they can. When the time has elapsed, ask the group(s) with section 1 to present and describe its illustration to the class. Continue with the rest of the sections, in order, until all the illustrations have been displayed. At this point, a lively discussion can ensue about the details of the story that were correctly or incorrectly illustrated.

Make your own quiz

You will need at least two different texts to do this activity. Give students copies of the different reading selections as homework. Have them read the passage and create six multiple-choice questions. Ask them to turn in a separate answer key so that you can check their work. The next day, collect the texts and questions and redistribute them to other students. Have

students complete the quizzes. Then, allow students time to discuss their results with the author of their quiz. Have volunteers share some sample questions and answers, as well as strategies that they used to take the quiz.

Sample activity to accompany *REALIDADES* reading

Have students choose the best answer in a sample multiple-choice activity that you create using the *Lecturas* in the *REALIDADES* student editions. Review the answers in class, making sure that students detail their strategy for finding each answer. The following activity assesses students' comprehension of *La mariposa monarca* found in *REALIDADES 3* student edition, pp. 422–424.

1. ¿Cuál es una de las diferencias principales entre la mariposa monarca y las otras mariposas?
   a. Es una polinizadora importante.
   b. Es más bello.
   c. Llega a vivir nueve meses.
   d. Tres cuartas partes de los animales que viven en la Tierra son insectos.
2. ¿Qué causa que la mariposa monarca sea desagradable para los otros animales?
   a. su dieta
   b. su resistencia a los cambios de clima
   c. es venenosa
   d. su polinización
3. ¿Por qué le gusta a la mariposa monarca la zona entre Michoacán y el estado de México?
   a. Hay una gran variedad de plantas.
   b. Es una zona tropical.
   c. Es boscosa con valles.
   d. Hay mucho oxígeno y protección del viento polar.
4. ¿Cuál elemento <u>no</u> amenaza la vida de la mariposa monarca?
   a. las asclepias
   b. el clima extremadamente frío
   c. los depredadores
   d. los ataques por otros bichos

5. ¿Cuántas mariposas monarca suelen sobrevivir el invierno en México?
   a. entre 100 y 400 millones
   b. casi 65%
   c. casi 35%
   d. aproximadamente 50%

6. Las mariposas monarca se reproducen
   a. donde hay aire polar y cambios de clima.
   b. durante tormentas de nieve en el Canadá.
   c. en el invierno en los refugios de México.
   d. a mediados de abril durante el viaje de regreso.

7. ¿Por qué no sufrieron daños las mariposas monarca durante el incendio de 2001?
   a. El fuego afectó hectáreas localizadas a 500 metros de altura sobre el nivel del mar.
   b. Un grupo de turistas lo apagaron.
   c. La población de mariposas recuperó su nivel de años anteriores.
   d. Ya habían salido para el Canadá.

Using student work

With their permission, use students' own writing samples as reading material for the class. Have students sit in a circle of 4 people, with their own corrected writing pieces in hand. Students pass the writing to the right and read the piece they have received. They continue passing and reading until they have received their own work back. This exercise serves as a confidence-builder. If students do not want to share their writing, give them a copy of a different text to pass through the circle. After everyone has read all of the selections, encourage students to discuss the work in small groups.

Student Strategy

When answering multiple-choice questions about a reading, remind students to skim through the passage once to gain a general sense of the passage. Next, encourage them to read the questions, but not the answers. Suggest that they re-read the passage for the answer and have them write it on a separate paper. Finally, have them compare the answer they got to the multiple-choice options, and select the option that most closely matches the written answer.

Student experts

When reading a longer piece, assign each pair of students a specific section. All students should read the entire piece, but only be held responsible for the portions to which they are assigned. For their respective section, pairs of students should:

- Write, in their own words, a brief summary of the main points or actions.
- Decode any unfamiliar vocabulary and be ready to share their strategies with the class.
- Create questions with multiple-choice answers to be shared with the class.

Once students have finished their preparations, have the class retell the story by going around the room and asking each pair, in order, to share their summary. Collect all of the multiple-choice questions and compile them into a longer activity that students can complete in class or as a homework assignment.

Preparing for Written and Print Interpretive Communication

There are many different activities in the *REALIDADES* Student Editions and program components that develop the reading interpretive skill.

Student Edition

- Various reading activities: *REALIDADES* A/B/1-4
- Lectura: *REALIDADES* A/B/1-3
- Puente a la cultura: *REALIDADES* 3
- Preparación para el examen: *REALIDADES* A/B/1-3
- Páginas: *REALIDADES* 4

Communication Workbook with Test Preparation

- Reading Skills Worksheets: *REALIDADES* A/B/1-3
- Practice Tests: *REALIDADES* A/B/1-3
- Integrated Performance Assessments: *REALIDADES* A/B/1-3

Vocabulary, Grammar, and Communication Workbook

- Páginas–A leer: *REALIDADES* 4

REALIDADES para hispanohablantes

- Lecturas: *REALIDADES* A/B/1-3

TPR Stories

- Stories: *REALIDADES* A/B/1-2

Lecturas

- Selecciones (varias): *REALIDADES* A/B/1-3

realidades.com

- Online Cultural Readings: *REALIDADES* A/B/1-3

Assessment Program

- Reading tasks: *REALIDADES* A/B/1-4

Writing

The AP Spanish Language and Culture Exam requires that students write in both the Interpersonal and Presentational modes of communication. In the Interpersonal mode students read and reply to an e-mail message. In the Presentational mode they write a persuasive essay based on a topic and three sources representing different points of view on the topic. The sources include print and audio material. Students must determine their own point of view and reference all sources as they support and defend it.

Preparing for Interpersonal Writing

Teaching Tips

Using *REALIDADES* resources

The *REALIDADES* series provides many resources for students to develop their interpersonal writing skills. The Communication Workbook for *REALIDADES* A/B/1 1-3 includes activities where students write notes, letters and e-mail messages. In addition, several *Presentación escrita* activities in *REALIDADES* A/B/1-3 ask students to write e-mail messages and letters. After students complete these activities, teachers can distribute them and ask students to write responses to complete the interpersonal communication. The interpersonal writing in the AP* Exam asks students to use a formal form of address, so it is important for students to learn to use the conventions of formal as well as informal communication.

Teach Interpersonal Writing Strategies

Students should learn the elements of authentic interpersonal writing, including greetings and closings in letters and e-mails. In addition, they should learn to respond to questions and embed their answers in text which flows naturally through the use of appropriate transition words and expressions. They should also learn to include logical questions in their responses in order to enhance communication. Where possible, students should be encouraged to use current and appropriate social media sources to develop their interpersonal writing skills.

Journal Writing

Journal writing can be a very useful way to develop students' interpersonal writing skills when the journal entries become a dialogue between the writer and the reader. Under any circumstances, journal writing serves as a strategy to build students' overall writing skills.

Teaching Tips

Keeping a journal

Journal writing can be a very effective writing task. Even beginning students can make weekly journal entries using newly acquired words and phrases. Using a journal, students can express their thoughts and feelings in a private, non-intimidating way. Students will inevitably improve their writing skills with regular practice, especially when they choose topics that interest them.

When and where to write

Journaling can be done as homework. However, it can also be done in class. Students can write as a warm-up, at a learning station during an independent writing period, or after they finish an assignment that others are still working on. Have beginning students write directly into a section of their notebook that has been reserved for this purpose. You may choose to keep small notebooks in crates (separated by class) in the classroom for more advanced students who will most likely write longer entries. These students should also be held accountable for weekly journal entries done outside of class.

Electronic journals

If possible, have students e-mail you their journal entries. This way, you will be free from managing large stacks or bins of journals. Set up an electronic folder on your computer desktop for students' journal entries. If you decide that this is a better option for your class, be sure to also provide students with ample opportunities to write assignments by hand, as that is what they will have to do for the AP* Exam.

Journal topics

Every chapter of *REALIDADES* is packed with ideas for writing. By making use of these topics, you will reinforce the use of the current lesson's vocabulary. You may want to use the appendix for other ideas. Or, have students create a list of topics that interest them on the first page of their journal. Whenever they are at a loss for what to write about, have them refer to their lists and choose a topic.

Correcting student journals

As a teacher, your greatest challenge is finding time to do everything that is necessary for students to learn effectively. Often, teachers avoid having students create journals because it seems like an intense amount of extra work. However, if you serve as the audience for your students, instead of the editor, you'll find that journals can be fun to read and often only create a minimal amount of work. It is important to remember that you should *not* correct the students' journals, unless you expect them to publish a certain entry. If they are not publishing or re-writing the piece, they will most likely ignore your corrections. Furthermore, you run the risk of discouraging them from writing by sending them the message that they should focus on form over content. Remember that the journals are students' personal reflections, and you should focus on the content of what they are saying. Consider the following options to help you adopt the use of journals in your classroom:

- Quickly skim each journal entry and place a sticker or a rubber stamp on the page to show students that you are looking at their work. This can take less than 10 minutes per class.

- Write a comment back to students about the content of their entry and encourage them to write back to you if you posed a question.

- If you notice common errors in several students' journals, bring those to the whole class' attention without naming the students who committed them.

- If you see a student making the same mistake repeatedly, write a response to that student using the difficult word or structure correctly. You will be correcting their trouble spot subtly by providing an accurate model.

- Use a colored highlighter to highlight phrases in the journal that were extremely well done. Students will compare how much highlighting they have received and celebrate their successes.

- If you *must* make corrections, it is best to choose the worst error you see and correct it, but no more. Drawing students' attention to just one error per week can add up to gradual improvements in their writing without intimidating them. Tell students that you are not correcting every error in this environment, but that their best efforts are expected. Remind them, however, that you will be checking for correct work in other writing assignments, and that they will be scored on the precision of their writing on the AP* Exam. Keeping a journal is a safe way for them to practice their skills.

- Hold a short conference with students who have persistent problems writing in their journals.

- Check journals once a week, and make sure to hold students accountable for a certain number of entries. Develop a schedule that students can follow to work independently. Remind students to be on time. Likewise, it's important that you return the journals to students as soon as possible.

Grading journals

If journal writing is done in class, you may wish to include it as part of the class participation grade. Journals done at home can count as completed assignments. Journals should never be graded for a letter grade as one might grade a formal essay. However, it is often difficult to get students to do written

work without receiving a grade. To keep students motivated, assign a number from 1 to 4 to each of their entries (1 being little effort, 4 being strong effort). Write the numbers in your grade book to keep track of their independent writing efforts each week. Add these points up and develop an independent writing grade to factor into students' overall grade. You may wish to develop an independent writing rubric or find one on the Internet so that students are aware of your expectations. This way, students will be graded on their writing effort, not the final product. The purpose of journal writing is to provide a forum for practice. Writing should only be graded if students have the opportunity to review and edit their work.

Activities

Spanish only!

Remind students that they should never approach a composition using English vocabulary when the Spanish vocabulary is unknown. If they can't express their ideas due to a lack of vocabulary or structures, they should consider what other ideas related to the essay topic that they can express with the tools at their disposal. Likewise, encourage them to avoid writing an assignment in English and then translating it, which leads to reliance on a dictionary and an often-incomprehensible product. Have students limit themselves to only two or three words from the dictionary when writing.

Comic strip

Have students make a comic strip of a completed journal entry. Ask them to re-read their entries, choose one, and draw a four-panel strip depicting the events or words of the passage. Remind them to choose small excerpts to use in the speech bubbles for each panel. This activity encourages students to review their own work and practice visualizing their writing. It is an excellent step to complete before revising a journal entry for publication.

Audio entries

Have students use a hand-held recorder to record one of their journal entries (see Speaking section of this book, p. 40 for instructions on how to record). As they read aloud and hear what they wrote, students may begin to notice things in their writing that doesn't "sound right." Consequently, they will begin to make their own corrections and monitor their writing more closely.

Preparing for Presentational Writing: The Writing Process

Teach students the steps to the writing process. Point out that they should apply the following steps when writing in Spanish. Remind them that they may already use these steps when they write in English.

- pre-write / brainstorm
- draft
- revise
- edit
- publish

Pre-Writing and Brainstorming

Teaching Tips

Organizers

Use the *REALIDADES* graphic organizers to help students collect and organize their ideas before they draft a passage. Choose a chart that is appropriate for the assigned task. For example, you may want to distribute Venn diagrams if students are preparing to write a compare and contrast essay. Other examples include a "sunburst" diagram, which helps students to add details to a main idea, and a flowchart that helps them to sequence events. These organizers can serve as brainstorming sheets to prepare students to write. See the organizers in the *Leveled Vocabulary and Grammar Workbook: Core Practice* for additional options. For example, the organizer on p. 174 of the *A/B Leveled Vocabulary and Grammar Workbook: Core Practice* could be a pre-writing activity for writing a piece about using electronics in our everyday lives.

Activities

Partner practice

Make several copies of the organizers found in the *REALIDADES* transparencies and

distribute them to the class. In pairs, have students complete the organizer as they share their ideas on the assigned topic. Have partners brainstorm their ideas as a class and write their suggestions on the appropriate transparency.

Student Strategy

Organize to write

Once students have finished brainstorming ideas on the topic, they can number their ideas in the order that they will appear in the essay. By following the ideas in numerical order, the draft will unfold in a logical manner. Remind students that they might not use every single idea that they created in the pre-writing activity, and that it is even helpful to eliminate some of the details that do not directly relate to the main idea. Students must also remember to plan for how they will include the references to the information received in the text and audio prompts when writing the formal essay.

Individual practice

After students have become familiar with how to use a graphic organizer to brainstorm their ideas on a topic, have them complete the organizer on their own. Then, have students convene in small groups to discuss their ideas. Encourage them to "borrow" ideas from classmates that will improve their own essays, and have them note those ideas in their organizers.

Drafting

Teaching Tips

Preparing a draft on the computer

If possible, have students write and store their formal essays on a computer. The essays should be double-spaced and typed for easy reading and editing. Having the drafts on the computer makes it easier for students to rework their writing after peer and teacher editing.

Taking the draft step by step

Trying to write a lengthy essay in Spanish can be intimidating to students. Have them break the draft into parts: the introduction, the

body, and the conclusion. Show them how to handle each part individually before having them organize their entire essay.

I. Introduction

For the purpose of the AP* essay, the introduction should serve two purposes: introduce the topic in the writers' own words, and state the plan for the remainder of the essay. The intro should serve as a sort of "road map" of where the essay will go. Remind students that they do not need to state all of their ideas in the introduction.

II. The body

As they draft each paragraph, remind students that it is essential that they focus on the content. Point out that they should not spend time on perfecting their grammar or spelling. Concentrating too much on the form may impede the message that students are trying to send. Remind them that editing will take place later in the writing process.

III. The conclusion

Point out to students that the conclusion must do more than merely restate what has already been stated in the body of the essay. The purpose of the conclusion is to close the essay. Possible ways of doing this include stating an opinion, creating a solution, making a recommendation, or providing a reflection on the topic.

Encourage use of connecting words

Have students practice using a minimum number of appropriate connecting words in each essay.

Common Connecting Words:

y / e	pero
o / u	sino
entonces	sin embargo
por eso	a lo menos
luego	porque
pues	a causa de
después	aunque
al principio	finalmente

Essay writing in Spanish

It is important that you recognize that some students may not be familiar with the essay as a genre. Students probably are more accustomed to writing personal narratives. Therefore, if you are having students draft essays, be sure that they understand some key aspects of the genre, such as the inclusion of the introduction, body, and conclusion. Also, remind them that essays are not generally written in the first person. Students often struggle with how to express an impersonal "you" in the essay. Before they begin to write the first draft, spend a moment reminding them how to use some common structures in Spanish essays, such as: *se* (impersonal), *ellos* (impersonal), *uno* as the impersonal subject of a reflexive verb, and *la gente* as opposed to *las personas*.

Activities

Writing an introduction

To get students accustomed to writing introductions, have them practice in pairs. Give pairs of students a body of text that doesn't have an introduction. Then, have students develop an introduction on transparencies to share with the rest of the class. Ask classmates to critique the introductions based on these criteria:

- Does the introduction state the theme of the essay?
- Does the introduction outline the plan for the essay?
- Does the author say too much in the introductory paragraph?

Writing a conclusion

You may wish to try a similar pair-work activity to get students on track with writing conclusions. As students share their work on transparencies, encourage others to use these criteria to determine if the conclusion is appropriate for the passage.

- Does the conclusion summarize the contents of the essay?
- Does the conclusion contain the authors' reflections about the topic?
- Does the conclusion "look ahead" to possible solutions or recommendations about the topic of the essay?

Revisions

Teaching Tips

Checklists

Give students a checklist that reflects your writing scoring guide or rubric. The checklist should be simple, but tailored to a specific activity. For example, sample checklist items for a memoir could include:

___ Did the student include an introduction, body, and conclusion?

___ Did the student successfully reflect on a personal experience?

___ Did the student consistently use the past tense?

Filling out a checklist like this helps you to provide students with quick feedback, and helps them to identify the areas that they need to improve.

Peer revisions

It is helpful for students to share their work with one another. Often, students feel comfortable taking and giving feedback with their peers. Allow time in class for students to sit together and read each other's essays and discuss their content. Students should consider the organization and comprehensibility of the piece and make any necessary suggestions. During the revision phase, urge students to ignore any possible grammatical errors in the writing that they are reading. This may be a welcome relief to them! The focus during this time is on meaning and content.

Activity

Self and peer revision

Have students re-read their own work, using a colored highlighter to mark areas in which they think they need to improve. Then, have them work together with a partner to discuss suggestions for the highlighted areas. Once students have feedback, ask them to write the changes into the essay and share it once more with their partner. After everybody has revised their works and received input from their partners, have a whole-class discussion about helpful strategies that surfaced during the discussions.

Student Strategy
Recommending changes
When students are peer editing, have them discuss any possible changes with the author, instead of writing them on the paper. This allows the author to ask for clarification and provide comments on the input. This discourse is much more effective in improving writing skills than written communication between the writer and the reader.

Editing and Publishing

Teaching Tips

Remind students that control of basic structures, such as orthography and agreement, is important when writing the essay for the AP* Spanish Exam. The following suggestions will help you to prepare students to edit their own work and write more accurately. Once students have an edited piece, have them carefully make changes to their work for publishing.

Peer editing

Peer editing is an excellent way to help students learn how to edit their own work and to be more conscious of common errors. The most fundamental types of errors that students need to overcome at the beginning and intermediate levels are regarding agreement. Basically, students need to watch for subject-verb agreement, as well as article and adjective agreement with nouns. Spelling problems can also require some attention. To teach students to manage these types of errors better, consider the following:

- Again, require that errors be discussed with a partner. Do not allow students to simply write on each other's papers.
- Encourage students to give themselves visual clues to help them identify the parts of speech in a sentence. Once they recognize the part of speech of an individual word, they will have an easier time understanding its role in the sentence, and how that role might affect other words based on grammar rules that students have learned.

Group revision

A great way to model essay revision is by using an essay from a student of a previous year or by gaining permission to use the work of one of your own students. Reproduce the typed essay (without the name) on a transparency and on sheets to distribute to students. Then, model a revision of the first two or three sentences of the essay, explaining your reasons for making changes as you go. Have a few student volunteers work on revising the next few sentences, and then have students finish the revision on their own. Afterwards, discuss the results as a class, focusing on strategies that students used to revise the work. Point out that they should look for content, flow, and organization as well as spelling and grammatical errors. Practicing and modeling in class will lead to more thorough student editors.

Activities

Timed practice

In order to acquaint students with the experience of writing with a limited amount of time, provide them with a writing prompt. (See p. 127 of the Level 3 Communication Workbook for an example.) Ask them to complete the task in 20–25 minutes. Remind them to use the writing process. Encourage them to take the time to scan their passages for agreement errors and other simple mistakes.

Parts of speech

Have students practice editing for agreement by identifying all of the parts of speech in a sentence. They might do this with different colored highlighters (pink for nouns, yellow for verbs, etc.) or with adhesive notes labeled with each part of speech. As a TPR activity, have students identify parts of speech by using the right index finger to touch the noun or the verb. Ask them to use the left index finger to touch the subject, adjective, or other related word. If the two do not agree, a change must be recommended. If the subject of the verb is understood, as is often the case in Spanish, students can just place the left index finger on their heads and *imagine* the subject. Once they have identified each part of speech, have them

check for agreement. Remind them of the different types of agreement by writing common relationships on the board.

Evaluating Students' Compositions

Teaching Tips

Making corrections

Only after students have completed peer revisions, editing, and have re-written the original draft, should you begin to correct their work. Do NOT assign a formal grade to any essay that has not had the benefit of revision, editing, and rewriting of the original draft. Having double-spaced essays makes correcting easier.

Correcting can take a variety of forms:

- Make the corrections directly on the students' essays. This is most helpful when students need to rework an entire phrase or require assistance with a complex structure.

- Establish a routine set of symbols to indicate the type of error to the students. For example: a circle for an agreement error, a box for an incorrectly conjugated verb, an underline for an incorrect vocabulary word choice, and so on. You may want to check with the Language Arts teachers at your school to see if students are already familiar with a set of correction symbols.

- Use highlighters of different colors. Errors of one type get the same color (i.e., agreement mistakes in blue, conjugation problems in green, etc.). When students receive their corrected essays, they can easily tell which type of error is the most problematic for them, based on which color they see most. You can also highlight students' papers on the computer if they send the works to you electronically.

- With electronically-submitted essays, you can use the "Insert Comment" function if available. Simply go to *insert*, and click on *comment*. Your comment will be inserted with your initials and a highlighted background.

Writing rubrics

By helping to familiarize students with the contents of the AP* Exam essay-grading rubrics in early levels of study, they can focus

Composition Rubrics				
Score	**4**	**3**	**2**	**1**
Structures	Excellent control of structures, almost no errors	Good control of structures with a few minor errors, or errors in complex structures	Weak control of structures with frequent errors in simple structures	Little to no control of structures with frequent, serious errors
Vocabulary	Rich, precise vocabulary and use of idiomatic expressions	Vocabulary is adequate for addressing the topic	Limited vocabulary with some interference from English	Poor vocabulary use with frequent interference from English
Organization and Content	Very clear introduction and conclusion with well-developed ideas overall	Basic organization and idea development	Not completely organized, some ideas fragmented	No clear organization, ideas are poorly developed

on mastering each element as they work to become better writers. Consider the following generic writing rubric and be sure to consult the *REALIDADES Assessment Program* for many task-specific writing rubrics.

Self-evaluation

In order to better acquaint students with the writing rubrics that are used for formal evaluation, allow them the opportunity to apply the rubrics to a practice piece of writing. Students could discuss in pairs or small groups how they would apply the rubrics to each other's work.

Producing the final product

After you have returned students' corrected and graded essays, there is great value in having them rewrite the essay once again. If not, all of your work is easily ignored. By rewriting, students learn from their revisions. You may wish to require a rewrite for an additional grade or an improved original grade. Or, offer incentives to students who are willing to rewrite an essay until it is perfect. This can take two or three tries and often leads to a conference regarding difficult errors. One-on-one consultations bring great rewards in terms of student improvement. Writing fewer compositions with more rewrites will likely improve students' writing more than writing multiple compositions without attention to revision, editing, and rewriting. As students submit rewritten essays, require that they attach the new version on top of the previous version(s) so that re-examination is made easier. As the essay nears perfection, you will need only to glance at the previous version to verify that the new corrections have been inserted.

Achieving Syntactic Control

Teaching Tips

The role of grammar

Having a grammatical framework can speed language acquisition at the secondary level as well as increase students' accuracy. Grammatical accuracy is taken into consideration in the speaking and writing portions of the exam. Providing students with brief linguistic explanations can be beneficial. Grammar should never replace communicative efforts in language teaching; however, it should be considered a significant component to the development of fluency.

Conjugation mastery

Students retain information when they have an opportunity to apply it. As students learn new verb tenses, it is important that they have the chance to continue practicing the tenses that they have already mastered. In this way, students will be able to have success speaking and writing using correct forms. Give frequent, quick verb quizzes in the early-intermediate and intermediate levels to help students use each tense that has been introduced.

- Change the quiz to reflect which tenses the students have learned and omit those that they have not yet learned. As students add new tenses, the length of the verb quiz can grow to reflect their learning.

- Give verb quizzes two or three times a week at the beginning of a class period during the second semester of the course. By then, students are probably trying to manage several tenses.

- Provide space in the quiz box for students to demonstrate the English equivalent of the tense you are focusing on in a particular lesson.

- You may want to assign a list of verbs to be studied as well as the desired tenses the night before the quiz, so that students can be well prepared.

- At the beginning, quiz regular *-ar*, *-er*, and *-ir* verbs. Next, work on verbs with stem changes and spelling changes. Finally, work through the verb appendix in *REALIDADES*, quizzing on the high frequency irregular verbs.

Correcting verb quizzes

You may wish to have students correct their own quizzes with colored pens by reviewing the answers on an overhead. This way, students are aware of their own errors. This can be time consuming to complete in class, until students are familiar with the system. Collect students' corrected work and hold them accountable for

both the completion of the test as well as their own corrections. If you do not want to correct the quizzes in class, it is still helpful to require students to correct all errors, even small accent errors. Return the graded quizzes and have students correct their work in a different color, directly on the quiz. Students can find correct answers by consulting with a peer or by using the *REALIDADES* verb appendix. Have students keep their quizzes in a folder. Check the folders periodically to monitor improvement and assess what areas you need to focus on in future lessons.

Activities on realidades.com

Students can complete assignments and take quizzes on **realidades.com.** Teachers may want to set their preferences to give beginning students more than one opportunity to complete an activity or quiz before submitting it for a final grade. In this way students can focus on correcting their mistakes and learn from them.

Activities

Board game

Students can practice verb tenses with a board game. Make a game board by drawing a series of small squares on a piece of paper. Inside of each square, write a verb tense that is familiar to students. You will need spaces for start and finish, and you may want to add other spaces to the game, such as *Pierde tu turno* and *Avance dos espacios*. Then, make a stack of twenty cards for each game board. On each card, write the present tense form of a verb that has been studied. You may want to have students do this to save time and give them further practice. To play, have students get into groups of two or three. The first student should take a card and move to the first space on the board. He or she should change the verb on the card into the tense on the board. (See blank game board template, p. 48.) A correct answer allows the student to advance to the next space and have another turn. Students can use the appendix of their *REALIDADES* textbook to check for correct answers after the answer has been given. A student's turn lasts until an incorrect answer is given, at which point play

goes to the next student. The first person to complete the game board wins.

Using *REALIDADES* resources
Teaching Tips

The *REALIDADES* series provides multiple opportunities for students to develop their presentational writing skills. In *REALIDADES* A/B/1-3 the performance-based tasks found in *Presentación escrita* prompt students to produce a variety of written material. Each task guides students through the writing process and supports the process with focused strategies. Rubrics are provided for each task so that the expectations are clear for the students and the teacher.

In *REALIDADES* 4 a series of creative writing assignments found in *Taller* further the development of students' presentational writing skills. Each assignment includes a step-by-step guide that follows the writing process and leads to effective completion of the task.

Activities

On the AP* exam students write an essay based on information from three sources: a printed text, an audio source, and a chart or other graphic. The sources present various points of view on a given topic. Students need to synthesize the information and write a persuasive essay on the topic, using information from all three sources. Students have six minutes to read the essay topic and the printed material. They hear the audio material twice and then have 40 minutes to write the essay. As a result, Pre-AP* students should learn to prepare and write essays using input from multiple sources. In *REALIDADES* A/B/1-3 teachers can use the Integrated Performance Assessments found in the Communication Workbook with Test Preparation. These assessments begin with an interpretive activity, move to an interpersonal activity, and culminate in a presentational activity. Rubrics are provided for the interpersonal and presentational activities. Each chapter of *REALIDADES* 3 includes a section called *Integración* where students hear an audio selection, read

printed material, and use information from the two sources in a culminating presentational activity. In *REALIDADES* 4 each chapter's thematic organization facilitates the use of a listening activity and a reading activity to prepare a written response. For example, students could listen to the description of an environmental problem in Nicaragua (Vocabulary, Grammar and Communication Workbook, Activity 2-9, p. 30), listen to a student discuss her plan to deal with the problem (Student Activity Manual, Activity 2-16, p. 33), and read the survey on page 40 of the Student Edition. As a result of what the students heard and read, they should select one environmental issue that they believe exists in their community. Have students write a paragraph identifying the problem, explaining why it is a problem in the community, and describing what their community should do to solve it.

Preparing for Written Interpersonal and Presentational Communication

There are many different activities in the *REALIDADES* Student Editions and program components that develop the writing skill.

Student Edition

- Various writing activities: *REALIDADES* A/B/1-4
- *Presentación escrita: REALIDADES* A/B/1-3
- *Preparación para el examen: REALIDADES* A/B/1-3
- *Taller: REALIDADES* 4

Communication Workbook with Test Preparation

- Writing Activities: *REALIDADES* A/B/1-3
- Integrated Performance Assessments: *REALIDADES* A/B/1-3

Vocabulary, Grammar, and Communication Workbook

- *Taller–A escribir: REALIDADES* 4

Assessment Program

- Writing tasks: *REALIDADES* A/B/1-4

Speaking

Since the AP* Spanish Language and Culture Exam is a proficiency–based exam, the types of preparation that might be included along the preparation continuum are not so very different from the strategies that might be included in any Spanish course where proficiency is the goal. This is especially true of speaking proficiency. On the AP* Exam, students complete two separate speaking tasks: the first focuses on the Interpersonal mode of communication and the second on the Presentational mode. In the interpersonal section students participate in a simulated conversation. They have 1 minute to read a preview, including an introduction and an outline of each turn in the conversation. During the conversation students hear recorded prompts and have 20 seconds to record each of their responses. They should give thorough and appropriate responses. In the presentational section students make an oral presentation in response to a prompt on a cultural topic. In the presentation they compare features of their community to those found in an area of the Spanish-speaking world with which they are familiar. Students have 4 minutes to read the presentation topic and prepare their presentation. It should be well organized. Then they have 2 minutes to record their presentation. The strategies in this section are designed to help students develop interpersonal and presentational skills, to train them to respond quickly so that they can be successful on the Speaking portion of the AP* Exam, and to help them with circumlocution skills. Helping students become accustomed to evaluating their speech performances with a rubric similar to the one used in grading the AP* Exam will serve to shape their efforts.

Preparing for Presentational Speaking

Teaching Tips

Using *REALIDADES* resources

The Presentational Speaking section of the AP* exam asks students to speak at length on a specific topic and expects them to make cultural comparisons between their community and an area of the Spanish-speaking world. The *REALIDADES* series teaches students how to make oral presentations. In *REALIDADES* A/B/1-3 the performance-based tasks found in *Presentación oral* prompt students to make a variety of oral presentations. Each task provides a step-by-step guide through the process and supports the process with focused strategies. Rubrics are provided for each task so that the expectations are clear for the students and the teacher. In *REALIDADES* 4 students express and explain their opinions on thought provoking issues in *En su opinión;* in *Debate* they present and defend their position on a topic of current interest. The series also provides many resources for teaching culture and having students make cultural comparisons. In *REALIDADES* 1 and 2 students view *Videoculturas* to learn more about the culture related to the theme of a chapter. *REALIDADES* 1 and 2 also include *La cultura en vivo* and *Perspectivas del mundo hispano,* activities and reading selections that focus on the practices, products, and perspectives of the Spanish-speaking world. In *REALIDADES* A/B/1-3 culture notes and standards-based questions are found in a section called *Fondo cultural.* Every chapter in *REALIDADES* A/B/1-3 includes a *Lectura,* a culture-based reading selection. Every chapter test in *REALIDADES* A/B/1-3 includes a section that asks students to make a cultural comparison. Additionally, every chapter in *REALIDADES* 4 includes *Conéctate,* where students make in-depth cultural comparisons.

Making cultural comparisons

Students should begin making cultural comparisons in their first year of study and continue through the advanced levels. Students can begin with short, simple comparisons and progress to more in-depth comparisons at the advanced levels. In *REALIDADES* A/B/1 students can view the Chapter 1A *Videocultura* and make a cultural comparison by comparing their interests with those of the young people in the video. They should prepare a list in Spanish of 1 or 2 activities they like to do and 1 or 2 activities they do not like to do. Each student can tell a partner about the activities they have selected and this can serve as the basis for a simple conversation. In *REALIDADES* 2 and 3 students can work with a partner or in a small group to discuss the answers to questions found in the *Fondo cultural* (see *REALIDADES* 2, page 25 or page 308). They can also discuss the *¡Compruébalo!* and *¿Qué te parece?* topics from *Perspectivas del mundo hispano*. At the end of the partner or group discussion teachers should ask several groups to share their answers with the class. In that way the class can hear a variety of responses, possibly leading to further discussion. Additionally, students should practice the Cultures activity found in *Repaso del capítulo* (see REALIDADES 2, page 69). In *REALIDADES* 3 and 4 students can discuss more in-depth comparisons in the *Puente a la cultura* (*REALIDADES* 3) and the *Conéctate* (*REALIDADES* 4) sections of the books.

Brainstorming

After providing the class with a speaking prompt on a cultural topic, have the class brainstorm together what the outline of a speech on the topic might be. Have students include cultural examples from the Spanish-speaking world in the outline. Having students brainstorm key vocabulary words on the topic can also be helpful.

Pair practice

Allow students to practice presentations in pairs. You may want to have the "stronger" student in the pair complete the presentation first, while the second student listens. Before the second student begins, the pair should discuss the strengths and weaknesses of the first presentation. In this way, the first student provides a successful model for the second student.

Time limits

In beginning level classes, allow students unlimited time to practice and complete presentations. As they progress to the intermediate level, begin to impose time limits on both preparation and execution of the presentations.

Avoid writing first

Discourage students from trying to write out complete scripts for their presentations, since they will not be able to write two minutes worth of speech. At most, they should develop an outline that includes their example(s) from the Spanish-speaking world as well as key vocabulary words and conjugated verb forms.

Strategy for Students
Say what you know

Learning to work with the language that students know will help them avoid reverting to English when speaking. A useful rule for students to follow: If you can't say it, don't.

Sample Activities

Strategy for Students
Circumlocution

A critical skill for AP* students, especially in oral production, is the ability to circumlocute, or to express an idea without knowing precise vocabulary words. Being able to get an idea across in the target language, without knowing the exact vocabulary word, is a valuable AP* skill. At the earliest levels, students can use *la cosa que...* or *la cosa +* (adjective).

Group crossword practice

A group crossword activity is an excellent way to foster the development of circumlocution skills. This activity is most useful after students become familiar with the chapter vocabulary. Prepare a crossword puzzle using vocabulary words currently being studied. Write the answer for each puzzle entry on a separate index card, then create a set of these cards for each group that you will have. Divide students into groups. Give each group a blank puzzle and a set of answers. Distribute the answers evenly among all the members of a group, or have students draw them from a pile. Students must explain their words to the rest of the group without using the words themselves. The other group members must determine the word being described and write it in the appropriate space on the

puzzle. Allow students plenty of time to express themselves. This exercise should be done entirely in the target language. The added benefit to this activity, in addition to building circumlocution skills, is practice with vocabulary words. You will find crossword puzzles already created in the *REALIDADES* Leveled Vocabulary and Grammar Workbook: Core Practice. You may also find it helpful to use one of the many crossword puzzle generators available on the Internet. You will find a sample group crossword puzzle activity at the end of the Speaking section on pp. 46–47.

Variation: Depending on how familiar your students are with the vocabulary, you may wish to allow them to have their word list available during the activity. This activity is best suited for intermediate level students, since beginning students lack the resources to conduct this activity entirely in Spanish.

Strategy for Students
Connecting words

Provide students with basic connecting words such as: *pues, entonces, después, por eso, sin embargo,* and *a causa de* to help them connect their ideas. You can find further connecting words in the *Integración* features in *REALIDADES 3*.

Preparing for Interpersonal Speaking

Teaching Tips

Use questions and answers

The Interpersonal Speaking portion of the AP* Exam asks students to respond to questions as part of a simulated conversation and focuses on two skills: listening and speaking. The conversation takes place in a context which is described to the students in the introduction. Students must be able to understand each question and respond quickly and thoroughly. They are expected to respond in five separate instances. In Pre-AP* classes students should build their communication skills by answering a variety of information-seeking questions related to a real-world context. As their knowledge of verb tenses grows, students should

learn to pay attention to the verb tense in the questions and reply in the same time frame, if appropriate. The *REALIDADES* series provides many opportunities for students to ask and answer questions; the questions found in *Y tú, ¿qué dices?* are particularly helpful.

Recycle questions

By continuing to recycle questions from previous chapters and levels, you can help enhance your students' long-term retention. Students will also gain confidence as they learn to respond with ease to familiar material.

Participation points

Give daily oral participation points based on students' ability to respond, as well as their participation in the activities that are described in the Sample Activities section. You may also want to include their participation in pair and group work.

Sample Activities

Strategy for Students
Understanding is key

Your students' ability to understand the question asked has a direct impact on their ability to respond appropriately. Building strong listening comprehension skills increases success on this task.

Preguntas rápidas

Create a bank of *preguntas rápidas* that reflect questions found in normal, everyday conversations. Take these open-ended questions from textbook activities found throughout *REALIDADES*, like the *Y tú ¿qué dices?* activities. Or you may use the bank of *preguntas rápidas* found on pp. 196–199 of the *REALIDADES* Pre-AP* Resource Book. Write each question on a separate index card (some teachers write them on other objects like tongue depressors) and store them in a filing box or jar for regular use in class. Continue to add to the bank with each new chapter covered. Be sure to limit the questions to vocabulary and topics that are appropriate to your students' level of Spanish. Use them as warm-up activities, end-of-class activities, for team competitions, or simply for a break in the middle of class.

Strategy for Students

Keep moving on

Remind students that if they hear themselves make an error, they should correct it quickly and move on.

Quick response game

Create game boards that incorporate quick responses to *preguntas rápidas*. This will allow students to practice responding to everyday questions in a fun and challenging activity. Have students use the game board on p. 48 as a template. You can set the game up like this:

1. Create a list of the *preguntas rápidas* or use the bank of *preguntas rápidas* found on pp. 196–199 and number them. Approximately 35–50 questions can be used in a game at a time.

2. Create a game board by putting numbers in most spaces and some other game terms such as *pierdes tu turno, avanza dos pasos,* and *tira los dados otra vez* in the remaining spaces. Each box can contain two numbers, one above the other. The first time through the game, students should refer to the top number. The second time through, they should refer to the bottom number.

3. Form groups of 3 or 4 students. Each group needs one game board and one set of numbered questions. One student rolls a die and moves to the appropriate space. If the space has numbers, another student in the group reads the question indicated by the number. The first student has 20 seconds (or more if necessary) to answer the question as completely as possible. The group judges if it was an adequate response. If it was not, the student returns to the space where he or she was before beginning the turn.

4. Play continues two times through the game board. The winner is the first player to reach *El fin.*

One minute of questions *(For Levels 1 and 2)*

Prepare a handout with 20 questions pertinent to the current lesson. Use vocabulary and structures from the lesson and vary the subject of the question so that not all questions are about "you and I." (See the

following list of *preguntas rápidas.*) Here is how the activity works:

Sample Activity

Preguntas rápidas: REALIDADES 2, Tema 4

1. ¿Cómo eras de niño(a)?
2. ¿Dónde vivía tu familia hace diez años?
3. De niño(a), ¿cuáles eran tus juguetes favoritos?
4. Por lo general, ¿qué te molesta más?
5. ¿Qué te regalaron tus padres para tu último cumpleaños?
6. ¿Cuáles programas de tele veías de pequeño(a)?
7. ¿Obedecías a tus padres siempre, a menudo o a veces?
8. ¿Qué clases te interesaban más en la escuela primaria?
9. ¿Les permitían correr en la escuela primaria?
10. ¿Te portabas bien en la casa de los vecinos?
11. De niño(a), ¿les prestabas tus juguetes a los demás?
12. ¿Cómo celebraba tu familia los cumpleaños?
13. ¿En qué días hay fuegos artificiales?
14. ¿Los miembros de tu familia se abrazan?
15. ¿Te despides de tus padres cuando sales para la escuela?
16. ¿Cuándo naciste?
17. ¿Dónde se reúnen tú y tus amigos?
18. ¿Llorabas a menudo de niño(a)?
19. ¿Les cuentas chistes a tus amigos durante la clase de español?
20. ¿Cuántos alumnos había en tu clase el año pasado?

Preparation

- As a homework assignment or together in class, have students make flashcards with the questions on one side and the correct response on the other side. Check that the answers are correct so students can use the cards effectively.

- Allow students several days to prepare for the evaluation. Give them time to practice the questions in class with a partner. You may also choose to allow students to work in teams to ask the questions on the list to the opposite team in an attempt to stump their opponents.

Activity

- This activity is very effective when done a few days prior to the unit test. Each student sits with you for one minute and answers as many questions as possible.
- When asking the questions, you should use a stopwatch or other timing device.
- Allow students to answer as many questions as possible. Tell them if they answer more than eight questions in a minute, they will receive extra credit or any other type of reward that you may use. Their performances will amaze you.
- If students have trouble understanding you, remind them to ask you to say the questions more slowly. Since repeating questions takes up more time, it's a good idea to encourage students to answer as quickly as possible.
- Students should be allowed to skip a question. The clock keeps ticking, so skipping too many questions isn't a good idea.
- You may choose to allow beginning students to have a second chance to repeat the assessment (on their own time after school) if they are unhappy with their performance.

Evaluation

- Eight questions is the minimum necessary for a perfect score.
- Questions are scored as follows:

  3 points for a correct answer
  2 points for an answer with one error
  1 point for a response that answers the question, but has major flaws
  0 points for an inappropriate or unrelated response or a skipped question

- For easy scoring, use a set of questions on index cards and as the student answers, divide the cards into four separate piles: one for 3-point answers, one for 2-point answers, and so on. Count the total when the student finishes. The scores can be incorporated into students' chapter test grades, or separate speaking assessment grades could be given. Remember to shuffle the questions after

each student performs so that questions are asked randomly.

- Because this assessment takes only one minute per student, it is fairly easy to speak with all of the students in your class during one period. Have a reading, writing, or quiet review activity to engage students while individuals come forward for assessment.
- Create a set of questions for each unit and reuse them from year to year. You may consider recycling the questions as part of the semester exam.

Teaching Tips

Build interpersonal speaking skills

Students should know the conventions and strategies for participating in an authentic interpersonal activity. They should know how to initiate, maintain, and close a conversation. They should be able to give and elicit information and opinions as well as clarify meaning. Students should be engaged in the conversation and work to sustain and advance it. In authentic communication students ask questions to clarify meaning if they do not understand a partner's comment. They should listen carefully to their partner and respond in a natural, logical, and appropriate way. In addition, students should know a variety of conversational expressions (see *Expresiones útiles para conversar,* Appendix, *REALIDADES* A/B/1).

Sample Activities

Using *REALIDADES* resources

Since the simulated conversation on the AP* exam is a kind of role-play, the teacher might want to use the Situation Cards found in the Teacher's Resource Book (*REALIDADES* A/B/1-3) to build students' interpersonal skills. These cards guide an exchange between two students. Although both students know what the general topic is, neither knows exactly what the other will say. Consequently, students have to listen carefully in order to respond appropriately. As early as the first chapters of *REALIDADES* 1/A/B students can begin to develop the skills they will need on the AP* Exam. At the beginning, when students are learning how to communicate effectively, it is a good idea to have the teacher play the role of a student and model the strategies of effective interpersonal communication. It is also a good idea to have two students model a conversation and let the class discuss the successful strategies they saw and those that could have been used. This is difficult for students, so the teacher might consider giving extra credit or some kind of reward to the students who agree to the performance. Additional sources of interpersonal communication can be found in the *Repaso del capítulo* (See *Preparación para el examen*) and the interpersonal portion of the Integrated Performance Assessments (see Communication Workbook with Test Preparation).

Strategy for Students

Use your imagination

Students should practice using their imaginations. Sometimes students get trapped trying to say what they *want* instead of what they *know*. Remind them that their answers don't have to be true, they just have to be correct. Fiction is fine! It is important that students show the language skills they have and not flounder as they reach for language that they have not yet acquired.

Practice in pairs

In levels 3 and 4 students can work with the simulated conversation format on the AP* Exam. Have the students work in pairs. Provide them with the printed stimuli to read and have the opposite student provide the responses. Students should switch roles and repeat the exercise. Let students know that they should never fail to answer a question. Even if they are not sure of the answer, they should try to answer it by picking out something from the question and speaking about it. In this activity, where the purpose is to practice the exam format, the student who is reading the stimuli should not make any attempt to help the student who is responding.

Recording and Evaluating

Recording Students' Speech Samples

Recordings can be captured in a variety of ways:

- on **realidades.com**, using RealTalk
- in a language lab
- on individual recorders
- on a computer, using digital sound files

One of the most effective ways for your students to have their speech samples recorded is online at **realidades.com.** Using the RealTalk feature, *REALIDADES* 1/A/B- 3 students can record responses to the *Y tú, ¿qué dices?* questions, their Presentación oral, and the speaking sections of the chapter tests. In levels 1 and 2 students can record the *Pronunciación* activity; in level 3 they record *En voz alta* and hear themselves reading excerpts of literary selections. In REALIDADES 4 they record their responses in a variety of speaking activities called *Práctica oral*. Teachers can also create and upload their own speaking assignments. The recordings are saved online and can be exported to portfolios so that individual students can track their progress as they develop their speaking skills. If you have access to a language lab, students can record their speaking samples at the same time. If you have access to a few computers, students can work in groups. While one member of the group is recording, the other members could work quietly on an alternate activity. It is advisable to seat the students who have not recorded far enough away from the computers that they do not distract the speakers. If you do not have access to computers, you can use handheld recorders. Give each student a copy of the task to be recorded and follow the procedures for recording in groups. This is also a good way to allow all students enough time to make their recordings. If there are groups of five students and the recordings last two minutes each, the entire group can be finished in 15–20 minutes.

Intermediate and advanced students could be asked to make weekly two-minute recordings, completed outside of class as a homework assignment. They should follow one of the procedures described below. You may

choose to assign a homework completion credit for many of the recordings and formally evaluate the recordings as time allows. Students could also exchange recordings with a classmate for peer feedback.

Recordings can be captured in a variety of ways.

1. On individual recorders:
   a. Students can record, one at a time, one after another, on the same recorder in the classroom. Students can hear their own work and other students' work. You and the students can provide constructive feedback and suggestions for improvement as you listen to the recordings in class.
   b. To practice simulated conversations on an individual recorder, two machines are needed. A CD or DVD player plays the introduction and the prompts. On a second machine, students record their responses, one after another.
2. In a language lab:
   This is truly the most effective way to simulate proper AP* recordings. Each student records a speech sample under your direction or by listening to a master recording. Students can record onto a cassette tape, which they then give to you. Or, if the lab is digital, the sound files can all be burned on to one CD, making your load lighter by not having to carry bags or boxes of cassettes.
3. On voice-mail:
   Shorter recordings (six to seven sentences describing a given picture as a homework assignment) can be accomplished by recording it at a voicemail number that you have at your school. If possible, you can even set up different voicemail boxes for each class.
4. On a computer, using digital sound files:
   While there are programs available to compress and store sound files varying from setting to setting, the basic concept is to use the sound recording device on the computer and capture a recording. Hand–held computer microphones made for this purpose can be helpful. Once recorded, students can save their sound files in a designated folder on a school server for

you to access. Students can also save their sound files on a local machine and e-mail them to you as an attachment.

5. Students can record speaking samples online at **realidades.com**. Once a teacher has assigned a speaking activity, students login, click on the speaking assignment, activate the recorder, speak, and save the sample. Teachers and students can retrieve the sample for evaluation and discussion.

Evaluating Students' Speech Samples

Pair and group work practices can be very effective; however, by creating opportunities for students to record their speech samples, you will be able to provide easier and more thorough evaluations. Feedback is an invaluable step in helping your students improve their speaking skills. Once the recordings are done, you can either grade the samples yourself, or have your students grade them. Either way, an evaluation rubric is essential to insure consistency and fairness. Be sure students understand what is expected of them to successfully complete the task. Before recording, students should be given time to study the rubric and should understand how it applies to their task. This can be accomplished by playing a few sample recordings for the class, followed by a discussion about how each sample would be scored. Once trained, students can generally give each other appropriate feedback and become better prepared to meet your expectations. Student-evaluated samples should not be graded, but rather should serve as practice. You may choose to evaluate your students' speech samples yourself for a formal evaluation from time to time. Students could also save their recordings and choose their best sample to be submitted for a grade.

The rubric on p. 49 represents standards similar to those used to evaluate students' speech samples during the grading of the AP* Spanish Language and Culture Exam. Familiarizing students with AP* expectations from their first year of Spanish will help guide their efforts. The rubric can be used with *any* speech sample, regardless of the task.

Nombre

Clase

Fecha

Group Crossword Puzzle Clue Cards
REALIDADES 3, Capítulo 7

Horizontal 4. medir	Horizontal 7. cubrir	Horizontal 11. Luna	Horizontal 12. observatorio	Horizontal 14. escritura
Horizontal 15. mito	Horizontal 17. diseño	Horizontal 18. universo	Horizontal 19. sagrado	Horizontal 20. creencia
Vertical 1. excavar	Vertical 2. pesar	Vertical 3. arqueólogo	Vertical 5. Tierra	Vertical 6. ruinas
Vertical 8. redondo	Vertical 9. pirámide	Vertical 10. conejo	Vertical 13. inexplicable	Vertical 16. sombra

Realidades

Group Crossword Puzzle Activity
REALIDADES 3, Capítulo 7

Work in groups to complete this crossword puzzle. Take turns describing the words on the cards that you have been given without mentioning the words themselves. The other members of your group will try to fill in the crossword puzzle with the appropriate words based on your clues.

Realidades

Quick Response Game Board

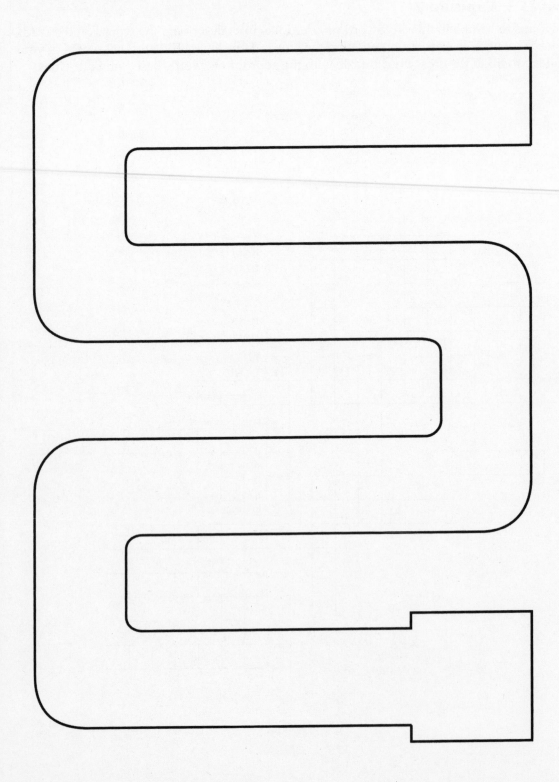

Realidades

Score	4	3	2	1
Content	Thoroughly and completely addresses the topic or task	Adequately completes the topic or task	Addresses the topic in a very basic, limited manner	Irrelevant to the topic or with a very limited amount of speech provided
Structures	Excellent control of structures	Good control of structures with a few minor errors	Weak control of structures with frequent errors	Little to no control of structures with frequent, serious errors
Vocabulary	Rich, precise vocabulary and use of idiomatic expressions	Vocabulary is adequate for addressing the topic	Limited vocabulary with some interference from English	Poor vocabulary use with frequent interference from English
Fluency**	Considerable ease; pronunciation is virtually free of of serious errors	Task completed with ease; good pronunciation	Some hesitation; possible pronunciation errors	Halting and hesitation; frequent serious pronunciation errors that interfere with communication

In *REALIDADES* 3 and 4 teachers may want to add rubrics for Culture if the speaking task asks students to make cultural comparisons.

**For the purpose of the AP* Examination, "fluency" is considered the ease and natural flow of speech, free of hesitation, halting, and groping for words. It encompasses how all of the parts of speech fit smoothly together. It does *not* imply the rate or speed of the speech sample.

Note: The *REALIDADES Assessment Program* contains several sets of rubrics to be applied to specific assessment tasks. Acquainting students with the use of rubrics sets the bar for their performance and helps them to understand the grading criteria.

Preparing for Spoken Interpersonal and Presentational Communication

There are many different activities in the *REALIDADES* Student Editions and program components that develop the speaking skill.

Student Edition

• Various paired and group activities: *REALIDADES* A/B/1-4
• *Y tú, ¿qué dices?: REALIDADES A/B/1-3*
• *Presentación oral: REALIDADES A/B/1-3*
• *Preparación para el examen: REALIDADES A/B/1-3*
• *Debate: REALIDADES 4*
• *En su opinión: REALIDADES 4*
• *¡Así lo expresamos!: REALIDADES 4*

Teacher's Resource Book and realidades.com

• Communicative Pair Activities: *REALIDADES* A/B/1-3
• Situation Cards: *REALIDADES* A/B/1-3

Communication Workbook with Test Preparation

• Integrated Performance Assessments: *REALIDADES* A/B/1-3

TPR Stories

• Stories: *REALIDADES* A/B/1-2

realidades.com: RealTalk!

• Paired practices: *REALIDADES* A/B/1-3
• *Presentación oral: REALIDADES A/B/1-3*
• *Práctica oral: REALIDADES 4*

Assessment Program

• Speaking tasks: *REALIDADES* A/B/1-4

Pre-AP* Vocabulary Building

One of the most fundamental elements for AP* success is quick access to a rich variety of vocabulary resources. A wide range of vocabulary is essential for successful performance on the interpretive listening and reading sections of the AP* Exam. Vocabulary is also a necessary tool for self-expression on the interpersonal writing and speaking as well as the presentational writing and speaking portions of the AP* Exam. The key to building lexical success is thorough learning that leads to long-term retention. By teaching students a variety of study skills, incorporating daily activities that focus on vocabulary acquisition, and testing vocabulary in ways that require higher order thinking skills, you can enhance students' in-depth vocabulary retention.

Effective Methods for Studying Vocabulary

Teaching Tips

Since students all have different learning styles, it is critical that you present a variety of strategies to help them to learn vocabulary effectively. Study skills should be directly taught in the first year of Spanish, and should be reinforced regularly throughout that year and at subsequent levels of study. Introduce the strategies discussed here (along with those that you know and find effective) directly to the students, and remind them of how to apply each one as they see new vocabulary in each chapter.

The very act of making the flashcards, tapes, or sheets causes students to interact with the vocabulary and allows them to begin to retain it. Have students try a variety of strategies at the beginning. For example, have them use one type of study strategy during the first chapter, a different type for the second chapter, and yet another type of strategy while working on the third chapter. After students have tried a variety of approaches,

allow them to choose which method works best for them.

Flashcards

Have students cut 3"x 5" index cards into thirds for the ideal size. Give students a rubber band to put around each lesson's cards or have students store them in a small resealable plastic bag. A hole can be punched in the bag so that the cards can be carried in students' notebooks. Have students store the cards from every lesson throughout the semester in a common place and encourage them to use the cards for an organized final exam review.

Have students make a new set of flashcards immediately after you present the information in the *Vocabulario en contexto* section of each *REALIDADES* chapter. Have students clearly print the Spanish vocabulary word or phrase on one side and write its English equivalent on the reverse side. It may be helpful if they create a color scheme to help them remember a word's part of speech (verbs / green, adjectives / purple, etc.). Also, students may find it helpful to write feminine nouns in one color and masculine nouns in another.

Students can work with the interactive flashcards found in the eText on **realidades .com**. As students work through the set of flashcards, they have a number of options. For example, they can choose to practice with the words and their meaning or the pictures of the words and their meaning. They can shuffle the deck to change the order of the flashcards. As the students learn the vocabulary, they can designate the words they have learned so that they focus on the words they have yet to learn. These options, and others, make the interactive flashcards an effective and engaging way to learn vocabulary. As an alternative, students can use PowerPoint to develop electronic flashcards. The first click makes the Spanish or English word appear, and after a delay, the translation can come onto the screen. Be sure that they make screens that work from Spanish to English as well as from English to Spanish. Have them duplicate the entire file so that one set of vocabulary words can be easily stored for exam review. Suggest that they have a second

set from which they can continually delete words as they memorize them. Students can also use clip art in place of English when creating electronic flashcards.

Suggest that students spend five minutes a day studying the flashcards. They can do this alone or with another person. Even if that other person does not speak Spanish, students can practice spelling the word to them after the other person says its English meaning. Point out to them that even though they may not be studying the cards for very long each day, they are becoming much more familiar with the vocabulary every time they use their flashcards. Have them study each side, so that they practice the Spanish to English as well as the English to Spanish. As they get to know certain words by heart, have them take those cards out of the pile so that they may focus on the more difficult words. In this way, students will eliminate the extra work of reviewing all words and will be able to focus on those that they require more practice to learn. Have them put all of the words back into the pile a day or two before a test for a final review.

Flashcards can be an extremely effective classroom management tool. If students finish a task before the rest of the class, have them use the class time to study their flashcards. They will get their study time in and you will have more time to focus on helping students finish a task instead of monitoring those who have already finished.

Audio vocabulary drills

Have students study vocabulary by listening to it being read repeatedly. Using the eText at **realidades.com**, students can play and replay the vocabulary presented in the *Vocabulario en contexto* and reviewed in the *Repaso del Capítulo* sections of their textbook. They can also download the audio files of these vocabulary sections for additional practice. At the beginning of a chapter, students may want to record the vocabulary on their own digital recorders. Suggest that they say the Spanish word first, pause for a few seconds, and then say the corresponding word in English. Whether they download the vocabulary from the eText or make their own recordings, encourage students to listen to the recordings on the bus, at home while they do chores, or when they are in the car. While auditory studying will provide extra vocabulary comprehension and retention, it does not give students the necessary spelling practice they need with new vocabulary. Therefore, it is wise to suggest that they combine this method with a visual form of studying. For that reason, students can view the Videohistoria, with the new vocabulary displayed, in their eText at **realidades.com**.

Studying vocabulary from a prepared list

It may be helpful for students to simply copy the words on a two-column chart and study them as a list. To make the chart, have them fold a lined piece of paper in half and print the vocabulary from the chapter in the two columns. Have them write one Spanish word per line going down the left side of the paper, and the corresponding English word going down the right side of the paper. (This can also be done electronically.) Make sure that students write the words close to the center-fold of the page, instead of on the left-hand side of each column. (See the sample on p. 49 for a clear picture of how to arrange the words on the page.) Students may want to use different colored pens or text fonts to distinguish gender, part of speech, or other vocabulary features.

To use the list, have students cover the folded paper with another paper or a book. Suggest that they look at only one word at a time, say the word, and then say its meaning. They should check for accuracy after each word. Encourage them to study from Spanish to English and vice-versa. Have them highlight the more difficult words that they need to spend more time on. It may be helpful for students to keep all of their vocabulary lists in a binder so that they can easily access them during other activities and use them to study for midterm or final exams.

Sample Vocabulary Study List
REALIDADES 1, Chapter 6A

la alfombra	rug
el armario	closet
la cama	bed
la cómoda	dresser
las cortinas	curtains
el cuadro	painting
el despertador	alarm clock
el dormitorio	bedroom
el espejo	mirror
el estante	shelf, bookshelf
la lámpara	lamp
la mesita	night table
la pared	wall
el disco compacto	compact disc
el equipo de sonido	sound (stereo) system
el lector DVD	DVD player
el televisor	television set
el video	videocassette
la videocasetera	VCR
¿De qué color...?	What color . . . .?
los colores	colors
amarillo, -a	yellow
anaranjado, -a	orange
azul	blue
blanco, -a	white
gris	gray
marrón	brown
morado, -a	purple
negro, -a	black
rojo, -a	red
rosado, -a	pink
verde	green
bonito, -a	pretty
feo, -a	ugly
grande	large
importante	important
mismo, -a	same
pequeño, -a	small
propio, -a	own
a la derecha (de)	to the right (of)
a la izquierda (de)	to the left (of)
mejor(es) que	better than
el, la mejor	the best
los, las mejores	the best
menos...que	less, fewer . . . than
peor(es) que	worse than
el, la peor	the worst
los, las peores	the worst
la cosa	thing
para mí	in my opinion, for me
para ti	in your opinion, for you
la posesión	possession

Activities

Quiz Show

Have students work in groups of four and use their flashcards to host a quiz show. Three students are contestants and one is the host. The host will use his or her flashcards to quiz the other three students for two rounds. Each correct answer gets those students a point. A new host is chosen every two rounds. After all eight rounds, the student with the most points wins the game.

Student Strategy

Study aloud

Remind students that they shouldn't just think the words as they study. Instead, they should say them out loud. This helps them to get auditory reinforcement of their learning.

Self-quiz

Have students place their flashcards in a stack, English side up. Then, have them write the correct corresponding word for each card on a separate piece of paper. Have them check for accuracy and correctly rewrite any words they missed.

Beat the clock

If students have made audio recordings of the vocabulary, have them use the recordings for a game in class. Give pairs of students a cassette or CD player to play one of the recordings. Have them play the recording and take turns trying to say the meaning of the word on the tape during the pause. Students who identify the meaning before it is given on the recording are given a point. The student with the most points at the end of the vocabulary list wins.

Classroom Vocabulary Practice

Vocabulary is one area where students can have fun and be actively engaged in their learning. Hands-on vocabulary activities that are incorporated into the daily lesson make class fun and foster long-term vocabulary retention.

Teaching Tips

Games

Try to play vocabulary games with your students at least once per chapter. Students learn more easily in the low-stress environment that games provide. As long as students are engaged in the activity, it tends to benefit them as much as, if not more than, controlled academic activities. Prizes are a great motivator for students, too. Whether they are in the sixth grade or seniors in high school, students are always eager to win and receive a prize or extra credit point.

Make it a race

Consider making any vocabulary activity (such as a crossword puzzle or a vocabulary cloze passage using a word bank from the Leveled Vocabulary and Grammar Workbook: Core Practice as a race. Allow students to work in pairs and reward the first two or three pairs who finish correctly. Once the winners have been determined, quickly bring the activity to a close by having the winners share the correct answers with the rest of the class. Since all of the sections of the AP* Exam are timed, teaching students to work quickly and under the pressure of time is very beneficial.

Cut-apart cards

For each chapter, prepare a handout on which you have 25 squares, with one vocabulary word written in Spanish on each square. When possible, you may want to include pictures of vocabulary words instead. (See the *REALIDADES Teacher's Resource Book* for

chapter-specific clip art.) You could also have students print the Spanish words in each of the 25 squares. Give each student a handout and a pair of scissors. Have them cut the squares apart and put their initials on each card, so that they can distinguish their own from a partner's. The students should keep the cards in a small plastic bag to use for each of the activities below. Keep a separate shoe-box for each chapter to store the students' cut-apart cards in your classroom.

Activities Using Cut-Apart Cards

Rápido

Have students work in pairs and place one set of cards face down on the desk. To play, have one student flip the top card over. The first student to say the meaning of what is on the card keeps the card. If neither student knows the word on the card, they look it up in their chapter vocabulary list and then place it back on the bottom of the pile. Students play until the pile is gone. The person with the most cards is the winner.

Pescar

Have students place two sets of cards face down in a scrambled pile. Each student takes three cards. The goal is to find a match for each card. To play, one student asks his or her partner if they have a certain card. For example: *¿Tienes "alfombra"?* The partner either hands over the card and says, *Aquí la tienes*, or says, *No. Ve a pescar*. If students get a match, they go again. Students play until the pile is gone. If a student runs out of cards, he or she takes another from the pile. The winner is the student that has the most matched pairs when the time is up.

Memoria

Have students work in pairs to play this memory game. Pairs should mix their cards and put them face down in rows on the desk. One at a time, students turn over one card from the desks, trying to make a match. Have students say the word out loud as they turn the picture over. If a match is made, an extra turn is granted. Students can play under a time limit or until all pairs have been matched. The student with the most matches wins. However, students must be able to identify the meaning of each matched pair in order for the pair to count!

Bingo

Ask students to place their own cards face up on their desks in five rows of five. Then, call out words from the vocabulary list. Students turn cards over, face down, when a word on their desk has been called out. A complete row of face down cards is a "bingo."

Definiciones

When students have finished using the cards for other activities, challenge them to a definition race. Use a stopwatch to time students in a race for who can write the meanings of the words on the back of each card the fastest. For pictures, students should write the word in Spanish. For words in Spanish, students should write the English meaning. Give each student their time, and have them log their times in their notebooks. Challenge them to improve their times after each chapter. The cards can also be used as flashcards for study.

Additional Vocabulary Activities

The Elimination Game

Using a permanent marker, write a list of current vocabulary on a transparency. Be sure to have at least one word for each student in the class. If your class has fewer students than there are words on the vocabulary list, it is wise to choose the words that require extra practice. As a warm-up to the game, have students work in pairs to quickly say what each word means. Next, each student secretly writes any two Spanish words from the list on a tiny slip of paper. When play begins, students hold their papers in their hands and stand next to their desks. Go around to the individual students, and call out one of the words on the overhead and the English meaning of that word. When a word is said, cross it off of the list. Once both of the words on a student's papers have been called, that student must sit down; he or she has been eliminated. Continue around the room. Even students that have been eliminated are allowed their turn to call out a word still remaining on the list. If a student doesn't know any of the remaining words on the list, the play passes to the next student, who then chooses a word from the list. The winner is the last student still standing with a word that hasn't been called.

As a follow-up, circle the four most difficult words to remember. Ask students to work in pairs and use each of the four words in a complete sentence. Have pairs share their sentences with the class.

Draw and Guess

Have students work with a partner. All pairs should be lined up in a straight row facing each other. Give each pair of students scrap paper to draw on. Stand on one side of the room and hold up a vocabulary word in Spanish from the current *REALIDADES* chapter. Be sure to write in big, bold letters. Those students facing you must draw the picture of the word for their partner. Those students with their backs to you must guess what their partner has drawn. The first person to guess the word wins the point for their pair. Have students stand and say the word loudly so that you are sure who was first to respond correctly. After the first round, move to the opposite side of the room and hold up a new word. Play continues with the opposite person drawing and the partner guessing. The pair with the most points wins.

Matamoscas

Enlarge the clip art images from the *Teacher's Resource Book* and tape them to the chalkboard or display the clip art from the Presentation Express Premium DVD. Divide the class into two teams. One member from each team approaches the images holding a fly swatter. Call out a word in Spanish that represents one of the pictures being displayed. The student who swats the corresponding picture first scores a point for the team. Tell students to leave the swatter in place so that you can tell which picture was swatted. Once a student wins two points in a row, a new team member moves forward to swat. The team with the most points after you have called out all of the vocabulary words wins. As an alternative, you can write the words in Spanish on the board and play as above, calling out the word in English.

Testing Vocabulary

Teaching Tips

When to test vocabulary

Consider giving a short vocabulary quiz two or three days prior to each chapter test. This allows students to focus on vocabulary first. Then for the chapter test, they can focus more on structures and on the bigger picture of putting the chapter elements together. Creating a vocabulary test that encompasses all of the vocabulary covered during half of the year and another one just prior to the final exam is an excellent way to reinforce long-term recall of vocabulary.

How to test vocabulary

It is beneficial for students if you move beyond any sort of simple vocabulary assessments, such as writing the word which corresponds to a picture, giving the Spanish definitions for a list of words in English, or matching Spanish words with given definitions in English. Testing in a way that causes students to *use* vocabulary, synthesize meaning, and move beyond mere recall will enhance their retention. A vocabulary quiz should be an opportunity to *use* vocabulary, rather than a memorization drill. A chapter vocabulary quiz might include some or all of the following:

- Banks of words that are used to complete sentences or paragraphs (see examples on p. 40 of the *REALIDADES 2* Leveled Vocabulary and Grammar Workbook: Core Practice or pp. 171–173 of the *REALIDADES 3 Assessment Program*)

- Multiple-choice sentence completions (see p. 136 of the *REALIDADES 3 Assessment Program* or the *ExamView* Test Banks multiple-choice segments)

- True and False sentences that contain vocabulary from the current chapters

- A short list of vocabulary words in Spanish that students are asked to use in a sentence or paragraph (When testing in this fashion, it is important that you make students understand that their sentence must *clearly* demonstrate the meaning of the word for credit.)

- Groups of four or five words in Spanish with one word that does not logically belong to the group because of its meaning (not because of its gender or part of speech)

- Matching activities for synonyms or antonyms in Spanish

Grading techniques will vary depending on what types of quiz you decide to give. Be sure to consider students' use of the word as well as the accuracy with which they write it.

Levels A/B/1
Resource Support

Introduction: Pre-AP* Student and Teacher Activity Sheets

The activities in this section are intended as simulations of the types of tasks and skills that students are asked to engage in on the AP* Spanish Language and Culture Exam. The level of difficulty has been adjusted to meet students' AP* abilities and obtained skills along their journey through *Realidades* 1, 2, 3, and 4. Some of the activities will cause students to stretch themselves, but this sort of rigor will serve to prepare students for the challenge of AP*. The activities themselves can be used as such—classroom exercises. Or, they can be used as additions to a chapter assessment. If they are used as assessments, it is recommended that students have had practice accomplishing a similar exercise in class, first.

Using rubrics, or as they are called by the AP* Program, scoring guidelines, is an essential component to familiarizing students with the caliber of work that is expected of them. Time used in class to allow students to critique each others' work in groups using scoring guidelines is time well spent. Once students are familiar with this sort of evaluation, the teacher can assign and collect a task for formal grading, using the same types of scoring guidelines.

For Level 1, the timed nature of the activities is left very open, building gradually to suggested time and length of the final student products. At first, the goal should be to familiarize students with the types of tasks they will need to be able to do. As students' skills mature and improve, it will be essential to require that the tasks be performed within a given amount of time and that the tasks produced conform to a specified length.

Finally, the many exercises across the *Realidades* suite of activities and components, when used together, will be vital for the preparation of successful future AP* students. AP* is about moving beyond the memorization of lists of vocabulary and verbs and into language use situations. It is about what students know and can do with the Spanish that they have learned.

Realidades A/B/1

Para empezar

Pre-AP* Resource Chart

	Teacher's Edition		Ancillaries
	Page #	Activity	
Vocabulary	p. 8	Pre-AP* Support	*realidades.com*
Listening	p. 8	Pre-AP* Support	*Pre-AP* Resource Book:* p. 61
Reading			*Teacher's Resource Book:* Situation cards, p. 16 *Pre-AP* Resource Book:* p. 61
Speaking			*Pre-AP* Resource Book:* p. 61
Writing	p. 14	Differentiated Instruction: Advanced Learners/Pre-AP*	*Pre-AP* Resource Book:* p. 61
	p. 18	Differentiated Instruction: Advanced Learners/Pre-AP*	
Integrated Skills	p. 13 p. 20 p. 21	Act. 7 Act. 4 Act. 5	*Communication Workbook:* Integrated Performance Assessment, p. 226

Student Activity 1
Interpersonal Writing

Directions: Read the comments that Joaquín posted on his blog. Write a short comment to post on his blog. Tell him about yourself and be sure to answer his questions.

¡Hola! Soy Joaquín. ¿Cómo te llamas tú? Mi cumpleaños es el 19 de septiembre. ¿Cuál es la fecha de tu cumpleaños? Soy estudiante en la escuela secundaria. Tengo siete clases. Como hoy es jueves, tengo la clase de matemáticas. Mi clase es a las ocho y media. El profesor de la clase es el Señor Martínez. Y tú, ¿cuántas clases tienes?

Student Activity 2
Interpersonal Speaking

Directions: Practice the following with a classmate. Imagine that you just won a radio call-in contest. Give the spelling of your name and your telephone number to the radio station employee so that someone may contact you to arrange for you to pick up your prize.

Student Activity 3
Interpersonal Speaking

Practice this exercise aloud with a classmate, switching roles so that each may have a turn being Student A and Student B, respectively.

Directions: Imagine that it is the first day of class and your teacher has asked you to get to know one other person in the room. A classmate will ask you several questions. Respond to his or her questions:

STUDENT A: Buenas tardes. Me llamo _____. Y tú, ¿cómo te llamas?

STUDENT B: _____

STUDENT A: ¿Cómo estás hoy?

STUDENT B: _____

STUDENT A: ¿Cuál es la fecha de tu cumpleaños?

STUDENT B: _____

STUDENT A: Repite, por favor.

STUDENT B: _____

STUDENT A: Muy bien. ¿Qué hora es?

STUDENT B: _____

STUDENT A: Pues, adiós.

STUDENT B: _____

Pre-AP* Resource Chart

	Teacher's Edition		Ancillaries
	Page #	**Activity**	
Vocabulary	p. 29	Pre-AP* Support	*Assessment Program:* Prueba 1A-2, pp. 15–16
			realidades.com
Listening	p. 35	Pre-AP* Support	*Video Program* Chapter 1A
			Video Teacher's Guide Chapter 1A
			Communication Workbook: Act. 6, p. 11
			Pre-AP Resource Book:* pp. 64–65
Reading	p. 35	Pre-AP* Support	*TPR Stories,* El día horrible de Juan Pablo, p. 22
	p. 38	Act. 19	*Realidades* para hispanohablantes: ¡Adelante!, Lectura 1, p. 22
			Realidades para hispanohablantes: Lectura 2, p. 24
			Pre-AP Resource Book:* pp. 64–65
Speaking	p. 29	Pre-AP* Support	*Assessment Program*: Examen de 1A, Hablar, p. 22
	p. 43	🗨 Presentación oral	*Teacher's Resource Book, Para empezar–Tema 4:* Communicative Activities, pp. 50–53
			Teacher's Resource Book, Para empezar–Tema 4: Situation cards, p. 54
			Realidades para hispanohablantes: Presentación oral, p. 27
			TPR Stories: Personalized Mini-situations, pp. 18–21
			Pre-AP Resource Book:* pp. 64–65
Writing	p. 35	Pre-AP* Support	realidades.com
	p. 36	Differentiated Instruction: Advanced Learners/Pre-AP*	*Realidades* para hispanohablantes: Act. O, p. 25
			Assessment Program: Examen 1A, Escribir, p. 22
	p. 38	Act. 19	*Communication Workbook:* Act. 13, p.17
	p. 41	Supplemental Pre-AP* Activity	*Communication Workbook:* Practice Test, pp. 230–232
			ExamView: Pre-AP* Question Bank
			Pre-AP Resource Book:* pp. 64–65
Integrated Skills	p. 33	Act. 12	*Communication Workbook: Integrated Performance Assessment,* p. 229
	p. 35	Act. 14	

	Teacher's Edition		Ancillaries
	Page #	**Activity**	
Vocabulary	p. 57	Pre-AP* Support	*Realidades* para hispanohablantes: Act. B, p. 19 *Assessment Program:* Prueba 1B-2, p. 28–29 *realidades.com*
Listening	p. 57	Pre-AP* Support	*Communication Workbook:* Act. 9, p. 24 *Video Program* Chapter 1B *Video Teacher's Guide* Chapter 1B *Pre-AP* Resource Book:* pp. 64–65
Reading			*Realidades* para hispanohablantes: Lectura 1, p. 42 *Realidades* para hispanohablantes: Lectura 2, p. 44 *Communication Workbook:* Practice Test, pp. 236–238 *realidades.com* *TPR Stories:* ¡Marilú no es simpática!, p. 27 *Pre-AP* Resource Book:* pp. 64–65
Speaking	p. 57 p. 60	Pre-AP* Support Differentiated Instruction: Advanced Learners/Pre-AP*	*Assessment Program:* Examen 1B, Hablar, p. 36 *Teacher's Resource Book, Para empezar–Tema 4:* Communicative Activities, pp. 84–87 *Teacher's Resource Book, Para empezar–Tema 4:* Situation cards, p. 88 *TPR Stories:* Personalized Mini-situations, pp. 24–26 *Pre-AP* Resource Book:* pp. 64–65
Writing	p. 53 p. 60 p. 63 p. 65 p. 67	Pre-AP* Support Differentiated Instruction: Advanced Learners/Pre-AP* Act. 21 Pre-AP* Support Presentación escrita	*Communication workbook:* Act. 13, p. 28 *Communication Workbook:* Practice Test, pp. 236–238 *Realidades* para hispanohablantes: Presentación escrita, p. 47 *Assessment Program:* Examen 1B, Escribir, p. 36 *realidades.com* *ExamView:* Pre-AP* Question Bank *Pre-AP* Resource Book:* pp. 64–65
Integrated Skills	p. 56 p. 57	Act. 10, Act. 11, 12	*Communication Workbook:* Integrated Performance Assessment, p. 235

Teacher Activity 1
Interpretive Communication, Audio and Audiovisual Texts

Before the students watch the *Realidades* Video for *Capítulo* 1A, play the video with the TV screen covered. Use the audio portion to engage students in the Dictogloss activity on p. 15. Once the students have completed the steps to the Dictogloss activity, uncover the TV screen, watch the video, then have them complete the video activities on pp. 8-9 of the *Realidades* Writing, Audio & Video Workbook.

Teacher Activity 2
Interpretive Communication, Print Texts

As an alternative, photocopy the *Realidades* Video Script for *Capítulo* 1A, *A primera vista: Y tú, ¿cómo eres?* Distribute the copies to students. In pairs, have students read the script aloud with a classmate and subsequently complete the video activities on pp. 8-9 of the *Realidades* Writing, Audio & Video Workbook. For follow-up and closure, allow students to watch the *Realidades* Video.

Teacher Activity 3
Special Focus, Scoring Guidelines and Writing Tasks

Have students complete the *Amigo por correspondencia* assignment found on p. 67 of the *Realidades* Student Textbook. Collect the assignment and select four or five student samples. Type those samples for photocopying so that the work will be anonymous. Distribute copies of the sample student work to the class. Distribute copies of the scoring guidelines found on p. 49 of this book. Since this is a writing task, the *Fluency* category on the bottom row can be ignored at this time. Have students read the first sample aloud with a partner. As a class, discuss where on the range of scoring guidelines the particular piece falls. Repeat this activity with subsequent samples. Making students familiar with how to apply scoring guidelines will help them engage more effectively in group evaluations to take place later during the course.

Student Activity 1
Presentational Speaking

Listen to the "match up" recording that accompanies the *Examen* 1A, pp. T60-T61 in the *Realidades* Assessment Program. Decide which one of the five people, based on their voicemail messages, you would most like to be friends with. Be sure to cite reasons for your choices based on what you heard as well as on your own likes and dislikes. You will have three minutes to prepare your answer and one minute to present your response to a classmate.

Student Activity 2
Interpersonal Speaking

Work with a partner to write complete-sentence answers to the following questions. Be sure to verify the correctness of your answers. Then, use the questions (and answers) to play *Preguntas rápidas* (see p. 41) or to prepare for *One minute of questions* (For Levels 1 and 2) (see p. 41).

1. ¿Cómo te llamas? _____
2. ¿Cómo eres? _____
3. Según tus amigos, ¿cómo eres? _____
4. ¿Eres más serio(a) o más gracioso(a)? _____
5. ¿Qué te gusta hacer? _____
6. ¿Qué no te gusta hacer? _____
7. ¿Te gusta pasar tiempo con tu familia? _____
8. ¿Cuál deporte te gusta practicar? _____
9. ¿Te gusta cantar o dibujar? _____
10. ¿Te gusta trabajar mucho? _____
11. ¿Cómo es tu profesor(a) favorito(a)? _____
12. ¿Como es tu mejor amigo(a)? _____
13. ¿Cómo se llama tu amigo(a)? _____
14. ¿Cómo es un buen estudiante? _____
15. ¿Cuál color te gusta más? _____
16. ¿Te gusta hablar por teléfono con amigos? _____
17. ¿Te gusta ir a la escuela? _____
18. ¿Eres trabajador(a) en la clase? _____
19. ¿Quién es deportista? _____
20. ¿Quién es perezoso(a)? _____

Pre-AP* Resource Chart

	Teacher's Edition		Ancillaries
	Page #	**Activity**	
Vocabulary	p. 77	Pre-AP* Support	*Assessment Program:* Prueba 2A-2, p. 43–44 *realidades.com* *Realidades* para hispanohablantes: Act. 2A-1, p. 21
Listening			*Communication Workbook:* Act. 9, p. 34 *Video Program* Chapter 2A *Video Teacher's Guide* Chapter 2A *Pre-AP* Resource Book:* pp. 68–69
Reading	p. 81 p. 91	Pre-AP* Support Pre-AP* Support	*Realidades* para hispanohablantes: Lectura 1, p. 62 *Realidades* para hispanohablantes: Lectura 2, p. 64 *TPR Stories:* Pepe el desordenado, p. 33 *Pre-AP* Resource Book:* pp. 68–69
Speaking	p. 77 p. 81 p. 93	Pre-AP* Support Pre-AP* Support (Talk!) Presentación oral	*TPR Stories:* Personalized Mini-situations, pp. 30–32 *Assessment Program:* Examen 2A, Hablar, p. 50 *Teacher's Resource Book, Para empezar–Tema 4:* Communicastive Activities, pp. 120–123 *Teacher's Resource Book, Para empezar–Tema 4:* Situation cards, p. 124 *Realidades* para hispanohablantes: Presentación oral, p. 67 *Pre-AP* Resource Book:* p. 68
Writing	p. 74 p. 81 p. 87	Differentiated Instruction: Advanced Learners/Pre-AP* Pre-AP* Support Act. 19	*Communication Workbook:* Act.13, p. 38 *Realidades* para hispanohablantes: Act. M, p. 65 *Communication Workbook:* Practice Test, pp. 242–244 *realidades.com* *ExamView:* Pre-AP* Question Bank *Assessment Program:* Examen 2A, Escribir, p. 49 *Pre-AP* Resource Book:* pp. 68–69
Integrated Skills	p. 87	Act. 18, 19	*Communication Workbook:* Integrated Performance Assessment, p. 241

	Teacher's Edition		Ancillaries
	Page #	**Activity**	
Vocabulary	p. 103	Pre-AP* Support	*realidades.com*
Listening	p. 103 p. 115	Pre-AP* Support Pre-AP* Support	*Communication Workbook:* Act. 6, p. 42 *Video Program* Chapter 2B *Video Teacher's Guide* Chapter 2B *Pre-AP* Resource Book:* pp. 68–69
Reading	p. 115	Pre-AP* Support	*Communication Workbook:* Practice Test, pp. 248–250 *Realidades* para hispanohablantes: Lectura 1, p. 82 *Realidades* para hispanohablantes: Lectura 2, p. 84 *TPR Stories:* La clase de fobias, p. 35 *Pre-AP* Resource Book:* pp. 68–69

Speaking	p. 105
	p. 107
		Pre-AP* Support
		Pre-AP* Support
			TPR Stories: Personalized Mini-situations,
			  pp. 30–32
			Assessment Program: Examen de 2B, Hablar, p. 63
			Teacher's Resource Book, Para empezar–Tema 4:
			  Communicative Activities, pp. 152–155
			Teacher's Resource Book, Para empezar–Tema 4:
			  Situation cards, p. 156
			Pre-AP Resource Book:* p. 68

Writing	p. 103
	p. 105
	p. 112
	p. 117
		Pre-AP* Support
		Pre-AP* Support
		Act. 20
		Presentación escrita
			Assessment Program: Examen de 2B, Escribir, p. 63
			Communication Workbook: Act. 13, p. 48
			Communication Workbook: Practice Test,
			  pp. 248–250
			Realidades para hispanohablantes: Act. P, p. 83
			Realidades para hispanohablantes: Act. R, p. 85
			Realidades para hispanohablantes: Presentación
			  escrita, p. 87
			realidades.com
			ExamView: Pre-AP* Question Bank
			Pre-AP Resource Book:* pp. 68–69

Integrated Skills	p. 105 p. 112	Act. 7 Act. 19	*Communication Workbook:* Integrated Performance Assessment, p. 247

Teacher Activity 1
Presentational Speaking

1. Have students listen to Audio Activity 9 on p. 34 in the *Realidades* Communication Workbook.

2. Next, have students prepare a one-minute talk about which of the four students they would most like to host as an exchange student, giving reasons to justify their choice and comparing their own likes and dislikes with the potential guest.

3. The amount of preparation time can vary, but should not be longer than three or four minutes.

4. Students are then allowed one minute to record their presentations, or they may make their presentations to a group of three or four students.

5. In groups of three or four, students should listen to each recording (or hear each presentation) and discuss the content and quality using the scoring guidelines on p. 49 of this book.

Teacher Activity 2
Presentational Writing

As students learn to compare facts and ideas, show them how to use graphic organizers, such as a Venn diagram, to organize information. For this activity, give students a Venn diagram. Have them label the first section *La Escuela Español Vivo*, the middle section *Las dos escuelas,* and the last section *Mi escuela.* As they read the *Lectura* on p. 90 of *Realidades* A/B/1, they should write some special features of *La Escuela Español Vivo* in the first section. Then they should note some special features of their school in the last section. As they think about the similarities between *La Escuela Español Vivo* and their school, they should write them in the middle section. In all cases, students should write key words only; they should not write sentences. The teacher may want to ask the class to brainstorm features for each section as they complete the Venn Diagram. It is important to teach the students to begin their paragraph with a simple topic sentence and to use appropriate vocabulary such as: *una diferencia, un parecido, diferente, parecido.* Remind them to use connecting words they have learned such as: *y, pero, también, o, ni ... ni ,*and *más ... que* so that the paragraph has structure and is not just a list. Ask students to use the information in the Venn diagram to write a short paragraph comparing the two schools. How are they similar? How are they different?

Teacher Activity 3
Interpretive Communication, Print Texts

After students have completed Student Activity 3 on the following page, make three photocopies of each student's written work. Place students in groups of four. Distribute copies of the scoring guidelines found on p. 49 of this book. (Since this is a writing task, the *Fluency* category on the bottom row can be ignored at this time.) Distribute the copies of the students' work within each group. Have each student read his or her writing aloud to the group, one piece at a time, and discuss the content and quality of each writing piece using the scoring guidelines. Each group may select one sample to share with the whole class.

Student Activity 1
Interpretive Communication, Audio Texts

Select the correct answer for each of the multiple-choice questions below after listening to Audio Activity 7 on p. 32 in the *Realidades* Communication Workbook.

1. ¿Cuándo tiene Diana la clase de español?
   a. a la primera hora
   b. a la segunda hora
   c. a la quinta hora

2. ¿Cuál clase es difícil para Diana?
   a. la de español
   b. la de arte
   c. la de matemáticas

3. ¿Por qué estudian mucho Diana y Emilio?
   a. Son divertidos.
   b. Son trabajadores.
   c. Son atléticos.

Student Activity 2
Presentational Writing

Directions: Imagine that you spent two weeks last summer at *La Escuela Español Vivo.* Your school newspaper has asked you to write a brief comparison of that school and your school. Use a Venn diagram and label the first section *La Escuela Español Vivo,* the middle section *Las dos escuelas,* and the last section *Mi escuela.* As you read the *Lectura* on pp. 90-91, write special features of *La Escuela Español Vivo* in the first section. Use key words only; do not write complete sentences. Think about your school and, using key words only, write some special features of it in the last section of your Venn diagram. Write features that both schools have in common in the middle section. Use the notes from your Venn diagram to write a paragraph comparing the two schools. How are they similar? How are they different?

Student Activity 3
Interpersonal Writing

Write an e-mail to a cousin in another state or town describing your favorite class. The message should include:

- The name of the subject
- Which period the class meets and at what time
- A description of the teacher
- Why it is your favorite class
- What items are needed for the class
- At least one question for your cousin to answer.

	Teacher's Edition		Ancillaries
	Page #	Activity	
Vocabulary	p. 126	Pre-AP* Support	*realidades.com*
Listening	p. 128	Differentiated Instruction: Advanced Learners/Pre-AP*	*Communication Workbook:* Act. 6, p. 52 *Video Program* Chapter 3A *Video Teacher's Guide* Chapter 3A
	p. 138	Pre-AP* Support	*Pre-AP* Resource Book:* pp. 72–73
Reading	p. 137	Act. 20	*Realidades* para hispanohablantes: Lectura 1, p. 102 *Realidades* para hispanohablantes: Lectura 2, p. 104 *TPR Stories:* La buena comida de todos los días, p. 42 *Pre-AP* Resource Book:* pp. 72–73
Speaking	p. 126 p. 128 p. 137 p. 141	Pre-AP* Support Differentiated Instruction: Advanced Learners/Pre-AP* Act. 20 🗨 Presentación oral	*Realidades* para hispanohablantes: Presentación oral, p. 107 *Assessment Program:* Examen de 3A, Parte II, Hablar, p. 77 *Teacher's Resource Book, Para empezar–Tema 4:* Communicative Activities, pp. 188–191 *Teacher's Resource Book, Para empezar–Tema 4:* Situation cards, p. 192 *TPR Stories:* Personalized Mini-situations, pp. 38–41 *Pre-AP* Resource Book:* pp. 72–73
Writing	p. 132 p. 137	Pre-AP* Support Act. 20	*Realidades* para hispanohablantes: Act. P, p. 103 *Assessment Program:* Examen de 3A, Parte II, Escribir, p. 76 *Communication Workbook:* Act. 13, p. 59 *Communication Workbook:* Practice Test, pp. 254–256 *realidades.com* *ExamView:* Pre-AP* Question Bank *Pre-AP* Resource Book:* pp. 72–73
Integrated Skills	p. 134 p. 136	Act. 15, 16 Act. 19	*Communication Workbook:* Integrated Performance Assessment, p. 253

Pre-AP* Resource Chart

	Teacher's Edition		Ancillaries
	Page #	**Activity**	
Vocabulary	p. 153	Pre-AP* Support	*realidades.com*
Listening	p. 151	Pre-AP* Support	*Video Program* Chapter 3B
	p. 153	Pre-AP* Support	*Video Teacher's Guide* Chapter 3B
	p. 162	Pre-AP* Support	*Communication Workbook:* Act. 9, p. 65
			Pre-AP Resource Book:* pp. 72–73
Reading	p. 161	Act. 19	*Realidades* para hispanohablantes: Lectura 1, p. 122
	p. 162	Pre-AP* Support	*Realidades* para hispanohablantes: Lectura 2, p. 124
			Communication Workbook: Practice Test, pp. 260–262
			TPR Stories: El camarero horrible, p. 47
			Pre-AP Resource Book:* pp. 72–73
Speaking	p. 151	Pre-AP* Support	*TPR Stories:* Personalized Mini-situations, pp. 44–46
	p. 153	Pre-AP* Support	*Teacher's Resource Book, Para empezar–Tema 4:* Communicative Activities, pp. 222–225
			Teacher's Resource Book, Para empezar–Tema 4: Situation cards, p. 226
			Assessment Program: Examen de capítulo 3B, Parte II, Hablar, p. 89
			Pre-AP Resource Book:* pp. 72–73
Writing	p. 151	Pre-AP* Support	*Communication Workbook:* Act. 13, p. 69
	p. 153	Pre-AP* Support	*Realidades* para hispanohablantes: Act. R, p. 125
	p. 161	Act. 19	*Realidades* para hispanohablantes: Presentación escrita, p. 127
	p. 162	Pre-AP* Support	*Communication Workbook:* Practice Test, pp. 260–262
	p. 165	Presentación escrita	*realidades.com*
			ExamView: Pre-AP* Question Bank
			Assessment Program: Examen de capítulo 3B, Parte C. Escribir, p. 89
			Pre-AP Resource Book:* pp. 72–73
Integrated Skills	p. 155	Act. 11	*Communication Workbook:* Integrated Performance Assessment, p. 259
	p. 157	Act. 14	

Teacher Activity 1
Interpersonal Speaking

Use the questions in Student Activity 1 to teach the students the elements of authentic interpersonal communication. Have each student select 5 questions to guide a conversation with his/her partner. Student A begins the conversation with a greeting and asks the first question. Student A listens to his/her partner's response and reacts to it in a natural and logical way, furthering the conversation. Student A continues with the next question and, once again, reacts to his/her partner's response naturally. The conversation continues until Student A has asked all his/her questions and ends the conversation. At that point, Student B begins his/her conversation and follows the same procedure. It is important to encourage students to let the conversation develop and flow naturally and to point out that the activity is a conversation with an exchange of information; it is not an interview. It is often helpful to select two students and have them do a sample conversation in English, using a few questions from Student Activity 1. When students focus on the elements of interpersonal communication in English, they are more likely to remember to use these elements in Spanish.

Teacher Activity 2
Presentational Writing

Provide students with the printed listening script for *Examen del capítulo,* 3B (See p. T63 of the *Realidades* Assessment Program.) Students should write two paragraphs describing what they believe to be a healthy lifestyle, including diet and activities, using the students in the reading (listening script) as examples to support their opinions. Then make three photocopies of each student's written work. Place students in groups of four. Distribute copies of the scoring guidelines found on p. 49 of this book. (Since this is a writing task, the *Fluency* category on the bottom row can be ignored at this time.) Distribute the copies of the students' work within each group. Have each student read his or her writing aloud to the group, one piece at a time, and discuss the content and quality of each writing piece using the scoring guidelines. Each group may select one sample to share with the whole class.

Student Activity 1
Interpersonal Speaking

Work with a partner to write complete-sentence answers to the following questions. Be sure to verify the correctness of your answers. Then, use the questions (and answers) to play *Preguntas rápidas* (see p. 41) or to prepare for *One minute of questions* (For Levels 1 and 2) (see p. 42).

1. ¿Cómo es tu dieta?
   _____

2. ¿Qué frutas te gustan más?
   _____

3. Describe tu sándwich favorito.
   _____

4. ¿Prefieres el desayuno o el almuerzo? ¿Por qué?
   _____

5. ¿Qué almuerzas los sábados?
   _____

6. ¿Qué bebida tomas con la pizza?
   _____

7. ¿Qué postre le gusta más a tu mejor amigo?
   _____

8. ¿Qué hay de almorzar en la cafetería de tu escuela?
   _____

9. ¿A tus amigos les gusta comer verduras?
   _____

10. ¿Qué tipo de sopa prefieres?
    _____

11. ¿En cuál restaurante te gusta comer? ¿Por qué?
    _____

12. ¿Compartes tu postre favorito con un amigo?
    _____

13. ¿Qué tipo de ejercicios haces?
    _____

14. ¿Qué haces para mantener la salud?
    _____

15. ¿Crees que es importante comer bien?
    _____

16. ¿Tomas vitaminas cada día?
    _____

	Teacher's Edition		Ancillaries
	Page #	**Activity**	
Vocabulary	p. 172	Pre-AP* Support	*realidades.com* *Assessment Program:* Prueba 4A-2, pp. 95–96
Listening	p. 172	Pre-AP* Support	*Video Program* Chapter 4A *Video Teacher's Guide* Chapter 4A *Communication Workbook:* Act. 6, p. 73 *Pre-AP* Resource Book:* pp. 76–77
Reading			*Realidades* para hispanohablantes: Lectura 1, p. 142 *Realidades* para hispanohablantes: Lectura 2, p. 144 *TPR Stories:* ¡Vamos a la playa!, p. 54 *Pre-AP* Resource Book:* pp. 76–77

Speaking	p. 172
	p. 182
	p. 186
	p. 191
		Pre-AP* Support
		Pre-AP* Support
		Act. 18
		Presentación oral
			TPR Stories: Personalized Mini-situations,
			  pp. 50–53
			Realidades para hispanohablantes: Presentación
			  oral, p. 147
			Teacher's Resource Book, Para empezar–Tema 4:
			  Communicative Activities, pp. 258–262
			Teacher's Resource Book, Para empezar–Tema 4:
			  Situation cards, p. 262
			Assessment Program: Parte II, Hablar, p. 102
			Pre-AP* Resource Book: pp. 76–77

Writing	p. 176
	
	p. 182
	p. 186
	p. 188
		Differentiated Instruction:
		  Advanced Learners/Pre-AP*
		Pre-AP* Support
		Act. 18
		Pre-AP* Support
			Communication Workbook: Act. 13, p. 77
			Realidades para hispanohablantes: Act. Ñ, p. 143
			Communication Workbook; Practice Test,
			  pp. 266–268
			realidades.com
			ExamView: Pre-AP* Question Bank
			Assessment Program: Parte II, Escribir, p. 102
			Pre-AP* Resource Book: pp. 76–77

Integrated Skills	p. 179 p. 182	Act. 9 Act. 14	*Communication Workbook:* Integrated Performance Assessment, p. 265

	Teacher's Edition		Ancillaries
	Page #	**Activity**	
Vocabulary	p. 201	Pre-AP* Support	*realidades.com* *Assesssment Program:* Prueba 4B-2, pp. 107–108
Listening	p. 201 p. 212	Pre-AP* Support Pre-AP* Support	*Video Program* Chapter 4B *Video Teacher's Guide* Chapter 4B *Communication Workbook:* Act. 9, p. 83 *Pre-AP* Resource Book:* pp. 76–77
Reading	p. 209	Act. 20	*Communication Workbook:* Practice Test, pp. 272–274 *TPR Stories:* A Jorge le gusta besar, pp. 60–61 *Realidades* para hispanohablantes: Lectura 1, p. 162 *Realidades* para hispanohablantes: Lectura 2, p. 164 *Pre-AP* Resource Book:* pp. 76–77

Speaking	p. 201
	 p. 204
	 p. 209
		Pre-AP* Support
		 Pre-AP* Support
		 Act. 20
			TPR Stories: Personalized Mini-situations, pp. 56–59
			 Teacher's Resource Book, Para empezar–Tema 4:
			    Communicative Activities, pp. 292–295
			 Teacher's Resource Book, Para empezar–Tema 4:
			    Situation cards, p. 296
			 Assessment Program: Parte II, Hablar, p. 113
			 Pre-AP* Resource Book: p. 77

Writing	p. 206
	
	 p. 209
	 p. 212
	 p. 215
		Differentiated Instruction:
		    Advanced Learners/Pre-AP*
		 Act. 20
		 Pre-AP* Support
		 Presentación escrita
			Communication Workbook: Act. 13, p. 87
			 Realidades para hispanohablantes: Act. N, p. 163
			 Realidades para hispanohablantes: Presentación
			    escrita, p. 167
			 Communication Workbook: Practice Test,
			    pp. 272–274
			 realidades.com
			 ExamView: Pre-AP* Question Bank
			 Assessment Program: Parte II, Escribir, p. 113
			 Pre-AP* Resource Book: pp. 76–77

Integrated Skills	p. 209 p. 211	Act. 19 Act. 21	*Communication Workbook:* Integrated Performance Assessment, p. 271

Teacher Activity 1
Presentational Speaking

As students learn to give oral presentations that focus on making comparisons, it is important to give them graphic organizers to use before and during their presentations. It is also important to teach students some useful vocabulary such as: *una diferencia, un parecido, diferente, parecido, tener en común,* and *por ejemplo.* In addition, remind the students to use adverbs (*también, nunca, siempre, todos los días, generalmente*) and conjunctions (*y, pero, cuando, porque, o, ni … ni*) they have learned to improve the flow of information in their presentation. For this activity, give students a Venn diagram to help them prepare for an oral presentation comparing their free time activities with those of students in the Spanish-speaking world. Have the students label the first section *Los estudiantes hispanos,* the middle section *Los dos grupos,* and the last section *Mis amigos y yo.* Have them review the *Videocultura* for *Tema* 4 and the *Videohistorias* for *Capítulos* 4A and 4B. Students should write a list of the activities presented under *Los estudiantes hispanos.* Then have them write the activities they do with their friends in their free time in the last section. In the middle section students write the activities that both groups do in their free time. In all cases, students should write key words only; they should not write sentences. When the preparations have been completed, have the students use the information in their Venn diagram to make an oral presentation in Spanish comparing their free time activities with those of students in the Spanish-speaking world. How are they similar? How are they different? Students should have three minutes to organize their thoughts and one minute to record their presentations or make them to a group of three or four students. If the activity has been recorded, students should work in groups of three or four to listen to each recording and discuss the content and quality using the scoring guidelines on p. 49 of this book.

Teacher Activity 2
Interpersonal Speaking

Continue to develop students' interpersonal speaking skills using the questions in Student Activity 1. Have each student select 5 questions to guide a conversation with his/her partner. Student A begins the conversation with a greeting and asks the first question. Student A listens to his/her partner's response and reacts to it in a natural and logical way, furthering the conversation. Student A continues with the next question and, once again, reacts to his/her partner's response naturally. The conversation continues until Student A has asked all his/her questions and ends the conversation. At that point, Student B begins his/her conversation and follows the same procedure. It is important to encourage students to let the conversation develop and flow naturally and to point out that the activity is a conversation with an exchange of information; it is not an interview. Remind the students to include useful expressions they have studied, such as ¡*genial*! ¡*qué buena idea*! ¡*qué asco*! ¡*no me digas*! (*no*) *estoy de acuerdo, por supuesto.* Adverbial expressions, such as *generalmente, cada día, todos los días, nunca, siempre, a veces* will also help advance the conversation. A list of additional expressions can be found on p. 483 of *Realidades* A/B/1.

Student Activity 1
Interpersonal Speaking

Work with a partner to write complete-sentence answers to the following questions. Be sure to verify the correctness of your answers. Then, use the questions (and answers) to play *Preguntas rápidas* (see p. 41) or to prepare for *One minute of questions* (For Levels 1 and 2) (see p. 41).

1. ¿Cuándo estás cansado(a)?

   _____

2. ¿Adónde vas los domingos?

   _____

3. ¿A qué deporte juegas?

   _____

4. ¿Qué quieres comer después de ver una película?

   _____

5. ¿De dónde eres?

   _____

6. ¿Con quién vas al parque?

   _____

7. ¿Cuántas carpetas tienes?

   _____

8. ¿Por qué tienes que estudiar mucho?

   _____

9. ¿Sabes jugar al vóleibol?

   _____

10. ¿Te gustaría ir de pesca conmigo?

    _____

11. ¿Qué haces en tu tiempo libre?

    _____

12. ¿Qué vas a hacer mañana por la tarde?

    _____

13. ¿Cuándo empiezan las vacaciones?

    _____

14. ¿A qué hora vas a la escuela?

    _____

15. ¿Cuántas personas hay en tu clase de español?

    _____

16. ¿Qué clase te gusta más? ¿Por qué?

    _____

Pre-AP* Resource Chart

	Teacher's Edition		Ancillaries
	Page #	**Activity**	
Vocabulary	p. 225	Pre-AP* Support	*realidades.com*
Listening	p. 238	Pre-AP* Support	*Video Program* Chapter 5A *Video Teacher's Guide* Chapter 5A *Communication Workbook:* Act. 9, p. 94 *Pre-AP* Resource Book:* p. 80–81
Reading			*TPR Stories:* La fiesta de sorpresa, p. 67 *Realidades* para hispanohablantes: Lectura 1, p. 182 *Realidades* para hispanohablantes: Lectura 2, p. 184 *Pre-AP* Resource Book:* pp. 80–81
Speaking	p. 233 p. 237 p. 241	Pre-AP* Support Act. 25 (Talk!) Presentación oral	*TPR Stories:* Personalized Mini-situations, pp. 64–66 *Realidades* para hispanohablantes: Presentación oral, p. 187 *Teacher's Resource Book, Temas 5–9:* Communicative Activities, pp. 12–15 *Teacher's Resource Book, Temas 5–9:* Situation cards, p. 16 *Assessment Program:* Parte II, Hablar, p. 129 *Pre-AP* Resource Book:* p. 80–81
Writing	p. 225 p. 232 p. 237	Pre-AP* Support Differentiated Instruction: Advanced Learners/Pre-AP* Act. 25	*Communication Workbook:* Act. 13, p. 98 *Communication Workbook:* Practice Test, pp. 278–280 *Realidades* para hispanohablantes: Act. L, p. 183 *Realidades* para hispanohablantes: Act. O, p. 185 *realidades.com* *ExamView:* Pre-AP* Question Bank *Assessment Program:* Parte II, Escribir, p. 128 *Pre-AP* Resource Book:* pp. 80–81
Integrated Skills	p. 235 p. 237	Act. 23, 24 Act. 25, 26	*Communication Workbook:* Integrated Performance Assessment, p. 277

	Teacher's Edition		Ancillaries
	Page #	**Activity**	
Vocabulary	p. 251	Pre-AP* Support	*realidades.com*
Listening	p. 251 p. 261 p. 278	Pre-AP* Support Pre-AP* Support Pre-AP* Support	*Video Program* Chapter 5B *Video Teacher's Guide* Chapter 5B *Communication Workbook:* Act. 8, p. 103 *Pre-AP* Resource Book:* p. 80–81
Reading			*Communication Workbook:* Practice Test, p. 285–287 *TPR Stories:* El jugo de aguacate, p. 75 *Realidades* para hispanohablantes: Lectura 1, p. 202 *Realidades* para hispanohablantes: Lectura 2, p. 204 *Pre-AP* Resource Book:* pp. 80–81

Speaking	p. 261
	p. 262
		Act. 20
		Pre-AP* Support
			TPR Stories: Personalized Mini-situations, pp. 71–74
			Teacher's Resource book, Temas 5–9:
			  Communicative Activities, pp. 46–49
			Teacher's Resource Book, Temas 5–9: Situation
			  cards, p. 50
			Assessment Program: Parte II, Hablar, p. 142
			Pre-AP Resource Book:* p. 80–81

Writing	p. 256
	
	p. 261
	p. 261
	p. 262
		Differentiated Instruction:
		  Advanced Learners/Pre-AP*
		Pre-AP* Support
		Act. 20
		Pre-AP* Support
			Communication Workbook: Act. 10, p. 105
			Realidades para hispanohablantes: Act. N, p. 203
			Realidades para hispanohablantes: Act. O, p. 205
			Realidades para hispanohablantes: Presentación
			  escrita, p. 207
			Communication Workbook: Practice Test,
			  pp. 285–287
			realidades.com
			ExamView: Pre-AP* Question Bank
			Assessment Program: Parte II, Escribir, p. 142
			Pre-AP Resource Book:* pp. 80–81

Integrated Skills	p. 255 p. 261	Act. 10 Act. 20, 21	*Communication Workbook:* Integrated Performance Assessment, p. 284

Teacher Activity 1
Interpersonal Speaking, Conversation

1. Based on the *Hablar* activity p. 269 in the **Realidades** Student Textbook, have students read the given scenario, and then prepare how they would fill in the following conversation. Teachers may wish to ask the class to brainstorm together some possible responses to the waiter's questions, but ultimately, the preparation should be accomplished individually in no longer than three or four minutes.

Conversation:

CAMARERO: Buenas noches. ¿A que hora tiene Ud. reservación?

ESTUDIANTE: (20-30 second response)

CAMARERO: ¿Hay otros que cenan con Ud. esta noche?

ESTUDIANTE: (20-30 second response)

CAMARERO: ¿Cómo es su tío?

ESTUDIANTE: (20-30 second response)

CAMARERO: ¿Y su tía?

ESTUDIANTE: (20-30 second response)

CAMARERO: Bueno, le aviso cuando lleguen.

2. Students then record their conversations. (See Recording and Evaluating on p. 44.) The teacher can be the voice of the waiter, allowing 30 seconds for each response.

3. In groups of three or four, students should listen to each recording and discuss the content and quality using the scoring guidelines on p. 49 of this book.

Teacher Activity 2
Presentational Speaking

As students continue to focus on making comparisons and develop their presentational speaking skills, it is important to give them graphic organizers to use before and during their presentations. It is also important to teach them some useful vocabulary. Remind students to use adverbs (*también, nunca, a veces*) and conjunctions (*y, pero, porque*) they have learned to improve the flow of information in their presentations. For this activity, students should have viewed and discussed the *Videocultura* for *Tema 5*, the painting *Barbacoa para cumpleaños* (**Realidades** A/B/1, p. 220 and PresentationeExpress Premium, Resources), the *Fondo cultural* on p. 226, and read the *Lectura* on p. 238 prior to the activity. Give the students a Venn diagram. Have them label the first section *Las celebraciones de familias hispanas,* the middle section *Las dos familias,* and the last section *Las celebraciones de mi familia.* Brainstorm birthday traditions that families in the Spanish-speaking world observe. Then have students think about birthday traditions in their families. In the middle section students write key words that represent birthday celebrations of both families. Have them use the information in their diagrams to make an oral presentation in Spanish comparing their family birthday celebrations with those of other Spanish-speaking families. Students have three minutes to organize their thoughts and one minute to record their presentations or make them to a group of three or four students.

Student Activity 1
Interpersonal Writing, E-mail Reply

Directions: Read the following e-mail message and write a response to it. Your reply should include a greeting and a closing. Be sure to answer all the questions that Miguel asks. You should also ask him at least one question.

Hola,

¿Cómo estás? Estoy muy contento porque voy a celebrar mi cumpleaños en dos semanas. Siempre voy con mi familia a mi restaurante favorito, pero este año quiero celebrar en casa con mi familia y mis amigos. Ahora tengo que hacer los planes para mi fiesta y necesito tu opinión. Primero, ¿qué día prefieres, el viernes o el sábado? ¿Por qué? Segundo, ¿qué comida debo servir? Mis abuelos, mis tíos y mis primos que tienen siete y once años van a venir. También voy a invitar a unos diez amigos. Vamos a escuchar música, jugar al fútbol y romper una piñata. ¿Crees que va a ser una fiesta divertida?

Hasta pronto,

Miguel

Student Activity 2
Presentational Speaking

Directions: Your teacher will give you a Venn diagram or ask you to draw one. Label the first section: *Las celebraciones de familias hispanas*, the middle section *Las dos familias*, and the last section *Las celebraciones de mi familia*. Think about the traditions that families in the Spanish-speaking world observe when they celebrate birthdays. In the first section write down key words that represent these traditions. Do not write complete sentences. Then think about the traditions of your family for birthday celebrations and write key words to represent them in the last section. In the middle section write key words that represent birthday celebrations of both families. Using your Venn diagram, give an oral presentation in Spanish comparing birthday celebrations of families in the Spanish-speaking world with those of your family. You have three minutes to prepare and one minute to speak.

	Teacher's Edition		Ancillaries
	Page #	Activity	
Vocabulary	p. 275	Pre-AP* Support	*realidades.com*
Listening	p. 275	Pre-AP* Support	*Video Program* Chapter 6A
	p. 278	Pre-AP* Support	*Video Teacher's Guide* Chapter 6A
			Pre-AP* Resource Book: pp. 84–85
Reading			*TPR Stories:* Buffy tiene sueño, p. 83
			Realidades para hispanohablantes: Lectura 1, p. 222
			Realidades para hispanohablantes: Lectura 2, p. 224
			Pre-AP* Resource Book: pp. 84–85
Speaking	p. 275	Pre-AP* Support	*TPR Stories:* Personalized Mini-situations, pp. 79–82
	p. 287	Act. 28	*Teacher's Resource Book, Temas 5–9:* Communicative Activities, pp. 86–89
	p. 288	Pre-AP* Support	*Teacher's Resource Book, Temas 5–9:* Situation cards, p. 90
	p. 291	(talk!) Presentación oral	*Realidades* para hispanohablantes: Presentación oral, p. 227
			Assessment Program: Parte II, Hablar, p. 157
			Pre-AP* Resource Book: p. 84
Writing	p. 278	Pre-AP* Support	*Communication Workbook:* Act. 13, p. 119
	p. 286	Differentiated Instruction: Advanced Learners/Pre-AP*	*Realidades* para hispanohablantes: Act. N, p. 223
			Communication Workbook: Practice Test, pp. 291–293
	p. 287	Act. 28	*realidades.com*
	p. 288	Pre-AP* Support	*ExamView:* Pre-AP* Question Bank
			Assessment Program: Parte II, Escribir, p. 157
			Pre-AP* Resource Book: pp. 84–85
Integrated Skills	p. 281	Act. 15	*Communication Workbook:* Integrated Performance Assessment, p. 290
	p. 286	Act. 26	
	p. 287	Act. 28	

	Teacher's Edition		Ancillaries
	Page #	**Activity**	
Vocabulary	p. 301	Pre-AP* Support	*realidades.com*
Listening	p. 301	Pre-AP* Support	*Video Program* Chapter 6B
	p. 311	Pre-AP* Support	*Video Teacher's Guide* Chapter 6B
			Communication Workbook: Act. 5, p. 123
			Communication Workbook: Act. 9, p. 125
			Pre-AP* Resource Book: pp. 84–85
Reading			*Realidades* para hispanohablantes: Lectura 1, p. 242
			Realidades para hispanohablantes: Lectura 2, p. 244
			Communication Workbook: Practice Test, pp. 297–299
			TPR Stories: Bellasucia, p. 90
			Pre-AP* Resource Book: pp. 84–85
Speaking	p. 301	Pre-AP* Support	*TPR Stories:* Personalized Mini-situations, pp. 86–89
	p. 304	Differentiated Instruction: Advanced Learners/Pre-AP*	*Teacher's Resource Book, Temas 5–9:* Communicative Activities, pp. 120–123
	p. 309	Act. 20	*Teacher's Resource Book, Temas 5–9:* Situation cards, p. 124
	p. 312	Pre-AP* Support	*Assessment Program:* Parte II, Hablar, p. 171
			Pre-AP* Resource Book: p. 84
Writing	p. 309	Act. 20	*Communication Workbook:* Act. 13, p. 129
	p. 311	Pre-AP* Support	*Communication workbook:* Practice Test, pp. 297–299
	p. 315	Presentación escrita	*Realidades* para hispanohablantes: Act. N, p. 243
			Realidades para hispanohablantes: Presentación escrita, p. 247
			realidades.com
			ExamView: Pre-AP* Question Bank
			Assessment Program: Parte II, Escribir p. 171
			Pre-AP* Resource Book: pp. 84–85
Integrated Skills	p. 306	Act. 13	*Communication Workbook:* Integrated Performance Assessment, p. 296
	p. 310	Act. 21	

Teacher Activity 1
Interpretive Communication, Audio Texts

The teacher should read aloud *El desastre en mi dormitorio* from p. 288 of the *Realidades* Student Textbook to engage students in the Dictogloss activity on p.15. Once students have completed the steps to the Dictogloss activity, have them read aloud to a partner the reply from Magdalena and follow-up with the *¿Comprendes?* and *Y tú, ¿qué dices?* activities found on p. 289 of the *Realidades* Student Textbook.

Teacher Activity 2
Evaluating with Rubrics

The teacher should make three photocopies of each student's written work for Student Activities 2 and 3 on the next page. Place students in groups of four. Distribute copies of the scoring guidelines found on p. 49 of this book. (Since this is a writing task, the *Fluency* category on the bottom row can be ignored at this time.) Distribute the copies of the students' work within each group. Have each student read his or her writing aloud to the group, one piece at a time, and discuss the content and quality of each writing piece using the scoring guidelines. Each group may select one sample to share with the whole class.

Student Activity 1
Interpretive Communication, Audiovisual Texts

After listening to the *Videohistoria* for *Capítulo* 6A (see *Realidades* Teacher's Resource Book, p. 83), have students select the most appropriate answer to the following:

1. ¿Por qué está mamá en el cuarto de Ignacio?
   a. Es la hora de la escuela.
   b. Necesita un disco compacto.
   c. Pone en orden el cuarto.

2. ¿Por qué está descontento Ignacio?
   a. Siempre duerme bien.
   b. Tiene muchas cosas encima de la cama.
   c. No sabe donde están sus cosas.

3. ¿Cuál es la mejor solución del problema, según mamá?
   a. Cerrar la puerta para no ver todas las cosas.
   b. Organizar el cuarto.
   c. Poner los libros y las revistas en el estante.

Student Activity 2
Interpersonal Writing

Imagine that you have just moved to a different state. Write an e-mail to your best friend at your former school describing to him or her your new house. Be sure to describe the rooms, the furniture, the colors, etc. Then, compare your new house to your old house. Include a question or two for your friend to answer.

Student Activity 3
Presentational Writing

Consider the two different houses on p. 168 of the *Realidades* Assessment Program and on p. 124 of the *Realidades* Communication Workbook. Imagine that you are a real estate agent needing to write an article to compare the two houses and the advantages of each, in order to attract potential buyers. Write your article of at least 100 words with a thorough description of each house. Consider the selling points of each property.

	Teacher's Edition		Ancillaries
	Page #	**Activity**	
Vocabulary	p. 325	Pre-AP* Support	*realidades.com* *Assessment Program:* Prueba 7A-2, pp. 177–78
Listening			*Video Program* Chapter 7A *Video Teacher's Guide* Chapter 7A *Communication Workbook:* Act. 7, p. 134 *Communication Workbook:* Act. 9, p. 135 *Pre-AP* Resource Book:* p. 88
Reading			*TPR Stories:* El viaje de Rosa, p. 99 *Realidades* para hispanohablantes: Lectura 1, p. 262 *Realidades* para hispanohablantes: Lectura 2, p. 264 *Pre-AP* Resource Book:* pp. 88–89
Speaking	p. 325 p. 330 p. 333 p. 336 p. 339	Pre-AP* Support Differentiated Instruction: Advanced Learners/Pre-AP* Act. 19 Pre-AP* Support (Talk!) Presentación oral	*TPR Stories:* Personalized Mini-situations, pp. 95–98 *Teacher's Resource Book, Temas 5–9:* Communicative Activities, pp. 158–161 *Teacher's Resource Book, Temas 5–9:* Situation cards, p. 162 *Realidades* para hispanohablantes: Presentación oral, p. 267 *Assessment Program:* Parte II, Hablar, p. 184 *Pre-AP* Resource Book:* pp. 88–89
Writing	p. 325 p. 330 p. 333 p. 336	Pre-AP* Support Differentiated Instruction: Advanced Learners/Pre-AP* Act. 19 Pre-AP* Support	*Communication Workbook:* Act. 13, p. 139 *Communication Workbook:* Practice Test, p. 303–305 *realidades.com* *ExamView:* Pre-AP* Question Bank *Assessment Program:* Parte II, Escribir, p. 183 *Pre-AP* Resource Book:* pp. 88–89
Integrated Skills	p. 334 p. 335	Act. 20, 21 Act. 22	*Communication Workbook:* Integrated Performance Assessment, p. 302

	Teacher's Edition		Ancillaries
	Page #	**Activity**	
Vocabulary	p. 349	Pre-AP* Support	*realidades.com*
Listening	p. 365	Pre-AP* Support	*Video Program* Chapter 7B *Video Teacher's Guide* Chapter 7B *Communication workbook:* Act. 9, p. 145 *Pre-AP* Resource Book:* p. 88
Reading			*Communication Workbook:* Practice test, pp. 309–311 *TPR Stories:* El regalo de Pepita, p. 105 *Realidades* para hispanohablantes: Lectura 1, p. 282 *Realidades* para hispanohablantes: Lectura 2, p. 284 *Pre-AP* Resource Book:* pp. 88–89

Speaking	p. 349
	p. 353
	p. 355
		Pre-AP* Support
		Pre-AP* Support
		Act. 14
			TPR Stories: Personalized Mini-situations,
			  pp. 101–104
			Teacher's Resource Book, Temas 5–9:
			  Communicative Activities, pp. 194–197
			Teacher's Resource Book, Temas 5–9: Situation
			  cards, p. 198
			Assessment Program: Parte II, Hablar, p. 198
			Pre-AP Resource Book:* pp. 88–89

Writing	p. 355
	p. 358
	
	p. 367
		Act. 14
		Differentiated Instruction:
		  Advanced Learners/Pre-AP*
		Presentación escrita
			Communication Workbook: Act. 12,
			  pp. 148–149
			Realidades para hispanohablantes: Act. L, p. 283
			Realidades para hispanohablantes: Act. N, p. 285
			Realidades para hispanohablantes: Presentación
			  escrita, p. 287
			Communication Workbook: Practice Test,
			  pp. 309–311
			realidades.com
			ExamView: Pre-AP* Question Bank
			Assessment Program: Parte II, Escribir, p. 197
			Pre-AP Resource Book:* pp. 88–89

Integrated Skills	p. 352 p. 358 p. 361	Act. 9 Act. 17 Act. 20	*Communication Workbook:* Integrated Performance Assessment, p. 308

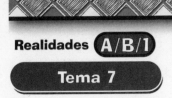

Teacher Activity 1
Interpretive Communication, Print Texts

Provide students with the printed Video Script 7B on p. 191 of the *Realidades* Teacher's Resource Book. Have students read the script out loud with a partner, each taking one of the roles. After the reading, ask the partners to answer the questions on pp. 140-141 of the *Realidades* Communication Workbook. Lastly, students should view the video.

Teacher Activity 2
Interpretive Communication, Audio and Audiovisual Texts

As an alternative to the above activity, play the *Realidades* Video to accompany *Tema* 7B with the TV screen covered. Students should have the *Realidades* Communication workbook open to p. 140. The first time they listen, ask students to complete *Actividad* 2, p. 140 of the Communication Workbook. Rewind the video and play it again, asking students to answer the questions in *Actividad* 3, p. 141 of the Communication Workbook. After listening, they may confer with a partner to consider the correct answer choices. Finally, rewind the video and allow students to view the scene as a means to verify their responses to the two activities.

Teacher Activity 3
Interpersonal Speaking, Conversation

Directions for Student Activity 1, p. 85

1. Teachers may wish to ask the class to brainstorm together about some possible responses, but ultimately, the preparation should be accomplished individually. The amount of preparation time can vary, but should not be longer than three or four minutes.

2. Students are then allowed to record their conversations. (See Recording and Evaluating on p. 44.) The teacher can be the voice of Mamá, allowing no more than 30 seconds for each response from the students.

3. In groups of three or four, students should listen to each recording and discuss the content and quality using the scoring guidelines on p. 49 of this book.

Student Activity 1
Interpersonal Speaking: Conversation

Scenario: You are back-to-school shopping in a department store with your mom.

Read the conversation framework below, and then prepare (by writing down key words), how you would fill in the following conversation with rich and full responses to the questions. (The goal is to provide as much speech as possible in the time provided, rather than to settle on a basic but short response that is appropriate.)

Conversation:

MAMÁ: ¿Qué artículos de ropa necesitas más este año?

ESTUDIANTE: (20-30 second response)

MAMÁ: ¿No quieres buscar zapatos?

ESTUDIANTE: (20-30 second response)

MAMÁ: Pues, ¿qué te parece esta camisa?

ESTUDIANTE: (20-30 second response)

MAMÁ: ¿Cuánto cuesta cada artículo?

ESTUDIANTE: (20-30 second response)

MAMÁ: Bueno, pero prefiero buscar mejores precios.

Student Activity 2
Interpersonal Writing

Directions: Read the following e-mail message and write a response to it. Your reply should include a greeting and a closing. Be sure to answer all the questions that Silvia asks. You should also ask her at least one question.

Hola,

¿Qué tal? Tengo un problema y necesito tu ayuda. Es que mis abuelos me regalaron dinero para mi cumpleaños. Con ese dinero, compré un reloj pulsera. Pagué treinta y cinco dólares por él. El problema es que no necesito otro reloj pulsera porque ya tengo uno que me gusta mucho. ¡No sé por qué lo compré! ¿Crees que es buena idea venderlo en e-Bay? ¿Por qué? Si lo vendo, puedo comprarme algo diferente, como ropa nueva o un videojuego. ¿Qué debo hacer?

Gracias por darme tu opinión,

Silvia

	Teacher's Edition		Ancillaries
	Page #	**Activity**	
Vocabulary	p. 377	Pre-AP* Support	*realidades.com*
Listening			*Video Program* Chapter 8A *Video Teacher's Guide* Chapter 8A *Communication workbook:* Act. 6, p. 153 *Communication workbook:* Act. 9, p. 155 *Pre-AP* Resource Book:* pp. 92–93
Reading			*TPR Stories:* Los amigos, la cena y el campo, p. 113 *Realidades* para hispanohablantes: Lectura 1, p. 302 *Realidades* para hispanohablantes: Lectura 2, p. 304 *Pre-AP* Resource Book:* pp. 92–93

Speaking	p. 377
	p. 379
	p. 386
	p. 390
	p. 393
	p. 393
		Pre-AP* Support
		Pre-AP* Support
		Act. 18
		Pre-AP* Support
		Presentación oral
		(Talk!) Presentación oral
			TPR Stories: Personalized Mini-situations,
			  pp. 109–112
			Teacher's Resource Book, Temas 5–9:
			  Communicative Activities, pp. 230–233
			Teacher's Resource Book, Temas 5–9: Situation
			  cards, p. 234
			Realidades para hispanohablantes: Presentación
			  oral, p. 307
			Assessment Program: Parte II, Hablar, p. 211
			Pre-AP* Resource Book: p. 92

Writing	p. 379
	p. 384
	
	p. 386
	p. 390
		Pre-AP* Support
		Differentiated Instruction:
		  Advanced Learners/Pre-AP*
		Act. 18
		Pre-AP* Support
			Communication Workbook: Act. 12, pp. 158–159
			Communication Workbook: Act. 13, p. 159
			Communication Workbook: Practice Test,
			  pp. 315–317
			Realidades para hispanohablantes: Act. L, p. 303
			realidades.com
			ExamView: Pre-AP* Question Bank
			Assessment Program: Parte II, Escribir, p. 211
			Pre-AP* Resource Book: pp. 92–93

Integrated Skills	p. 384 p. 386	Act. 15 Act. 18	*Communication Workbook:* Integrated Performance Assessment, p. 314

	Teacher's Edition		Ancillaries
	Page #	Activity	
Vocabulary	p. 403	Pre-AP* Support	*realidades.com*
Listening	p. 416	Pre-AP* Support	*Video Program* Chapter 8B
			Video Teacher's Guide Chapter 8B
			Communication Workbook: Act. 7, p. 164
			Pre-AP Resource Book:* pp. 92–93
Reading			*Communication Workbook:* Practice Test, pp. 321–324
			Teacher's Resource Book, Temas 5–9: Communicative Activity 8B-2, pp. 210–211
			Realidades para hispanohablantes: Lectura 1, p. 322
			Realidades para hispanohablantes: Lectura 2, p. 324
			TPR Stories: Cómo ayudar el planeta, p. 120
			Pre-AP Resource Book:* pp. 92–93
Speaking	p. 403	Pre-AP* Support	*TPR Stories:* Personalized Mini-situations, pp. 116–119
	p. 409	Act. 11	*Teacher's Resource Book, Temas 5–9:* Communicative Activities, pp. 264–267
	p. 414	Pre-AP* Support	*Teacher's Resource Book, Temas 5–9:* Situation cards, p. 268
	p. 416	Pre-AP* Support	*Assessment Program:* Parte II, Hablar, p. 225
			Pre-AP Resource Book:* p. 92
Writing	p. 403	Pre-AP* Support	*Communication Workbook:* Act. 13, p. 169
	p. 408	Differentiated Instruction: Advanced Learners/Pre-AP*	*Realidades* para hispanohablantes: Presentación escrita, p. 327
	p. 409	Act. 11	*Communication Workbook:* Practice Test, pp. 322–324
	p. 416	Pre-AP* Support	*realidades.com*
	p. 419	Presentación escrita	*ExamView:* Pre-AP* Question Bank
			Assessment Program: Parte II, Escribir, p. 225
			Pre-AP Resource Book:* pp. 92–93
Integrated Skill	p. 409	Act. 12	*Communication Workbook:* Integrated Performance Assessment, p. 321
	p. 415	Act. 22	

Teacher Activity 1
Evaluating with Rubrics

The teacher should make three photocopies of each student's written work for Student Activity 1 on the next page. Place students in groups of four. Distribute copies of the scoring guidelines found on p. 49 of this book. (Since this is a writing task, the *Fluency* category on the bottom row can be ignored at this time.) Distribute the copies of the students' work within each group. Have each student read his or her writing aloud to the group, one piece at a time, and discuss the content and quality of each writing piece using the scoring guidelines. Each group may select one sample to share with the whole class.

Teacher Activity 2
Presentational Writing

1. Have students read *Hábitat para la Humanidad Internacional*, pp. 416-417 in the **Realidades** Student Textbook.

2. Have students watch the Video for *Capítulo* 8B. (See **Realidades** Teacher's Resource Book, p. 262.)

3. Ask students to write a composition of 100 words (minimum) in which they describe the benefits of different types of community service. They should cite the reading and the video using specific examples from each.

Teacher Activity 3
Presentational Speaking

As students continue to focus on making comparisons and develop their presentational speaking skills, it is important to give them graphic organizers to use before and during their presentations. It is also important to teach students some useful vocabulary and remind them to use adverbs and conjunctions they have already learned (see p. 80). Teach expressions such as *por eso, adem·s, por un lado, por otro (lado),* and *sin embargo.* Encourage the use a variety of transition words to improve the flow of information in their presentations. Tell them to use conjunctions to raise the level of discourse. In addition, students should learn to organize their presentations and to provide main ideas with supporting details. For this activity, give the students a Venn diagram. Have them label the first section *En San José, Costa Rica,* the middle section *En las dos comunidades,* and the last section *En mi comunidad.* Show the *Videohistoria* for *Capìtulo* 8B. As they view it, have them write the ways that students in San José help their community in the first section. Remind them to use key words only. Then have them think about ways that they and their friends can help their own community and write key words to represent them in the last section. In the middle section students write key words that represent what they do in both communities. Have students use the information in the diagram to make an oral presentation in Spanish comparing what students do to help their own community to what students do in San José, Costa Rica. Students should have three minutes to organize their thoughts and one minute to record their presentations or make them to a group of students. If the activity has been recorded, they should work in groups of three or four to listen to each recording and discuss the content using the scoring guidelines on p. 49 on this book.

Student Activity 1
Interpersonal Writing

Imagine that you just came home from working on a community volunteer project. E-mail a friend and tell him or her what you did, whom you helped, and why you got involved. Encourage him or her to engage in community service as well. Include a question or two for your friend to answer.

Student Activity 2
Interpretive Communication: Print Texts

Read *Las tortugas tinglar* on p. 415 of the *Realidades* Student Textbook. Then, respond to the following questions:

1. ¿Por qué es impresionante esta tortuga?
   a. Pone sus huevos entre febrero y julio.
   b. Vive en aguas frías cerca del Caribe.
   c. Es una de las tortugas más grandes del mundo.

2. ¿Por qué está en peligro de extinción la tortuga tinglar?
   a. Por falta de protección para los huevos.
   b. Por los voluntarios.
   c. Por los binoculares y las linternas.

3. ¿Cuánto tiempo pasan los huevos en el nido artificial?
   a. 28 horas
   b. dos meses
   c. el mes de febrero

Student Activity 3
Presentational Speaking

Directions: Your teacher will give you a Venn diagram or ask you to draw one. Label the first section: *En San José, Costa Rica,* the middle section *En las dos comunidades,* and the last section *En mi comunidad.* As you view the video *Cómo ayudamos a los demás,* write a list of the ways that the students in San José help their community in the first section of the diagram. Write key words only. Then think about what you and your friends can do to help your community and write key words to represent them in the last section. In the middle section write key words that represent what both groups do to help their communities. Using your Venn diagram, give an oral presentation in Spanish comparing what you and your friends do to help your community to what students in San José do to help theirs. You have three minutes to prepare and one minute to speak.

	Teacher's Edition		Ancillaries
	Page #	**Activity**	
Vocabulary	p. 429 p. 439	Pre-AP* Support Pre-AP* Support	*realidades.com* *Assessment Program:* Prueba 9A-2, pp. 231–232
Listening	p. 433 p. 436 p. 440	Pre-AP* Support Act. 14 Pre-AP* Support	*Video Program* Chapter 9A *Video Teacher's Guide* Chapter 9A *Communication Workbook:* Act. 9, p. 175 *Pre-AP* Resource Book:* p. 96
Reading	p. 440	Pre-AP* Support	*TPR Stories:* ¡Demasiada tele!, p. 127 *Realidades* para hispanohablantes: Lectura 1, p. 342 *Realidades* para hispanohablantes: Lectura 2, p. 344 *Pre-AP* Resource Book:* pp. 96–97
Speaking	p. 429 p. 443	Pre-AP* Support (talk!) Presentación oral	*TPR Stories:* Personalized Mini-situations, pp. 123–126 *Realidades* para hispanohablantes: Presentación oral, p. 347 *Teacher's Resource Book, Temas 5–9:* Communicative Activities, pp. 300–303 *Teacher's Resource Book, Temas 5–9:* Situation cards, p. 304 *Assessment Program:* Parte II, Hablar, p. 238 *Pre-AP* Resource Book:* p. 96
Writing	p. 429 p. 433 p. 436 p. 439 p. 440	Pre-AP* Support Pre-AP* Support Act. 14 Pre-AP* Support Pre-AP* Support	*Communication Workbook:* Act. 13, p. 179 *Communication Workbook:* Practice Test, pp. 328–330 *Realidades* para hispanohablantes: Act. M, p. 343 *Realidades* para hispanohablantes: Act. O, p. 345 *realidades.com* *ExamView:* Pre-AP* Question Bank *Assessment Program:* Parte II, Escribir, p. 237 *Pre-AP* Resource Book:* pp. 96–97
Integrated Skills	p. 433 p. 436 p. 439	Act. 11 Act. 15, 16 Act. 18	*Communication Workbook:* Integrated Performance Assessment, p. 327

	Teacher's Edition		Ancillaries
	Page #	Activity	
Vocabulary	p. 453	Pre-AP* Support	*realidades.com* *Assessment Program:* Prueba 9B-2, pp. 243–244
Listening	p. 460 p. 463 p. 465	Differentiated Instruction: Advanced Learners/Pre-AP* Pre-AP* Support Pre-AP* Support	*Video Program* Chapter 9B *Video Teacher's Guide* Chapter 9B *Communication Workbook:* Act. 9, p. 184 *Pre-AP* Resource Book:* p. 96
Reading	p. 454	Act. 4	*Communication Workbook:* Practice Test, pp. 334–336 *TPR Stories:* El regalo de los Reyes Magos, p. 130 *Realidades* para hispanohablantes: Lectura 1, p. 362 *Realidades* para hispanohablantes: Lectura 2, p. 364 *Pre-AP* Resource Book:* pp. 96–97

Speaking	p. 453
	p. 454
	p. 460
	
	p. 465
		Pre-AP* Support
		Act. 4
		Differentiated Instruction:
		  Advanced Learners/Pre-AP*
		Pre-AP* Support
			Teacher's Resource Book, Temas 5–9:
			  Communicative Activities, pp. 334–337
			Teacher's Resource Book, Temas 5–9: Situation
			  cards, p. 338
			Assessment Program: Parte II, Hablar, p. 250
			Pre-AP* Resource Book: p. 96

Writing	p. 460
	
	p. 463
	p. 465
	p. 467
		Differentiated Instruction:
		  Advanced Learners/Pre-AP*
		Pre-AP* Support
		Pre-AP* Support
		Presentación escrita
			Communication Workbook: Act. 13, p. 188
			Communication Workbook: Practice Test,
			  pp. 334–336
			Realidades para hispanohablantes: Act. O, p. 363
			Realidades para hispanohablantes: Presentación
			  escrita, p. 367
			realidades.com
			ExamView: Pre-AP* Question Bank
			Assessment Program: Parte II, Escribir, p. 250
			Pre-AP* Resource Book: pp. 96–97

Integrated Skills	p. 459 p. 463	Act. 12 Act. 19	*Communication Workbook:* Integrated Performance Assessment, p. 333

Teacher Activity 1
Interpretive Communication, Audio and Print Texts

Use the first portion of the reading *La invasión del ciberspanglish*, p. 464 of the *Realidades* Student Textbook, to engage students in the Dictogloss activity on p. 15. (Read aloud the first two paragraphs on p. 464, not the entire reading.) Once students have completed the steps to the Dictogloss activity, have them open their texts to p. 464, read the entire passage aloud with a partner, then work as a class to answer the *¿Comprendes?* questions.

Teacher Activity 2
Presentational Writing

1. Have students watch the Videohistoria for *Capítulo* 9B. (See *Realidades* Teacher's Resource Book, p. 251.)

2. Have students take the quiz *La computadora y tú* on p. 454 and read *A sus teclados, listos a navegar* on p. 456 of the *Realidades* A/B/1 Student Textbook.

3. Next, have students write a composition of 100 words (minimum) about the pros and cons of communicating via traditional methods (telephone, mail) vs. cyber methods. They should provide examples from the text and video sources in their composition.

Teacher Activity 3
Interpersonal Speaking, Conversation

Directions for Student Activity 1, p. 93.

1. Give students one or two minutes to read the introduction and the outline of the conversation and to think about their responses. They may write down key words, but should not write complete answers.

2. Students should record their conversation, responding to a master tape (the teacher can be the voice of Mario) with 20 second pauses after each question to allow time for the students to respond.

3. Students should be encouraged to give full and rich responses.

4. In groups of three or four, students should listen to each recording and discuss the content and quality using the scoring guidelines on p. 49 of this book.

Student Activity 1
Interpersonal Speaking, Conversation

Directions: You will participate in a conversation with Mario, a classmate. You will have one minute to read the introduction and the outline of the conversation below and think about your responses. You may write down key words, but do not write complete answers to the questions. When the conversation begins, you will have up to 20 seconds to respond to each question. Give full and appropriate responses.

Introduction

This is a conversation with Mario, a classmate. He wants to talk about watching television.

MARIO: Hola, ¿qué tal? Oye, ¿crees que los jóvenes pasan demasiado tiempo viendo la televisión?

TÚ: Greet him and answer his questions.

MARIO: Y tú, ¿cuántas horas ves la tele durante una semana típica?

TÚ: Answer his question.

MARIO: En tu opinión, ¿qué clase de programas son buenos para los jóvenes? ¿Por qué?

TÚ: Answer his question fully and explain why.

MARIO: Y, ¿qué clase de programas son malos? ¿Por qué?

TÚ: Answer his question fully and explain why.

MARIO: Finalmente, ¿cuáles son tus programas favoritos? ¿Cómo son?

TÚ: Answer his questions fully.

MARIO: Gracias por darme tu opinión. ¡Hasta luego!

TÚ: Respond to his comments.

Student Activity 2
Interpersonal Writing

Write an e-mail to a classmate to tell him or her about a movie you just saw. Give the title, describe the main characters, and tell about the main plot points. Tell your friend if you liked the movie or not, and why. Include a question or two for your friend to answer. Suggested writing time: 10 minutes.

Level 2
Resource Support

Realidades ❷

Capítulo 1A

Pre-AP* Resource Chart

	Teacher's Edition		**Ancillaries**
	Page #	**Activity**	
Vocabulary	p. 20	Pre-AP* Support	*realidades.com*
Listening	pp. 20–21	Videohistoria	*Video Program* Chapter 1A
	p. 35	Pre-AP* Support	*Video Teacher's Guide* Chapter 1A
			Communication Workbook: Act. 2, pp. 6–7
			Pre-AP Resource Book:* p. 103
Reading	p. 16	Fondo cultural	*TPR Stories:* Juanito el ocupado, p. 10
	p. 25	Fondo cultural	*TPR Stories:* El elefante sin memoria, p. 16
	p. 30	Act. 18	*Realidades* para hispanohablantes: Act. K, p. 20
	p. 32	Fondo cultural	*Realidades* para hispanohablantes: Lectura 1, pp. 22–23
	p. 33	Act. 23	
	p. 34	Fondo cultural	*Realidades* para hispanohablantes: Lectura 2, pp. 24–25
	p. 35	Fondo cultural	
	p. 35	Pre-AP* Support	*Realidades* para hispanohablantes: La cultura en vivo, p. 26
			Pre-AP Resource Book:* pp. 102–103
Speaking	p. 20	Pre-AP* Support	*Assessment Program:* Examen de 1A, Parte II, Hablar, p. 22
	p. 22	Differentiated Instruction, Advanced Learners/Pre-AP*	*Teacher's Resource Book, Para empezar–Tema 4:* Communicative Activities, pp. 36-39
	p. 35	Pre-AP* Support	*Teacher's Resource Book, Para empezar–Tema 4:* Situation cards, p. 40
	p. 37	⬤ Presentación oral	*Realidades* para hispanohablantes: Presentación oral, p. 27
			TPR Stories: pp. 11–15
			Pre-AP Resource Book:* pp. 102–103
Writing	p. 30	Act. 18	*realidades.com*
	p. 33	Act. 23	*Assessment Program:* Examen 1A, Parte II, Escribir, p. 21
	p. 22	Differentiated Instruction, Advanced Learners/Pre-AP*	*Communication Workbook:* Act. 13, p.15
	p. 30	Pre-AP* Support	*ExamView:* Pre-AP* Question Bank
	p. 35	Pre-AP* Support	*Realidades* para hispanohablantes: Act. K, L, p. 20
			Realidades para hispanohablantes: Act. Ñ, O, p. 23
			Realidades para hispanohablantes: Act. Q, p. 25
			Pre-AP Resource Book:* pp. 102–103
Integrated Skills	p. 26	Act. 13	*Communication Workbook:* Integrated Performance Assessment, p. 213
	p. 28	Act. 16	
	p. 30	Act. 18	

	Teacher's Edition		Ancillaries
	Page #	**Activity**	
Vocabulary	p. 48	Pre-AP* Support	*realidades.com*
Listening	pp. 48–49	Videohistoria	*Communication Workbook:* Act. 7, p. 19
	p. 48	Pre-AP* Support	*Video Program* Chapter 1B
			Video Teacher's Guide Chapter 1B
			Pre-AP Resource Book:* p. 103
Reading	p. 44	Fondo cultural	*Realidades* para hispanohablantes; Lectura 1, p. 42
	p. 51	Fondo cultural	*Realidades* para hispanohablantes: Lectura 2, p. 44
	p. 54	Fondo cultural	*Realidades* para hispanohablantes: Perspectivas del
	p. 55	Fondo cultural	mundo hispano, p. 46
	p. 60	Act. 22	*Communication Workbook:* Practice Test,
	p. 61	Act. 23	pp. 217-219
	p. 62	Fondo cultural	*realidades.com*
	p. 64	Perspectivas del mundo hispano	*TPR Stories:* La vida en Colorado, p. 18
			TPR Stories: Tito lo hace todo, p. 22
			Realidades para hispanohablantes: Perspectivas del mundo hispano, p. 46
			Pre-AP Resource Book:* pp. 102–103
Speaking	p. 57	Pre-AP* Support	*Assessment Program:* Examen 1B, Parte II,
	p. 58	Differentiated Instruction: Advanced Learners/Pre-AP*	Hablar, p. 36
			Teacher's Resource Book, Para empezar–Tema 4: Communicative Activities, pp. 70-73
	p. 60	Act. 22	*Teacher's Resource Book, Para empezar–Tema 4:* Situation cards, p. 74
			TPR Stories: pp. 19–21
			Pre-AP Resource Book:* pp. 102–103
Writing	p. 58	Differentiated Instruction: Advanced Learners/Pre-AP*	*Communication Workbook:* Act .13, p. 24
			Communication Workbook: Practice Test,
	p. 60	Act. 22	pp. 217-219
	p. 62	Pre-AP* Support	*Realidades* para hispanohablantes: Presentación
	p. 65	Presentación escrita	escrita, p. 47
			Assessment Program: Examen 1B, Parte II, Escribir, pp. 36, 39
			realidades.com
			ExamView: Pre-AP* Question Bank
			Realidades para hispanohablantes: Act. P, Q, R, S, pp. 42-43
			Realidades para hispanohablantes: Act. U, V, W, p. 45
			Pre-AP Resource Book:* pp. 102–103
Integrated Skills	p. 54	Act. 13	*Communication Workbook:* Integrated Performance
	p. 55	Act. 14	Assessment, p. 216

Teacher Activity 1
Presentational Writing

Have students read *Un anuncio* on p. 61 of the *Realidades* Student Textbook. Students should then write three paragraphs describing how they believe people can remain in good physical condition throughout life citing activities from the reading as examples to support their ideas. Then make three photocopies of each student's written work. Place students in groups of four. Distribute copies of the scoring guidelines found on p. 49 of this book. (Since this is a writing task, the *Fluency* category on the bottom row can be ignored at this time.) Distribute the copies of the students' work within each group. Have each student read his or her writing aloud to the group, one piece at a time, and discuss the content and quality of each writing piece using the scoring guidelines. Each group may select one sample to share with the whole class.

Teacher Activity 2
Interpersonal Speaking

Use the questions in Student Activity 1 to develop students' interpersonal speaking skills. Have each student select 5 questions to guide a conversation with a partner. Student A begins the conversation with a greeting and asks the first question. Student A listens to his/her partner's response and reacts to it in a natural and logical way, furthering the conversation. Student A continues with the next question and reacts to his/her partner's response naturally. The conversation continues until Student A has asked all his/her questions and ends the conversation. At that point, Student B begins his/her conversation and follows the same procedure. It is important to encourage students to let the conversation flow naturally and to point out that the activity is a conversation; it is not an interview. Remind the students to use expressions they have studied, such as *¡genial! ¡qué buena idea! ¡qué pena! (no) estoy de acuerdo, ¡no me digas! ¿de veras?* and *¡uf!* Adverbial expressions, such as *generalmente, también, todos los días, nunca, siempre, a veces, ayer, el año pasado,* will also help advance the conversation. In addition, students should be encouraged to use conjunctions, such as *y, pero, cuando, porque, o aunque,* to form multi-clause sentences and raise their level of discourse.

Teacher Activity 3
Using the *Fondo cultural*

The *Fondo cultural* activities of each chapter offer additional insight into the cultures of the Spanish-speaking world. Because the information is in Spanish and the questions typically involve a comparison to the students' own culture, these activities can be a very effective tool for partner, small group, and whole class discussions. Teachers might want to have students read the information and write an answer to the question. Students can then read and discuss their answers with a partner or in a small group. Or teachers might have small groups read the information and use the question to prompt a group discussion. Each group should prepare a short answer to present to the class. The teacher can then guide a class discussion, comparing and commenting on each group's answer.

Student Activity 1
Interpersonal Speaking

Work with a partner to write complete-sentence answers to the following questions. Be sure to verify the correctness of your answers. Then, use the questions (and answers) to participate in a conversation with your partner, play *Preguntas rápidas* (see p. 41) or to prepare for *One minute of questions* (For Levels 1 and 2) (see p. 42).

1. ¿Qué tienes que hacer para tus clases?

   _____

2. ¿Qué se prohíbe en tu escuela?

   _____

3. ¿Cuáles reglas de tu escuela no te gustan?

   _____

4. ¿Con quiénes almuerzas?

   _____

5. ¿A qué hora empiezan tus clases? ¿Es temprano?

   _____

6. ¿Conoces a alguien en tu clase de matemáticas?

   _____

7. ¿Te dan muchas tareas algunos profesores?

   _____

8. ¿Comprendes lo que te dice tu profesor(a) de español?

   _____

9. ¿Quién es tan amable como tú?

   _____

10. ¿Qué piensas de las artes marciales?

    _____

11. ¿Cuánto tiempo hace que conoces a tu mejor amigo(a)?

    _____

12. ¿Cuánto tiempo hace que asistes a tu escuela?

    _____

13. ¿Cuántas horas pasas al día navegando en la Red?

    _____

14. ¿Eres miembro de algún club o equipo?

    _____

15. ¿Qué vas a hacer hoy después de las clases?

    _____

16. ¿Sabes jugar algún deporte? ¿Cuál?

    _____

	Teacher's Edition		Ancillaries
	Page #	**Activity**	
Vocabulary	p. 87	Act. 21	*realidades.com*
Listening	pp. 76–77	Videohistoria	*Communication Workbook:* Act. 3, pp. 26–27
			Communication Workbook: Act. 7, p. 29
			Communication Workbook: Act. 8, p. 30
			Video Program Chapter 2A
			Video Teacher's Guide Chapter 2A
			Pre-AP* Resource Book: p. 106
Reading	p. 72	Fondo cultural	*TPR Stories:* Las audiciones de Santiago, p. 25
	p. 79	Fondo cultural	*TPR Stories:* La vida de una actriz, pp. *29*
	p. 84	Fondo cultural	*Realidades* para hispanohablantes*:* Lectura 1, p. 62
	p. 91	Fondo cultural	*Realidades* para hispanohablantes: Lectura 2, p. 64
			Realidades para hispanohablantes: La cultura en vivo, p. 66
			Pre-AP* Resource Book: pp. 106–107
Speaking	p. 76	Pre-AP* Support	*Assessment Program:* Examen 2A, Parte II, Hablar, p. 51
	p. 78	Differentiated Instruction: Advanced Learners/Pre-AP*	*Teacher's Resource Book, Para empezar–Tema 4:* Communicative Activities, pp. 109–111
	p. 87	Act. 21	*Teacher's Resource Book, Para empezar–Tema 4:* Situation cards, p. 112
	p. 90	Pre-AP* Support	*Realidades* para hispanohablantes: Presentación oral, p. 67
	p. 93	(Talk!) Presentación oral	*TPR Stories:* pp. 26–28
			Pre-AP* Resource Book: pp. 106–107
Writing	p. 76	Pre-AP* Support	*Communication Workbook:* Act. 13, p. 34
	p. 85	Pre-AP* Support	*realidades.com*
	p. 87	Act. 21	*ExamView:* Pre-AP* Question Bank
			Assessment Program: Examen 2A, Parte II, Escribir, p. 51
			Realidades para hispanohablantes: Act Ñ, O, p. 63
			Realidades para hispanohablantes: Act. Q, pp. 64–65
			Pre-AP* Resource Book: pp. 106–107
Integrated Skills	p. 82	Act. 13	*Communication Workbook:* Integrated Performance Assessment, p. 222

	Teacher's Edition		Ancillaries
	Page #	Activity	
Vocabulary	p. 104	Pre-AP* Support	*realidades.com*
Listening	pp. 104–105	Videohistoria	*Writing, Audio & Video Workbook:* Act. 2, pp. 35–36
	p. 108	Pre-AP* Support	*Video Program* Chapter 2B
	p. 120	Pre-AP* Support	*Video Teacher's Guide* Chapter 2B
			Pre-AP Resource Book:* p. 106
Reading	p. 100	Fondo cultural	*Communication workbook:* Practice Test, pp. 226-228
	p. 108	Pre-AP* Support	*TPR Stories:* Princesita y el agua, p. 31
	p. 109	Fondo cultural	*TPR Stories:* La Tienda "Variedad", pp. 35
	p. 117	Fondo cultural	*Realidades* para hispanohablantes: Lectura 1, p. 82
	p. 118	Fondo cultural	*Realidades* para hispanohablantes: Lectura 2, p. 84
	p. 120	Pre-AP* Support	*Realidades* para hispanohablantes: Perspectivas del mundo hispano, p. 86
	p. 120	Perspectivas del mundo hispano	*Pre-AP* Resource Book:* p. 107
Speaking	p. 104	Differentiated Instruction: Advanced Learners/Pre-AP*	*Assessment Program:* Examen de 2B, Parte II, Hablar, p. 65
	p.104	Pre-AP* Support	*Teacher's Resource Book, Para empezar–Tema 4:* Communicative Activities, pp. 146–149
	p. 117	Act. 24	*Teacher's Resource Book, Para empezar–Tema 4:* Situation cards, p. 150
	p. 118	Pre-AP* Support	*TPR Stories:* pp. 32–34
	p. 120	Pre-AP* Support	*Pre-AP* Resource Book,* pp. 106–107
Writing	p. 108	Pre-AP* Support	*Assessment Program:* Examen de 2B, Parte II, Escribir, p. 65
	p. 116	Differentiated Instruction: Advanced Learners/Pre-AP*	*Communication Workbook:* Act. 12, p. 44
	p. 117	Act. 24	*Comunication workbook:* Practice Test, pp. 226-228
	p. 121	Presentación escrita	*Realidades* para hispanohablantes: Presentación escrita, p. 87
			realidades.com
			ExamView: Pre-AP* Question Bank
			Realidades para hispanohablantes: Acts. R, S, T, U, p. 83
			Realidades para hispanohablantes: Act. V, pp. 84–85
			Pre-AP Resource Book,* pp. 106–107
Integrated Skills	p. 112	Act. 18	*Communication workbook:* Integrated Performance Assessment, p. 226
	p. 117	Act. 24	

Teacher Activity 1
Circumlocution

Place students in pairs and provide each one with one of the following lists of words. Allow 4-5 minutes for each individual to write definitions in Spanish for the given words. Next, partners take turns expressing the meaning of the word to each other, with the opposite partner trying to guess the word that is being defined. After the partners have concluded by guessing the words for all of the definitions, allow a few students to share some of the "best" definitions with the class.

Directions: Write a definition in Spanish for each of the following words without using the word or similar root words in the definition.

Student A—List 1
1. lentamente
2. toalla
3. pedir prestado
4. ganga
5. mediano
6. cuero

Student B—List 2
1. el desodorante
2. despertarse
3. salón de belleza
4. flojo
5. encontrar
6. vivo

Teacher Activity 2
Interpersonal Speaking, Conversation

Directions:

1. Make a transparency of the following scenario: Your first-period teacher wants to understand why you arrive late to class almost every day.

   Conversation:
   PROFESOR: Mira, ¿por qué sueles llegar tarde a mi clase?
   ESTUDIANTE: (20 second response)
   PROFESOR: ¿A qué hora te despiertas y qué haces después?
   ESTUDIANTE: (20 second response)
   PROFESOR: ¿Qué desayunas? ¿Cómo llegas a la escuela?
   ESTUDIANTE: (20 second response)
   PROFESOR: Pues, ¿cómo piensas resolver el problema?
   ESTUDIANTE: (20 second response)
   PROFESOR: De acuerdo. Vamos a ver si la situación mejora o no.

2. Have students read the conversation framework above, and then prepare (by writing down key words), how they would fill in the following conversation with rich and full responses to the questions. The goal is to provide as much speech as possible in the time provided, rather than to settle on a basic, short appropriate response.

3. Teachers may wish to ask the class to brainstorm together about some possible responses, but ultimately, the preparation should be accomplished individually. Students should have one minute to read the outline of the conversation and think about their responses.

4. Students are then allowed to record their conversations. (See Recording and Evaluating on p. 44.) The teacher can be the voice of the *Profesor*, allowing no more than 20 seconds for each response from the students.

5. In groups of three or four, students should listen to each recording and discuss the content and quality using the scoring guidelines on p. 49 of this book.

Student Activity 1
Presentational Speaking

Directions: Your teacher will give you a Venn diagram or ask you to draw one. Label the first section: *Las parrandas,* the middle section *Las dos fiestas,* and the last section *Las fiestas de mi familia.* As you read *Perspectivas del mundo hispano* (REALIDADES 2, p. 120), write a list of features of the celebration described in the reading selection in the first section of the Venn diagram. Be sure to write key words only. Then think about parties that your family gives and write key words to represent their features in the last section. In the middle section write key words that represent what both parties have in common. Using your Venn diagram, give an oral presentation in Spanish in which you compare parties that your family gives to family parties in the Spanish-speaking world. How are they similar? How are they different? After reading *La parranda* and completing the first section of the Venn diagram, you will have three minutes to complete your Venn diagram and organize your thoughts. Then you will have one minute to speak. Be sure to include appropriate transition words to facilitate the flow of information in your presentation.

Student Activity 2
Interpersonal Writing

Directions: Read the following e-mail message and write a response to it. Your reply should include a greeting and a closing. Be sure to answer all the questions that Ana asks. You should also ask her at least one or two questions.

¡Hola!

¿Cómo estás? Como ya sabes, voy a ir a tu escuela en septiembre para estudiar por tres meses. ¡Estoy muy entusiasmada porque sé que será una experiencia especial! Ayer recibí el calendario escolar que incluye la fecha de *Homecoming.* ¿Qué es *Homecoming?* Para mí es algo nuevo. El calendario también menciona el baile de *Homecoming* y dice que todos los estudiantes pueden asistir. ¿Qué ropa necesito llevar al baile? Te tengo que decir que me encanta ir de compras y que paso mucho tiempo buscando liquidaciones y gangas. Por eso me gustaría saber cómo son las tiendas en tu comunidad. Gracias por la información que me enviaste la semana pasada.

Un saludo,

Ana

	Teacher's Edition		Ancillaries
	Page #	**Activity**	
Vocabulary	p. 132	Pre-AP* Support	*realidades.com*
Listening	pp. 132–133	Videohistoria	*Communication Workbook:* Act. 9, p. 51
	p. 132	Pre-AP* Support	*Video Program* Chapter 3A
			Video Teacher's Guide Chapter 3A
			Pre-AP* Resource Book, p. 111
Reading	p. 140	Pre-AP* Support	*TPR Stories: ¡Se me olvido!,* p. 38
	p. 141	Act. 16	*TPR Stories: La vida sin crema de afeitar,* p. 42
	p. 146	Pre-AP* Support	*Realidades* para hispanohablantes: Lectura 1, p. 102
	p. 128	Fondo cultural	
	p. 135	Fondo cultural	*Realidades* para hispanohablantes: Lectura 2, p. 104
	p. 137	Fondo cultural	
	p. 144	Fondo cultural	*Realidades* para hispanohablantes: La cultura en vivo, p. 106
	p. 145	Fondo cultural	*Pre-AP* Resource Book:* pp. 110–111
Speaking	p. 132	Pre-AP* Support	*Assessment Program:* Examen de 3A, Parte II, Hablar, p. 79
	p. 140	Pre-AP* Support	*Teacher's Resource Book, Para empezar–Tema 4:* Communicative Activities, pp. 188–190
	p. 142	Differentiated Instruction: Advanced Learners/Pre-AP*	*Teacher's Resource Book, Para empezar–Tema 4:* Situation cards, p. 191
	p. 145	Act. 24	*TPR Stories:* pp. 39–41
	p. 149	⟨Talk!⟩ Presentación oral	*Realidades* para hispanohablantes: Presentación oral, p. 107
			Pre-AP Resource Book:* p. 111
Writing	p. 132	Pre-AP* Support	*Assessment Program:* Examen de 3A, Parte II, Escribir, p. 79
	p. 140	Pre-AP* Support	
	p. 142	Differentiated Instruction: Advanced Learners/Pre-AP*	*Communication workbook:* Act. 13, p. 55
			realidades.com
	p. 145	Pre-AP* Support	*ExamView:* Pre-AP* Question Bank
	p. 146	Act. 24	*Realidades* para hispanohablantes: Act. O, P, p. 103
			Realidades para hispanohablantes: Act. R, S, p. 106
			Pre-AP Resource Book:* pp. 110–111
Integrated Skills	p. 143	Act. 21	*Communication Workbook:* Integrated Performance Assessment, p. 234
	p. 145	Act. 23, 24	

	Teacher's Edition		Ancillaries
	Page #	**Activity**	
Vocabulary	p. 160	Pre-AP* Support	*realidades.com*
Listening	pp. 160–161	Videohistoria	*Video Program* Chapter 3B
			Video Teacher's Guide Chapter 3B
	p. 174	Pre-AP* Support	*Communication Workbook:* Act. 3, p. 58
			Pre-AP* Resource Book, p. 111
Reading	p. 156	*Fondo cultural*	*Communication Workbook:* Practice Test, pp. 235–237
	p. 165	*Fondo cultural*	*TPR Stories:* Una aventura en la calle, p. 44
	p. 169	*Fondo cultural*	*TPR Stories:* Manejando con Desi, p. 48
	p. 172	*Fondo cultural*	*Realidades* para hispanohablantes: Lectura 1, p. 122
	p. 174	Pre-AP* Support	*Realidades* para hispanohablantes: Lectura 2, p. 124
	p. 175	*Fondo cultural*	*Realidades* para hispanohblantes: Perspectivas del mundo hispano, p. 126
	p. 176	Perspectivas del mundo hispano	Pre-AP* Resource Book: pp. 110–111
Speaking	p. 160	Pre-AP* Support	*TPR Stories:* pp. 45–47
	p. 169	Pre-AP* Support	*Teacher's Resource Book, Para empezar–Tema 4:* Communicative Activities, pp. 226–229
	p. 173	Act. 22	*Teacher's Resource Book, Para empezar–Tema 4:* Situation cards, p. 230
			Assessment Program: Examen de capítulo 3B, Parte II, Hablar, p. 93
			Pre-AP* Resource Book: p. 111
Writing	p. 164	Differentiated Instruction: Advanced Learners/Pre-AP*	*Communication Workbook:* Act. 13, p. 66
			Communication Workbook: Practice Test, pp. 235–237
	p. 173	Act. 22	*realidades.com*
	p. 177	Presentación escrita	*Exam View:* Pre-AP* Question Bank
			Assessment Program: Examen de capítulo 3B, Parte II, Escribir, p. 93
			Realidades para hispanohablantes: Act. S, T, U, p. 123
			Realidades para hispanohablantes: Act. W, X, p. 125
			Realidades para hispanohablantes: Presentación escrita, p. 127
			Pre-AP* Resource Book: pp. 110–111
Integrated Skills	p. 173	Act. 21	*Communication Workbook:* Integrated Performance Assessment, p. 234
	p. 173	Act. 22	

Teacher Activity Sheet

Teacher Activity 1
Presentational Writing

Have students each choose a Spanish-speaking country they would like to visit. From the school library, a classroom reference, or the Internet, they should then find a publication about the country that includes: locations of cultural and historical significance, weather, and currency exchange rate. The publication will be needed in class on the day of the writing exercise.

In class, give students 30-40 minutes to write three paragraphs on the following topic:

- Explain what would be needed to prepare for a trip to [name of country]. Include details about:
- How long of a trip to plan based on the number of sites to see.
- Justify the places you would visit while there based on their cultural and / or historical significance.
- Tell how you would travel to and within the country.
- Describe the clothing you would need to pack based on where you will visit.
- Tell how much money you would need to take and why.
- Describe what you expect to be the highlight of this trip.

Students should cite facts from the publication to support their travel plans.

Next, make three photocopies of each student's written work. Place students in groups of four. Distribute copies of the scoring guidelines found on p. 49 of this book. (Since this is a writing task, the *Fluency* category on the bottom row can be ignored at this time.) Distribute the copies of the students' work within each group. Have each student read his or her writing aloud to the group, one piece at a time, and discuss the content and quality of each writing piece using the scoring guidelines. Each group may select one sample to share with the whole class.

Teacher Activity 2
Interpersonal Speaking

Directions:

1. Give students one minute to read the introduction and the outline of the conversation and to think about their responses. They may write down key words, but should not write complete answers.
2. Students should record their conversation, responding to a master recording (the teacher can be the voice of Mario) with 20-second pauses after each question to allow time for the students to respond.
3. Students should be encouraged to give full and rich responses.
4. In groups of three or four, students should listen to each recording and discuss content and quality using the scoring guidelines on p. 49 of this book.

Student Activity 1
Interpersonal Writing

Directions: Read the following e-mail message and write a response to it. Your reply should include a greeting and a closing. Be sure to answer all the questions that Andrés asks. You should also ask him at least one or two questions.

Hola,

¡Estoy muy contento! Mis padres acaban de decirme que puedo conseguir mi permiso de manejar. Primero, tengo que prepararme para un examen escrito. Estoy un poco nervioso porque no me gusta tomar exámenes. ¿Qué crees que debo hacer para salir bien en el examen? Después del examen, voy a aprender a manejar un coche con un instructor. Dicen que puedo tomar lecciones que duran una hora o media hora. En tu opinión, ¿qué es mejor? ¿Por qué? Yo sé que es importante tener mucho cuidado cuando manejo. Además, no quiero que el instructor se ponga nervioso. Por eso no voy a escuchar la radio ni hablar por teléfono celular durante las lecciones. ¿Estás de acuerdo? Te voy a enviar otro mensaje después de mi primera lección.

Hasta pronto,

Andrés

Student Activity 2
Interpersonal Speaking

Directions: You will participate in a conversation with Jorge, a classmate. You will have one minute to read the introduction and the outline of the conversation below and think about your responses. You may write down key words, but do not write complete answers to the questions. When the conversation begins, you will have up to 20 seconds to respond to each question. Give full and appropriate responses.

Introduction

This is a conversation with Jorge, a classmate. He wants to talk about your day yesterday.

JORGE: Hola, ¿qué tal? ¿Cómo fue tu día ayer?

TÚ: Greet him and answer his questions.

JORGE: Para mí fue un día típico. ¿Qué hiciste ayer por la mañana?

TÚ: Answer his question fully.

JORGE: ¿De veras? ¿Qué hiciste por la tarde?

TÚ: Answer his question fully.

JORGE: Y, ¿dónde cenaste? ¿Te gustó la comida?

TÚ: Answer his questions fully.

JORGE: Pues, me parece que fue un día interesante. Gracias por describírmelo. ¡Hasta pronto!

TÚ: Respond to his comments.

	Teacher's Edition		Ancillaries
	Page #	Activity	
Vocabulary	p. 188	Pre-AP* Support	*realidades.com*
Listening	pp. 188–189	Videohistoria	*Video Program* Chapter 4A *Video Teacher's Guide* Chapter 4A *Communication Workbook:* Act. 8, p. 72 *Pre-AP* Resource Book:* p. 114
Reading	p. 184 p. 190 p. 192 p. 194 p. 200 p. 201 p. 203	Fondo cultural Fondo cultural Fondo cultural Differentiated Instruction: Advanced Learners/Pre-AP* Fondo cultural Act. 26 Pre-AP* Support	*TPR Stories:* La educación de Burbuja, p. 52 *TPR Stories:* Magdalena, la mala educada, p. 56 *Realidades* para hispanohablantes: Lectura 1, p. 142 *Realidades* para hispanohablantes: Lectura 2, p. 144 *Realidades* para hispanohablantes: La cultura en vivo, p. 146 *Pre-AP* Resource Book:* pp. 114–115
Speaking	p. 201 p. 205	Act. 26 (talk!) Presentación oral	*TPR Stories:* pp. 53–55 *Teacher's Resource Book, Para empezar–Tema 4:* Communicative Activities, pp. 269-272 *Teacher's Resource Book, Para empezar–Tema 4:* Situation cards, p. 273 *Assessment Program:* Examen del capítulo 4A, Parte II, Hablar, p. 107 *Realidades* para hispanohablantes: Presentación oral, p. 147 *Pre-AP* Resource Book:* pp. 114–115
Writing	p. 188 p. 194 p. 197 p. 201	Pre-AP* Support Differentiated Instruction: Advanced Learners/Pre-AP* Pre-AP* Support Act. 26	*Communication Workbook:* Act. 12, p. 76 *realidades.com* *ExamView:* Pre-AP* Question Bank *Assessment Program:* Examen del capítulo 4A, Parte II, Escribir, p. 107 *Realidades* para hispanohablantes: Act. Ñ, p. 143 *Realidades* para hispanohablantes: Act. P, Q, p. 145 *Pre-AP* Resource Book:* pp. 114–115
Integrated Skills	p. 198 p. 200 p. 201	Act. 21 Act. 24 Act. 26	*Communication Workbook:* Integrated Performance Assessment, p. 240

	Teacher's Edition		Ancillaries
	Page #	**Activity**	
Vocabulary			*realidades.com*
Listening	pp. 214–215	Videohistoria	*Video Program* Chapter 4B
	p. 221	Pre-AP* Support	*Video Teacher's Guide* Chapter 4B
			Communication Workbook: Act. 9, p. 83
			Pre-AP Resource Book:* p. 114
Reading	p. 210	Fondo cultural	*Communication Workbook:* Practice Test, pp. 244–246
	p. 216	Fondo cultural	*TPR Stories:* María, Diego y los gatos, p. 58
	p. 218	Fondo cultural	*TPR Stories:* La boda de Héctor y Marisel, p. 62
	p. 220	Fondo cultural	*Realidades* para hispanohablantes: Lectura 1, p. 162
	p. 226	Fondo cultural	
	p. 226	Fondo cultural	*Realidades* para hispanohablantes: Lectura 2, p. 164
	p. 228	Pre-AP* Support	*Realidades* para hispanohablantes: Perspectivas del mundo hispano, p. 166
	p. 230	Perspectivas del mundo hispano	*Pre-AP* Resource Book:* pp. 114–115
Speaking	p. 214	Pre-AP* Support	*TPR Stories:* pp. 59–61
	p. 226	Act. 19	*Teacher's Resource Book, Para empezar–Tema 4:* Communicative Activities: pp. 303–306
			Teacher's Resource Book, Para empezar–Tema 4: Situation cards, p. 307
			Assessment Program: Parte II, Hablar, p. 120
			Pre-AP Resource Book:* pp. 114–115
Writing	p. 214	Pre-AP* Support	*Communication Workbook:* Act. 4, p. 80
	p. 221	Pre-AP* Support	*Communication Workbook:* Act. 13, p. 87
	p. 224	Differentiated Instruction: Advanced Learners/Pre-AP*	*Communication Workbook:* Practice Test, pp. 244–246
	p. 226	Act. 19	*realidades.com*
	p. 228	Pre-AP* Support	*ExamView:* Pre-AP* Question Bank
	p. 231	Presentación escrita	*Assessment Program:* Parte II, Escribir, p. 120
			Realidades para hispanohablantes: Acts. R and S, p. 163
			Realidades para hispanohablantes: Act. U, V, p. 165
			Realidades para hispanohablantes: Presentación escrita, p. 167
			Pre-AP Resource Book:* pp. 114–115
Integrated Skills	p. 226	Act. 19	*Communication Workbook:* Integrated Performance Assessment, p. 243
	p. 227	Act. 21	

Teacher Activity 1
Circumlocution

Place students in pairs and provide each one with one of the following lists of words. Allow 4–5 minutes for each individual to write definitions in Spanish for the given words. Next, partners take turns expressing the meaning of the word to each other, with the opposite partner trying to guess the word that is being defined. After the partners have concluded by guessing the words for all of the definitions, allow a few students to share some of the "best" definitions with the class.

Directions: Write a definition in Spanish for each of the following words without using the word or similar root words in the definition.

Student A—List 1
1. patio de recreo
2. portarse mal
3. los bloques
4. enorme
5. recordar
6. llorar

Student B—List 2
1. vecino
2. oso de peluche
3. dinosaurio
4. casarse con
5. despedirse de
6. la reunión

Teacher Activity 2
Interpretive Communication, Print Texts

Use the reading, *El grillo y el jaguar* from p. 202 in the *Realidades* Student Textbook to engage students in the Dictogloss activity on p. 14. It may be necessary to pre-teach some of the unfamiliar vocabulary (*grillo, tenían miedo, se escondieron,* etc.) using TPR or some other means in order to make the story more meaningful. Once students have completed the steps to the Dictogloss activity, have them open their books and read the selection aloud with a partner. Following the paired reading, students should continue working in pairs to answer and discuss the questions in *¿Comprendiste?* and *Y tú ¿qué dices?*

Teacher Activity 3
Interpretive Communication, Print Texts

Make a transparency of the following questions. After reading *El grillo y el jaguar*, pp. 202–203 in the *Realidades* Student Textbook, have students select the most appropriate answer to the following questions.

1. ¿Por qué salió el jaguar de su casa?
   a. Tenía sed.
   b. Tenía miedo.
   c. Le gustaba rugir.

2. ¿Por qué necesitaba el grillo que el jaguar lo perdonara?
   a. No se escondió.
   b. No oyó al jaguar.
   c. No saludó al rey.

3. ¿Por qué ganó el grillo la carrera?
   a. Era más rápido que el jaguar.
   b. Era más astuto que el jaguar.
   c. Siguió cantando.

Student Activity 1
Presentational Speaking

Directions: Your teacher will give you a Venn diagram or ask you to draw one. Label the first section: *La fiesta de San Pedro*, the middle section *Las dos fiestas*, and the last section *Mi día festivo*. As you view the *Capítulo* 4B *Videohistoria*, listen to Ignacio describe his childhood memories of the celebration of *La fiesta de San Pedro*. Write a list of the features of the celebration as Ignacio describes them in the first section of the Venn diagram. Be sure to write key words only. Then think about a holiday that was important to you in your childhood and write key words to represent its features in the last section. In the middle section write key words that represent features of both celebrations. Using your Venn diagram, give an oral presentation in Spanish in which you compare how you celebrated a special holiday in your childhood to Ignacio's childhood memories of the celebration of *La fiesta de San Pedro*. How were they similar? How were they different? After viewing the video and completing the first section of the Venn diagram, you will have three minutes to complete your Venn diagram and organize your thoughts. Then you will have 90 seconds to speak. Be sure to include appropriate transition words to facilitate the flow of information in your presentation.

Student Activity 2
Presentational Writing

Directions: Knowing that holidays are an important part of the life of a community, the lifestyle editor of a local Spanish language newspaper wants to create a new holiday called *El día del estudiante*. The newspaper is seeking input from students and is asking them to submit essays describing how and why the new holiday should be celebrated. The students who submit the best essays will be asked to serve on the committee that plans the celebration. Write a detailed essay that answers the question "How and why should our community celebrate *El día del estudiante?*

1. Use a graphic organizer to outline your main points. Why is it a good idea to celebrate *El día del estudiante?* What activities should the celebration include? Be sure to provide supporting details.
2. Begin the essay with an introductory paragraph and end with a concluding paragraph.
3. Remember to use a variety of transition words and expressions so that the information flows smoothly.
4. Use conjunctions and adverbial expressions to create multi-clause sentences to raise the level of discourse in the essay.

	Teacher's Edition		Ancillaries
	Page #	Activity	
Vocabulary	p. 242	Pre-AP* Support	*realidades.com*
Listening	pp. 242–243	Videohistoria	*Video Program* Chapter 5A
			Video Teacher's Guide Chapter 5A
	p. 242	Pre-AP* Support	*Communication Workbook:* Act. 5, p. 91
	p. 249	Pre-AP* Support	*Pre-AP* Resource Book:* pp. 118–119
Reading	p. 238	Fondo cultural	*TPR Stories:* La leyenda de José María, p. 66
	p. 245	Fondo cultural	*TPR Stories:* Guau, el héroe, p. 70
	p. 247	Fondo cultural	*Lecturas* para hispanohablantes: Lectura 1, p. 182
	p. 253	Act. 20	*Lecturas* para hispanohablantes: Lectura 2, p. 184
	p. 257	Fondo cultural	*Realidades para hispanohablantes:* La cultura en
	p. 257	Pre-AP* Support	vivo, p. 186
			Pre-AP Resource Book:* pp. 118–119
Speaking	p. 242	Pre-AP* Support	*TPR Stories:* pp. 67–69
	p. 249	Pre-AP* Support	*Teacher's Resource Book, Temas 5–9:* Communicative Activities, pp. 15–17
	p. 253	Act. 20	*Teacher's Resource Book, Temas 5–9:* Situation cards, p. 18
	p. 257	Pre-AP* Support	*Assessment Program:* Parte II, Hablar, p. 134
	p. 259	(Talk!) Presentación oral	*Realidades* para hispanohablantes: Presentación oral, p. 187
			Pre-AP Resource Book:* pp. 118–119
Writing	p. 242	Pre-AP* Support	*Communication Workbook:* Act. 4, p. 90
	p. 257	Pre-AP* Support	*Communication Workbook:* Act. 13, p. 97
			realidades.com
			ExamView: Pre-AP* Question Bank
			Assessment Program: Parte II, Escribir, p. 134
			Realidades para hispanohablantes: Act. Q, R, S, p. 183
			Realidades para hispanohablantes: Act. U, V, W, p. 185
			Pre-AP Resource Book:* pp. 118–119
Integrated Skills	p. 252	Act. 20	*Communication Workbook:* Integrated Performance Assessment, p. 249
	p. 254	Act. 22	
	p. 255	Act. 23	

Realidades 2

Capítulo 5B

Pre-AP* Resource Chart

	Teacher's Edition		Ancillaries
	Page #	Activity	
Vocabulary	p. 268	Pre-AP* Support	*realidades.com*
Listening	pp. 268–269	Videohistoria	*Video Program* Chapter 5B *Video Teacher's Guide* Chapter 5B *Communication Workbook:* Act. 9,10, p. 102 *Pre-AP* Resource Book:* pp. 118–119

Reading	p. 265
	p. 271
	p. 278
	p. 280
	p. 282
	p. 284
		Fondo cultural
		Fondo cultural
		Fondo cultural
		Fondo cultural
		Pre-AP* Support
		Perspectivas del mundo hispano
			Communication Workbook: Practice Test,
			  pp. 253–255
			TPR Stories: Alicia la alérgica, p. 72
			TPR Stories: El día terrible d la curandera, p. 76
			Realidades para hispanohablantes: Lectura 1,
			  p. 202
			Realidades para hispanohablantes: Lectura 2, p. 204
			Realidades para hispanohablantes: Perspectivas del
			  mundo hispano, p. 206
			Pre-AP Resource Book:* pp. 118–119

Speaking	p. 268
	p. 281
	p. 282
		Pre-AP* Support
		Act. 26
		Pre-AP* Support
			TPR Stories: pp. 73–75
			Teacher's Resource Book, Temas 5–9:
			  Communicative Activities, pp. 52–55
			Teacher's Resource Book, Temas 5–9: Situation
			  cards, p. 56
			Assessment Program: Parte II, Hablar, p. 147
			Pre-AP Resource Book:* p. 118–119

Writing	p. 272
	p. 272
	
	p. 285
		Pre-AP* Support
		Differentiated Instruction:
		  Advanced Learners/Pre-AP*
		Presentación escrita
			Communication Workbook: Act.13, p. 106
			Communication Workbook: Practice Test,
			  pp. 253–255
			realidades.com
			ExamView: Pre-AP* Question Bank
			Assessment Program: Parte II, Escribir, p. 147
			Realidades para hispanohablantes: Act. P, Q,
			  p. 203
			Realidades para hispanohablantes: Act. R, S, T,
			  p. 205
			Realidades para hispanohablantes: Presentación
			  escrita, p. 207
			Pre-AP Resource Book:* p. 119

Integrated Skills	p. 276 p. 279	Act. 16 Act. 21	*Communication Workbook:* Integrated Performance Assessment, p. 253

Teacher Activity 1
Presentational Speaking

1. Have students read the *Lectura* on pp. 256–257 of the *Realidades* Student Text Book silently.

2. Next, have students prepare a one-minute news commentary as if they were reporters in the field, citing data from the *Lectura*. The amount of preparation time can vary, but should not be longer than three minutes.

3. Students are then allowed one minute to record their presentations, or they may make their presentations to a group of three or four students.

4. In groups of three or four, students should listen to each recording (or hear each presentation) and discuss the content and quality using the scoring guidelines on p. 49 of this book.

Teacher Activity 2
Evaluating with Rubrics

After students have completed Student Activity 2 on the next page, make three photocopies of each student's written work. Place students in groups of four. Distribute copies of the scoring guidelines found on p. 49 of this book. (Since this is a writing task, the *Fluency* category on the bottom row can be ignored at this time.) Distribute the copies of the students' work within each group. Have each student read his or her writing aloud to the group, one piece at a time, and discuss the content and quality of each writing piece using the scoring guidelines. Each group may select one sample to share with the whole class.

Student Activity 1
Interpersonal Speaking

Directions: You will participate in a conversation with Rosa, a classmate. You will have one minute to read the introduction and the outline of the conversation below and think about your responses. You may write down key words, but do not write complete answers to the questions. When the conversation begins, you will have up to 20 seconds to respond to each question. Give full and appropriate responses.

Introduction

This is a conversation with Rosa, a classmate. She wants to talk about what happened to your brother yesterday.

ROSA: Hola, ¿cómo estás? Oye, oí que tu hermano tuvo un accidente ayer. ¿Dónde estaba él cuando ocurrió el accidente?

TÚ: Greet her and answer her questions.

ROSA: ¿Cómo ocurrió el accidente?

TÚ: Answer her question fully.

ROSA: ¡Qué pena! ¿Qué pasó después?

TÚ: Answer her question fully.

ROSA: Pobrecito. ¿Qué dijo el médico?

TÚ: Answer her question fully.

ROSA: Y, ¿cómo se siente tu hermano ahora?

TÚ: Answer her question fully.

ROSA: Bueno, mañana le escribiré un correo electrónico para ver cómo está. Hasta luego.

TÚ: Respond to her comments.

Student Activity 2
Interpersonal Writing

Imagine that you are at home recovering from a recent accident. Since you cannot go anywhere or do anything, write a short note to send to a friend in another town to let him or her know:

- What happened to you and when
- What the doctor said
- How long it will take you to recuperate
- What the first thing is that you will do when you are able

Include a question or two for your friend to answer.

Pre-AP* Resource Chart

	Teacher's Edition		Ancillaries
	Page #	**Activity**	
Vocabulary			*realidades.com* *Pre-AP* Resource Book:* p. 123
Listening	pp. 296–297	Videohistoria	*Video Program* Chapter 6A *Video Teacher's Guide* Chapter 6A
	p. 296	Pre-AP* Support	*Communication Workbook:* Act. 9, p.111
	p. 308	Pre-AP* Support	*Pre-AP* Resource Book:* p. 122
	p. 311	Pre-AP* Support	
Reading	p. 292	Fondo cultural	*TPR Stories:* En busca de una idea, p. 80
	p. 301	Fondo cultural	*TPR Stories:* Dora la entrenadora, p. 83
	p. 308	Fondo cultural	*Realidades* para hispanohablantes: Lectura 1, p. 222
	p. 311	Pre-AP* Support	*Realidades* para hispanohablantes: Lectura 2, p. 224
			Realidades para hispanohablantes: La cultura en vivo, p. 226
			Pre-AP Resource Book:* pp. 122–123
Speaking	p. 296	Pre-AP* Support	*TPR Stories:* pp. 81–82
	p. 308	Pre-AP* Support	*Teacher's Resource Book, Temas 5–9:* Communicative Activities, pp. 92–95
	p. 309	Act. 22, 23	*Teacher's Resource Book, Temas 5–9:* Situation cards, p. 96
	p. 313	(Talk!) Presentación oral	*Assessment Program:* Parte II, Hablar, p. 160
			Realidades para hispanohablantes: Presentación oral, p. 227
			Realidades para hispanohablantes: La cultura en vivo, p. 226
			Pre-AP Resource Book:* pp. 122–123
Writing	p. 296	Pre-AP* Support	*Communication Workbook:* Act. 4, p. 108
	p. 302	Differentiated Instruction: Advanced Learners/Pre-AP*	*Communication Workbook:* Act. 13, p. 115 *realidades.com*
	p. 308	Pre-AP* Support	*ExamView:* Pre-AP* Question Bank
	p. 309	Act. 22, 23	*Assessment Program:* Parte II, Escribir, p. 159
	p. 311	Pre-AP* Support	*Realidades* para hispanohablantes: Act. R, S, T, p. 223
			Realidades para hispanohablantes: Act. W, p. 225
			Pre-AP Resource Book:* pp. 122–123
Integrated Skills	p. 304	Act. 15	*Communication Workbook:* Integrated Performance Assessment, p. 258
	p. 309	Act. 22, 23	

	Teacher's Edition		Ancillaries
	Page #	Activity	
Vocabulary	p. 322	Pre-AP* Support	*realidades.com* *Pre-AP* Resource Book:* p. 123
Listening	pp. 322–323	Videohistoria	*Video Program* Chapter 6B
	p. 334	Pre-AP* Support	*Video Teacher's Guide* Chapter 6B
	p. 336	Pre-AP* Support	*Communication Workbook:* Act. 8, p. 120
			Communication Workbook: Act. 9, p. 121
			Pre-AP* Resource Book: p. 122
Reading	p. 318	Fondo cultural	*TPR Stories:* La película más violenta, p. 85
	p. 324	Differentiated Instruction: Advanced Learners/Pre-AP*	*TPR Stories:* Manuela y Manuel, p. 89
			Communication Workbook: Practice Test, pp. 262–264
	p. 325	Fondo cultural	*Realidades* para hispanohablantes: Lectura 1,
	p. 326	Fondo cultural	p. 242
	p. 330	Act. 16	*Realidades* para hispanohablantes: Lectura 2,
	p. 332	Fondo cultural	p. 244
	p. 334	Fondo cultural	*Realidades* para hispanohablantes: Perspectivas
	p. 336	Pre-AP* Support	del mundo hispano, p. 246
	p. 337	Fondo cultural	*Pre-AP* Resource Book:* pp. 122–123
	p. 338	Perspectivas del mundo hispano	
Speaking	p. 322	Pre-AP* Support	*TPR Stories:* pp. 86–88
	p. 336	Pre-AP* Support	*Teacher's Resource Book, Temas 5–9:* Communicative Activities, pp. 130–132
			Teacher's Resource Book, Temas 5–9: Situation cards, p. 133
			Assessment Program: Parte II, Hablar, p. 173
			Pre-AP* Resource Book: pp. 122–123
Writing	p. 324	Differentiated Instruction: Advanced Learners/Pre-AP*	*Communication Workbook:* Act. 4, p. 118
			Communication Workbook: Act. 13, p. 125
	p. 330	Act. 16	*Communication Workbook:* Practice Test,
	p. 336	Pre-AP* Support	pp. 262–264
	p. 339	Presentación escrita	*realidades.com*
			ExamView: Pre-AP* Question Bank
			Assessment Program: Parte II, Escribir, p. 173
			Realidades para hispanohablantes: Act. O, P, p. 243
			Realidades para hispanohablantes: Act. R, S, p. 245
			Realidades para hispanohablantes: Presentación escrita, p. 247
			Pre-AP* Resource Book: pp. 122–123
Integrated Skills	p. 334	Act. 22	*Communication Workbook:* Integrated Performance Assessment, p. 261
	p. 335	Act. 24, 25	

Teacher Activity
Circumlocution

Place students in groups of 3 or 4. Copy and cut apart the following four sets of words / clues, giving each student one set of the answers for the crossword puzzle in the Student Activity on the next page. Have students practice circumlocution skills in Spanish by engaging them in the Group Crossword Practice as outlined on p. 46.

Horizontal
1. metió un gol
5. galán
6. competir
7. se trata de
10. nos volvemos
14. extraterrestre

Vertical
2. estar enamorado de
4. devuelto
5. se aburren
6. concurso
8. robó
9. matar
11. puesto

Horizontal
16. me enojé
17. dicho
18. hizo el papel de
19. dormirse
21. fracaso

Vertical
12. tener éxito
13. argumento
15. escena
20. entrevista
22. reina
23. aplaudiste

Student Activity
Circumlocution

Directions: Taking turns, explain the vocabulary words on the answer sheet you have been given to the members of your group using Spanish only. You should not use any forms of the word as you try to explain what your word is. Be sure to use "horizontal" and "vertical" plus the number of the word in the puzzle to help your group members locate the correct placement of the word.

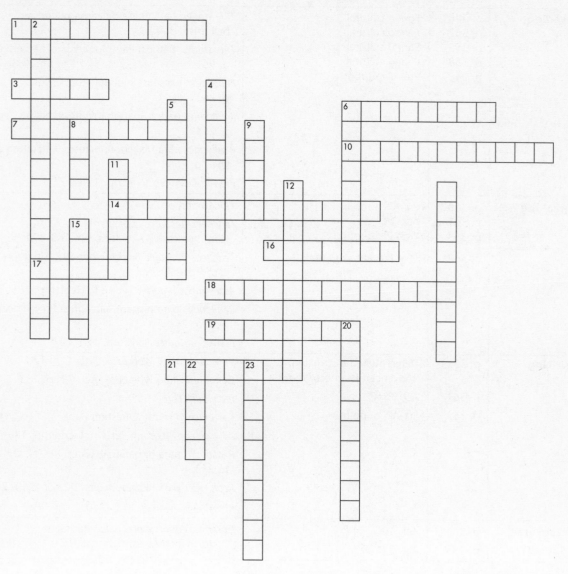

Pre-AP* Resource Chart

	Teacher's Edition		Ancillaries
	Page #	**Activity**	
Vocabulary	p. 350	Pre-AP* Support	*realidades.com*
Listening	pp. 350–351	Videohistoria	*Video Program* Chapter 7A *Video Teacher's Guide* Chapter 7A *Communication Workbook:* Act. 9, p. 131 *Pre-AP* Resource Book:* p. 127
Reading	p. 346 p. 352 p. 355 p. 358 p. 346	Fondo cultural Fondo cultural Fondo cultural Fondo cultural Pre-AP* Support	*TPR Stories:* La comida deliciosa puede ser peligrosa, p. 92 *TPR Stories:* Patricia Pamplona y la cena perfecta, p. 96 *Realidades* para hispanohablantes: Lectura 1, p. 262 *Realidades* para hispanohablantes: Lectura 2, p. 264 *Realidades* para hispanohablantes: La cultura en vivo, p. 266 *Pre-AP* Resource Book:* pp. 126–127
Speaking	p. 350 p. 361 p. 363 p. 367	Pre-AP* Support Act. 18 Pre-AP* Support (Talk!) Presentación oral	*TPR Stories:* pp. 93–95 *Teacher's Resource Book, Temas 5–9:* Communicative Activities, pp. 168–171 *Teacher's Resource Book, Temas 5–9:* Situation cards, p. 172 *Assessment Program:* Parte II, Hablar, p. 186 *Realidades* para hispanohablantes: Presentación oral, p. 267 *Pre-AP* Resource Book:* pp. 126–127
Writing	p. 356 p. 361 p. 365	Differentiated Instruction: Advanced Learners/Pre-AP* Act. 18 Pre-AP* Support	*Communication Workbook:* Act. 4, p. 128 *Communication Workbook:* Act. 13, p. 135 *realidades.com* *ExamView:* Pre-AP* Question Bank *Assessment Program:* Parte II, Escribir, p. 186 *Realidades* para hispanohablantes: Act. Ñ, O, p. 263 *Realidades* para hispanohablantes: Act. Q, p. 265 *Pre-AP* Resource Book:* p. 126
Integrated Skills	p. 360 p. 363	Act. 19 Act. 22, 23	*Communication Workbook:* Integrated Performance Assessment, p. 267

Pre-AP* Resource Chart

	Teacher's Edition		Ancillaries
	Page #	**Activity**	
Vocabulary	p. 376	Pre-AP* Support	*realidades.com*
Listening	pp. 376–377	Videohistoria	*Video Program* Chapter 7B
	p. 384	Pre-AP* Support	*Video Teacher's Guide* Chapter 7B
	p. 391	Pre-AP* Support	*Communication Workbook:* Act. 8, p. 141
			Pre-AP* Resource Book: p. 127
Reading	p. 392	Perspectivas del mundo hispano	*Communication Workbook:* Practice Test, pp. 271–273
	p. 372	Fondo cultural	*TPR Stories:* Un picnic en el parque, p. 98
	p. 378	Fondo cultural	*TPR Stories:* La sencillez del cámping, p. 102
	p. 381	Fondo cultural	*Realidades* para hispanohablantes: Lectura !, p. 282
	p. 384	Fondo cultural	
	p. 387	Fondo cultural	*Realidades* para hispanohablantes: Lectura 2, p. 284
	p. 391	Fondo cultural	*Realidades* para hispanohablantes: Perspectivas del mundo hispano, p. 286
			Pre-AP* Resource Book: pp. 126–127
Speaking	p. 376	Pre-AP* Support	*Teacher's Resource Book, Temas 5–9:* Communicative Activities, pp. 206–209
	p. 384	Pre-AP* Support	*Teacher's Resource Book, Temas 5–9:* Situation cards, p. 210
	p. 389	Act. 25	*TPR Stories:* pp. 99–101
			Assessment Program: Parte II, Hablar, p. 199
			Pre-AP* Resource Book: pp. 126–127
Writing	p. 382	Differentiated Instruction: Advanced Learners/Pre-AP*	*Communication Workbook:* Act. 13, p. 145
	p. 389	Act. 25	*Communication Workbook:* Practice Test, pp. 271–273
	p. 391	Pre-AP* Support	*realidades.com*
	p. 393	Presentación escrita	*ExamView:* Pre-AP* Question Bank
			Assessment Program: Parte II, Escribir, p. 199
			Realidades para hispanohablantes: Act. P, Q, p. 283
			Realidades para hispanohablantes: Act. S, T, p. 285
			Realidades para hispanohablantes: Presentación escrita, p. 287
			Pre-AP* Resource Book: p. 126
Integrated Skills	p. 383	Act. 14	*Communication Workbook:* Integrated Performance Assessment, p. 270
	p. 388	Act. 23	

Teacher Activity 1
Interpersonal Writing

Have students imagine that they just went on a family picnic and outing. They should write an e-mail to a friend describing the event. Students should include at least two questions in the e-mail for their friends to answer. After students have completed their writing, make three photocopies of each student's written work. Place students in groups of four. Distribute copies of the scoring guidelines found on p. 49 of this book. (Since this is a writing task, the *Fluency* category on the bottom row can be ignored at this time.) Distribute the copies of the students' work within each group. Have each student read his or her writing aloud to the group, one piece at a time, and discuss the content and quality of each writing piece using the scoring guidelines. Each group may select one sample to share with the whole class.

Teacher Activity 2
Building Speaking and Writing Skills

As students develop their language skills, there are a number of strategies that teachers should use to help students make their speaking and writing more effective. For example:

1. Remind students to use transition words they have learned to link ideas and improve the flow of information in their speaking and writing samples. Some useful transition words include: *también, por eso, por ejemplo, por lo general, en realidad, entonces, además, sin duda, sin embargo, primero, segundo,* and *tercero.*

2. Many adverbs can also be used to enrich the content of speaking and writing samples. They include: *nunca, siempre, a veces, todos los días, a menudo, otra vez, ya, todavía, de vez en cuando, afortunadamente, recientemente, en seguida, ahora, anoche, ayer, el año pasado,* and *la semana pasada.*

3. Students typically express themselves using short, simple sentences early in Spanish 1. However, they should gradually raise their level of discourse by using a variety of conjunctions to form multi-clause sentences. Common conjunctions include: *y, o, ni...ni, pero, porque, si, cuando,* and *mientras.*

4. To improve their interpersonal speaking skills students should learn to listen to each other and respond to each other's comments in a natural and authentic way. They should learn to clarify meaning, when necessary, and to provide additional information in order to advance the conversation. In addition, students should use rejoinders they have learned to enhance and enliven the conversation. Some useful rejoinders are: *pues, a ver, ¡no me digas! ¿de veras? por supuesto, ¡qué pena! ¡genial! lo siento, ¡Uf! ¡qué asco! ¿verdad?* and *(no) estoy de acuerdo.*

5. Regardless of the type of activity, students should always be encouraged to give rich and thorough responses. They should think of their speaking and writing samples as opportunities to show what they know and can do!

Student Activity 1
Presentational Speaking

Directions: Your teacher will give you a Venn diagram or ask you to draw one. Label the first section: *El Yunque*, the middle section *Los dos parques*, and the last section *El parque en mi comunidad*. As you read about El Yunque (REALIDADES 2, p. 390), make a list of its special features in the first section of the Venn diagram. Be sure to write key words only. Then think about a park in your community and write key words to represent its features in the last section. In the middle section write key words that represent features of both parks. Using your Venn diagram, give an oral presentation in Spanish in which you compare a park in your community with El Yunque. How are the plants and animals similar or different? How are the activities in the parks similar or different? After reading the *Lectura* and completing the first section of the Venn diagram, you will have three minutes to complete your Venn diagram and organize your thoughts. Then you will have 90 seconds to speak. Be sure to include appropriate transition words to facilitate the flow of information in your presentation.

Student Activity 2
Interpersonal Speaking

Directions: You will participate in a conversation with Manolo, a classmate. You will have one minute to read the introduction and the outline of the conversation below and think about your responses. You may write down key words, but do not write complete answers to the questions. When the conversation begins, you will have up to 20 seconds to respond to each question. Give full and appropriate responses.

Introduction

This is a conversation with Manolo, a classmate. He wants to talk about preparing a special meal.

MANOLO: Hola, ¿qué tal? Este fin de semana quiero preparar una cena especial para el cumpleaños de mi mamá. ¿Qué crees que debo preparar?

TÚ: Greet him and answer his questions.

MANOLO: Buena idea. ¿Es fácil o difícil de preparar? ¿Por qué?

TÚ: Answer his question and explain why.

MANOLO: Pues, ¿dónde puedo conseguir los ingredientes?

TÚ: Answer his question fully.

MANOLO: Y, ¿qué recomiendas de postre?

TÚ: Answer his question fully.

MANOLO: En tu opinión, ¿cuánto tiempo necesito para preparar todo eso?

TÚ: Answer his question fully.

MANOLO: Gracias por todo. ¡Estoy seguro de que a mi mamá le va a encantar la cena! Hasta luego.

TÚ: Respond to his comments.

	Teacher's Edition		Ancillaries
	Page #	Activity	
Vocabulary			*realidades.com* *Pre-AP* Resource Book:* p. 130 *Pre-AP* Resource Book:* p. 131
Listening	pp. 404–405	Videohistoria	*Video Program* Chapter 8A *Video Teacher's Guide* Chapter 8A *Communication Workbook:* Act. 9, p. 151 *Pre-AP* Resource Book:* p. 130
	p. 406	Differentiated Instruction: Advanced Learners/Pre-AP*	
	p. 408	Pre-AP* Support	
	p. 419	Pre-AP* Support	

Reading	p. 400	Fondo cultural	*TPR Stories:* Álvaro aburrido, p. 106
			TPR Stories: El viajero infeliz (Primera parte), p. 110
			Realidades para hispanohablantes: Lectura 1,
			  p. 302
			Realidades para hispanohablantes: Lectura 2,
			  p. 304
			Realidades para hispanohablantes: La cultura en
			  vivo, p. 306
			Pre-AP* Resource Book: pp. 130–131

	p. 406	Differentiated Instruction: Advanced Learners/Pre-AP*	
	p. 407	Fondo cultural	
	p. 409	Fondo cultural	
	p. 412	Fondo cultural	
	p. 419	Pre-AP* Support	
	p. 414	Act. 19	

Speaking	p. 414	Act. 19	*TPR Stories:* pp. 107–109
			Teacher's Resource Book, Temas 5–9:
			  Communicative Activities, pp. 246–249
			Teacher's Resource Book, Temas 5–9: Situation
			  cards, p. 250
			Assessment Program: Parte II, Hablar, p. 212
			Realidades para hispanohablantes: Presentación
			  oral, p. 307
			Pre-AP* Resource Book: pp. 130–131

	p. 419	Pre-AP* Support	
	p. 421	(Talk!) Presentación oral	
Writing	p. 404	Pre-AP* Support	*Communication Workbook:* Act. 13, p. 155 *realidades.com* *ExamView:* Pre-AP* Question Bank *Assessment Program:* Parte II, Escribir, p. 212 *Realidades* para hispanohablantes: Act. P, Q, p. 303 *Realidades* para hispanohablantes: Act. R, p. 305 *Pre-AP* Resource Book:* pp. 130–131
	p. 406	Differentiated Instruction: Advanced Learners/Pre-AP*	
	p. 408	Pre-AP* Support	
	p. 414	Act. 19	
Integrated Skills	p. 414	Act. 19	*Communication Workbook:* Integrated Performance Assessment, p. 276
	p. 417	Act. 23	

	Teacher's Edition		Ancillaries
	Page #	**Activity**	
Vocabulary			realidades.com Pre-AP* Resource Book: p. 130 Pre-AP* Resource Book: p. 131
Listening	pp. 428–429	Videohistoria	Video Program Chapter 8B
	p. 428	Pre-AP* Support	Video Teacher's Guide Chapter 8B
	p. 437	Pre-AP* Support	Communication Workbook: Act. 9, p. 161
	p. 443	Pre-AP* Support	Pre-AP* Resource Book: p. 130
Reading	p. 424	Fondo cultural	Communication Workbook: Practice Test, pp. 280–282
	p. 428	Pre-AP* Support	TPR Stories: La vida buena en San Juan, p. 112
	p. 431	Fondo cultural	TPR Stories: El viajero infeliz (Segunda parte), p. 117
	p. 433	Fondo cultural	Realidades para hispanohablantes: Lectura 1, p. 322
	p. 436	Fondo cultural	Realidades para hispanohablantes: Lectura 2, p. 324
	p. 440	Fondo cultural	Realidades para hispanohablantes: Perspectivas del mundo hispano, p. 326
	p. 441	Act. 21	Pre-AP* Resource Book: p. 131
	p. 444	Perspectivas del mundo hispano	
Speaking	p. 428	Pre-AP* Support	TPR Stories: pp. 113–116
	p. 437	Pre-AP* Support	Teacher's Resource Book, Temas 5–9: Communicative Activities, pp. 284–287
	p. 441	Act. 21	Teacher's Resource Book, Temas 5–9: Situation cards, p. 288
	p. 443	Pre-AP* Support	Assessment Program: Parte II, Hablar, p. 120
			Pre-AP* Resource Book: pp. 130–131
Writing	p. 424	Fondo cultural	Communication Workbook: Act. 4, p. 158
	p. 428	Pre-AP* Support	Communication Workbook: Act. 13, p. 165
	p. 431	Fondo cultural	Communication Workbook: Practice Test, pp. 280–282
	p. 433	Fondo cultural	realidades.com
	p. 436	Fondo cultural	ExamView: Pre-AP* Question Bank
	p. 437	Pre-AP* Support	Assessment Program: Parte II, Escribir, p. 120
	p. 438	Differentiated Instruction: Advanced Learners/Pre-AP*	Realidades para hispanohablantes: Act. O, P, p. 323
	p. 440	Fondo cultural	Realidades para hispanohablantes: Act. R, S, p. 325
	p. 441	Act. 21	Realidades para hispanohablantes: Presentación escrita, p. 327
	p. 445	Presentación escrita	Pre-AP* Resource Book: pp. 130–131
Integrated Skills	p. 441	Act. 21, 22	Communication Workbook: Integrated Performance Assessment, p. 279

Realidades 2

Tema 8

Teacher Activity
Circumlocution

Place students in groups of 3 or 4. Cut apart the following sets of words, giving each student one set of the answers for the crossword puzzle in the Student Activity on the next page. Have students practice circumlocution skills in Spanish by engaging them in the Group Crossword Practice as outlined on p. 47.

Horizontal
6. pasillo
8. habitación
9. extranjero
12. aduanera
14. Castillo
18. cortés
19. bote de vela

Vertical
1. cajero
2. puerta de embarque
3. planear
4. duró
5. hizo escala
7. de ida y vuelta
10. ruido

Horizontal
21. propina
23. abordaste
24. tal vez
25. registrar
26. sugerimos
27. regatear

Vertical
11. facturé
13. bello
15. siguiente
16. pasajero
17. conseguí
20. disfrutar de
22. retraso

Realidades 2

Tema 8

Student Activity
Circumlocution

Directions: Taking turns, explain the vocabulary words on the answer sheet you have been given to the members of your group using Spanish only. You should not use any forms of the word as you try to explain what your word is. Be sure to use "horizontal" and "vertical" plus the number of the word in the puzzle to help your group members locate the correct placement of the word.

	Teacher's Edition		Ancillaries
	Page #	Activity	
Vocabulary	p. 454	Pre-AP* Support	*realidades.com*
	p. 469	Pre-AP* Support	
Listening	pp. 454–455	Videohistoria	*Video Program* Chapter 9A
			Video Teacher's Guide Chapter 9A
	p. 460	Differentiated Instruction: Advanced Learners/Pre-AP*	*Communication Workbook:* Act. 8,9, p. 171
			Pre-AP* Resource Book: pp. 134–135
Reading	p. 450	Fondo cultural	*TPR Stories:* Algún día seré..., p. 120
	p. 458	Fondo cultural	*TPR Stories:* Algún día seré...(segunda parte), p. 125
	p. 463	Fondo cultural	*Realidades* para hispanohablantes: Lectura 1, p. 342
	p. 463	Pre-AP* Support	*Realidades* para hispanohablantes: Lectura 2, p. 344
	p. 466	Fondo cultural	*Realidades* para hispanohablantes: La cultura en vivo, p. 346
			Pre-AP* Resource Book: pp. 134–135
Speaking	p. 454	Pre-AP* Support	*TPR Stories:* pp. 121–124
	p. 467	Act. 25	*Teacher's Resource Book, Temas 5–9:* Communicative Activities, pp. 324–327
	p. 469	Pre-AP* Support	*Teacher's Resource Book, Temas 5–9:* Situation cards, p. 328
	p. 471	Presentación ora	*Assessment Program:* Parte II, Hablar, p. 238
			Realidades para hispanohablantes: Presentación oral, p. 347
			Pre-AP* Resource Book: pp. 134–135
Writing	p. 467	Act. 25	*Communication Workbook:* Act. 4, p. 168
	p. 463	Pre-AP* Support	*Communication Workbook:* Act. 13, p. 175
	p. 460	Differentiated Instruction: Advanced Learners/Pre-AP*	*realidades.com*
			ExamView: Pre-AP* Question Bank
	p. 469	Pre-AP* Support	*Assessment Program:* Parte II, Escribir, p. 238
			Realidades para hispanohablantes: Act. P, Q, p. 343
			Realidades para hispanohablantes: Act. S, T, p. 345
			Pre-AP* Resource Book: pp. 134–135
Integrated Skills	p. 464	Act. 19	*Communication Workbook:* Integrated Performance Assessment, p. 285
	p. 465	Act. 22	
	p. 467	Act. 25	

	Teacher's Edition		Ancillaries
	Page #	**Activity**	
Vocabulary	p. 478	Pre-AP* Support	*realidades.com*
	p. 482	Differentiated Instruction: Advanced Learners/Pre-AP*	
Listening	pp. 478–479	Videohistoria	*Video Program* Chapter 9B
	p. 490	Pre-AP* Support	*Video Teacher's Guide* Chapter 9B
			Communication Workbook: Act. 9, p. 180
			Pre-AP* Resource Book: pp. 134–135
Reading	p. 474	Fondo cultural	*Communication Workbook:* Practice Test, pp. 289–291
	p. 481	Fondo cultural	*TPR Stories:* El superhéroe del futuro, p. 127
	p. 483	Fondo cultural	
	p. 485	Fondo cultural	*TPR Stories:* El club de ecología, pp. 128–129
	p. 493	Pre-AP* Support	*Realidades* para hispanohablantes: Lectura 1, p. 362
	p. 494	Perspectivas del mundo hispano	*Realidades* para hispanohablantes: Lectura 2, p. 364
			Realidades para hispanohablantes: Perspectivas del mundo hispano, p. 366
			Pre-AP* Resource Book: pp. 134–135
Speaking	p. 478	Pre-AP* Support	*Teacher's Resource Book, Temas 5–9:* Communicative Activities, pp. 362–365
	p. 490	Pre-AP* Support	*Teacher's Resource Book, Temas 5–9:* Situation cards, p. 366
	p. 493	Pre-AP* Support	
			Assessment Program: Parte II, Hablar, p. 251
			Pre-AP* Resource Book: pp. 134–135
Writing	p. 474	Fondo cultural	*Communication Workbook:* Act.13, p. 184
	p. 481	Fondo cultural	*Communication Workbook:* Practice Test, pp. 289–291
	p. 482	Differentiated Instruction: Advanced Learners/Pre-AP*	*realidades.com*
	p. 483	Fondo cultural	*ExamView:* Pre-AP* Question Bank
	p. 485	Fondo cultural	*Assessment Program:* Parte II, Escribir, p. 251
	p. 490	Act. 22	*Realidades* para hispanohablantes: Act. P, Q, p. 363
	p. 490	Pre-AP* Support	
	p. 495	Presentación escrita	*Realidades* para hispanohablantes: Act. S, T, p. 365
			Realidades para hispanohablantes: Presentación escrita, p. 367
			Pre-AP* Resource Book: pp. 134–135
Integrated Skills	p. 488	Act. 19	*Communication Workbook:* Integrated Performance Assessment, p. 288
	p. 489	Act. 20	
	p. 491	Act. 24	

Teacher Activity 1
Presentational Speaking

1. Have students listen to Audio Activity 7 on p. 170 in the **Realidades** Communication Workbook.

2. Next, have students prepare a one-minute talk based on *Mi vida hoy y en el futuro* found on p. 471 of the **Realidades** Student Textbook. Like the teens speaking in Activity 7, students should give reasons for making the career choice that they present. The amount of preparation time can vary, but should not be longer than three or four minutes.

3. Students are then allowed one minute to record their presentations, or they may make their presentations to a group of three or four students.

4. In groups of three or four, students should listen to each recording (or hear each presentation) and discuss the content and quality using the scoring guidelines on p. 49 of this book.

Teacher Activity 2
Presentational Writing

Have students read *Animales en peligro de extinción* on p. 483 of the **Realidades** Student Textbook as well as *La contaminación acústica* on p. 489 of the **Realidades** Student Textbook. They should also listen to Audio Activity 9 on p. 180 of the **Realidades** Communication Workbook. Students should then write four paragraphs describing what they believe to be the most serious global environmental problem and propose solutions for resolving that problem. They should cite the two readings and audio text mentioned above as examples of ways to resolve environmental problems.

Then make three photocopies of each student's written work. Place students in groups of four. Distribute copies of the scoring guidelines found on p. 49 of this book. (Since this is a writing task, the *Fluency* category on the bottom row can be ignored at this time.) Distribute the copies of the students' work within each group. Have each student read his or her writing aloud to the group, one piece at a time, and discuss the content and quality of each writing piece using the scoring guidelines. Each group may select one sample to share with the whole class.

Teacher Activity 3
Interpersonal Writing

1. Have students imagine that they are spending a week away from home doing community service work. They should write a postcard to their parents telling them what they have been doing while on volunteer assignment.

2. After students have completed this activity, make three photocopies of each student's written work. Place students in groups of four. Distribute copies of the scoring guidelines found on p. 49 of this book. (Since this is a writing task, the *Fluency* category on the bottom row can be ignored at this time.) Distribute the copies of the students' work within each group. Have each student read his or her writing aloud to the group, one piece at a time, and discuss the content and quality of each writing piece using the scoring guidelines. Each group may select one sample to share with the whole class.

Student Activity 1
Interpersonal Speaking

Work with a partner to write complete-sentence answers to the following questions. Be sure to verify the correctness of your answers. Then, use the questions (and answers) to play *Preguntas rápidas* (see p. 41) or to prepare for *One minute of questions* (For Levels 1 and 2) (see p. 42).

1. ¿Te sugieren tus profesores que estudies durante las vacaciones?

2. ¿Les gusta a tus padres que vayas al extranjero?

3. ¿Por qué insiste tu amigo(a) para que le mandes una tarjeta postal?

4. ¿Cuánto tiempo dura un vuelo a España?

5. ¿Te diviertes mucho viajando en bote de vela?

6. ¿Es bueno que visites los sitios históricos?

7. ¿Adónde viajarás el verano próximo?

8. ¿Asistirás a la universidad después del colegio?

9. ¿Cómo te ganarás la vida en el futuro?

10. ¿Tendrás que estudiar muchos años para tu carrera futura?

11. ¿Seguirás una carrera militar?

12. ¿Será importante que hagamos mejores leyes para el medio ambiente?

13. Si reciclamos más, ¿podremos reducir la basura en el mundo?

14. ¿Dudas que haya soluciones fáciles para el medio ambiente?

15. ¿Qué harás después de salir de la escuela esta tarde?

16. ¿Cómo recomiendas que se resuelva el problema de la guerra?

PRENTICE HALL
Realidades

Level 3
Resource Support

	Teacher's Edition		Ancillaries
	Page #	**Activity**	
Vocabulary	p. 23	Pre-AP* Support	*realidades.com*
Listening	p. 38	Pre-AP* Support	*Video Program* Chapter 1
	p. 56	Pre-AP* Support	*Video Teacher's Guide* Chapter 1
			Communication Workbook: Act. 1, p. 8
			Communication Workbook: Act. 3, p. 9
			Communication Workbook: Act. 4, p. 10
			Pre-AP* Resource Book, pp. 139–140
Reading	p. 20	Fondo cultural	*Realidades* para hispanohablantes: Act. H, p. 19
	p. 27	Fondo cultural	*Realidades* para hispanohablantes: Fondo cultural, p. 28
	p. 38	Pre-AP* Support	*Realidades* para hispanohablantes: Puente a la
	p. 40	Fondo cultural	cultura, pp. 34–36
	p. 48–49	Puente a la cultura	*Communication Workbook:* Practice Test, p. 166
	p. 57	Fondo cultural	*realidades.com*
			Pre-AP* Resource Book: pp. 139–140
Speaking	p. 23	Pre-AP* Support	*Assessment Program:* Examen del capítulo 1,
	p. 42	Differentiated Instruction: Advanced Learners/Pre-AP*	Hablar, p. 33
	p. 44	Pre-AP* Support	*Teacher's Resource Book:* Communicative Activities, pp. 42–48
	p. 51	(Talk!) Presentación oral	*Teacher's Resource Book:* Situation cards, p. 49
	p. 56	Pre-AP* Support	*Realidades* para hispanohablantes: Presentación oral, p. 38
			Pre-AP* Resource Book, pp. 139–140
Writing	p. 23	Pre-AP* Support	*realidades.com*
	p. 34	Pre-AP* Support	*Assessment Program:* Examen del capítulo 1, Escribir, p. 33
	p. 36	Differentiated Instruction: Advanced Learners/Pre-AP*	*Assessment Program:* Examen del capítulo 1, Cultura, p. 33
	p. 42	Differentiated Instruction: Advanced Learners/Pre-AP*	*Communication Workbook:* Act. 12, p. 18
	p. 44	Pre-AP* Support	*Communication Workbook:* Act. 13, p. 19
	p. 52	Presentación escrita	*Realidades* para hispanohablantes: Fondo cultural, p. 13
	p. 56	Pre-AP* Support	*Realidades* para hispanohablantes:, Act. F, p. 16
			Realidades para hispanohablantes: Act. Q, p. 27
			Realidades para hispanohablantes: Act. X, p. 35
			Realidades para hispanohablantes: Presentación escrita, p. 39
			Communication Workbook: Practice Test, p. 166
			ExamView: Pre-AP* Question Bank
			Pre-AP* Resource Book: p. 139
Integrated Skills	p. 29	Act. 12	*Communication Workbook:* Integrated Performance Assessment, p. 165
	p. 43	Act. 38	
	p. 47	Act. 44	
	p. 50	Integración	

Teacher Activity 1
Interpersonal Speaking, Conversation

1. Allow students one minute to prepare to record the conversation. Allowing too much preparation time will lead to students' writing the script of what they want to say, and subsequently reading it. The purpose of the preparation time is to get a sense of the conversation and to generally gather thoughts.

2. Students should record their conversations. (See Recording and Evaluating on p. 44.) (See also "Administering the *Examen del capítulo* Speaking Proficiency Test" on p. T66 of the *Realidades* Assessment Program.) The teacher can be the voice of the other person in the conversation, allowing no more than 20 seconds for each response from students.

3. In groups of three or four, students should listen to each recording and discuss the content and quality using the scoring guidelines on p. 49 of this book. Teachers may also consider using the "Speaking and Writing Rubrics for the *Examen del capítulo*" available in the *Realidades* Assessment Program front matter. Near the end of *Realidades* 3, teachers might wish to begin using adapted versions of the official AP* Spanish Language and Culture Scoring Guidelines for the interpersonal speaking task found at: apcentral.collegeboard.com/spanlang.

Teacher Activity 2
Presentational Writing

For each of the Presentational Writing Student Activities, there is a prompt with recommended readings as well as a recommended listening selection that present different aspects of the prompt. Students should:

1. Listen to the indicated audio selection, taking notes as they listen.

2. Complete the two reading selections silently.

3. Prepare a written essay in response to the prompt citing information from the audio and reading sources. Students should state their own point of view and explain it thoroughly. By the end of the academic year, students should be given 40 minutes to prepare their essay and to write approximately 200 words. In addition, students should learn to save a few minutes before the end of the writing time to proofread their work.

Once students have finished writing, make three photocopies of each student's written work. Place students in groups of four. Distribute copies of the scoring guidelines found on p. 49 of this book. (Since this is a writing task, the *Fluency* category on the bottom row can be ignored at this time.) Distribute the copies of the students' work within each group. Have each student read his or her writing aloud to the group, one piece at a time, and discuss the content and quality of each writing piece using the scoring guidelines. Each group may select one sample to share with the whole class, as time permits. Near the end of *Realidades* 3, teachers might wish to begin using adapted versions of the official AP* Spanish Language and Culture Scoring Guidelines for the presentational writing task found at: apcentral.collegeboard.com/spanlang.

Note: Continue to consider and to bring to students' attention the many writing tips offered in the *Realidades* Student Textbook as well as in the "Preparing to Write an Essay" section of this Pre-AP* Resource Book.

Student Activity 1
Interpersonal Speaking, Conversation

Directions: You will now participate in a simulated telephone conversation before which you will have one minute to read the outline of the conversation. During that time, plan how you will respond by making brief notes to yourself. Do not try to write out your answers, as there will not be sufficient time, and the purpose of this exercise is to strengthen your ability to engage in sustained conversations in Spanish. After the preparation time ends, the phone conversation will begin. When it is your turn to speak, you will have 20 seconds to respond. Use your 20 seconds to give an appropriate and thorough response, using up the allocated time as fully as possible.

Scenario: You just returned from a two-week family vacation. Your friend, Nico, has called to ask if you enjoyed your trip.

NICO: ¿Qué tal, amigo? Hace mucho que no nos hablamos. ¿Cómo estás?

TÚ: _____

NICO: Pues, cuéntame algo de tus vacaciones. ¿Adónde fuiste?

TÚ: _____

NICO: ¿Cuál fue la mejor cosa que hiciste?

TÚ: _____

NICO: ¿Te aburriste en algún momento?

TÚ: _____

NICO: ¡Qué va! ¿Cuándo vamos a vernos? ¿Quieres hacer algo mañana?

TÚ: _____

NICO: Perfecto. Hasta entonces. Adiós.

TÚ: _____

Student Activity 2
Presentational Writing

Directions: First, you will hear an audio recording. You should take notes as you listen. Next, you will read the print articles. You will have a maximum of 15 minutes to accomplish these steps. Then, you will have 45 minutes to write a well-organized, formal essay on the topic below. Be sure to state your viewpoint clearly and explain it thoroughly, using information from all three sources to support your ideas. You should also cite the sources appropriately as they are used. Remember that this essay is not intended to be a summary of the three sources, but rather, an opportunity for you to synthesize these sources into your own ideas. Save a few minutes before the end of the writing time to proofread your work.

Topic: Explique el valor y los beneficios de viajar al extranjero.

Audio Source: Video Script, *Los deportes en el mundo hispano*, Capítulo 1 (*Realidades* TRB, p. 33)

Reading Source 1: *Parques nacionales de América del Sur* (*Realidades* Student Textbook, p. 27)

Reading Source 2: *El Camino de Santiago* (*Realidades* Student Textbook, pp. 48-49)

	Teacher's Edition		Ancillaries
	Page #	**Activity**	
Vocabulary	p. 69	Pre-AP* Support	*realidades.com*
Listening	p. 69	Pre-AP* Support	*Communication Workbook:* Act. 4, p. 24
	p. 75	Pre-AP* Support	*Communication Workbook:* Act. 5, p. 25
	p. 92	Pre-AP* Support	*Video Program* Chapter 2; *Video Teacher's Guide*
	p. 102	Pre-AP* Support	Chapter 2
			Pre-AP* Resource Book: pp. 142–143
Reading	p. 66	Fondo cultural	*Communication Workbook:* Practice Test, p. 173
	p. 78	Fondo cultural	*Realidades* para hispanohablantes: Puente a la
	p. 91	Fondo cultural	cultura, pp. 66–68
	p. 93	Fondo cultural	*realidades.com*
	pp. 94–95	Puente a la cultura	Pre-AP* Resource Book: pp. 142–143
	p. 103	Fondo cultural	
Speaking	p. 69	Pre-AP* Support	*Assessment Program:* Examen del capítulo 2,
	p. 75	Pre-AP* Support	Hablar, p. 56
	p. 84	Pre-AP* Support	*Teacher's Resource Book:* Communicative
	p. 92	Pre-AP* Support	Activities, pp. 101–108
	p. 97	Presentación oral	*Teacher's Resource Book:* Situation cards, p. 109
	p. 102	Pre-AP* Support	*Realidades* para hispanohablantes: Presentación
			oral, p. 70
			Pre-AP* Resource Book: pp. 142–143
Writing	p. 76	Differentiated Instruction: Advanced Learners/Pre-AP*	*Communication Workbook:* Act. 9, p. 29
			Communication Workbook: Act. 13, p. 33
	p. 84	Pre-AP* Support	*Communication Workbook:* Practice Test, p. 173
	p. 86	Differentiated Instruction: Advanced Learners/Pre-AP*	*Realidades* para hispanohablantes: Act. BB, p. 69; Presentación escrita, p. 71
	p. 92	Pre-AP* Support	*Assessment Program:* Examen del capítulo 2,
	p. 98	Presentación escrita	Escribir, p. 56
	p. 102	Pre-AP* Support	*Assessment Program:* Examen del capítulo 2,
			Cultura, p. 56
			realidades.com
			ExamView: Pre-AP* Question Bank
			Pre-AP* Resource Book: pp. 142–143
Integrated Skills	p. 74	Act. 11	*Communication Workbook:* Integrated Performance Assessment, p. 172
	p. 75	Act. 13	
	p. 89	Act. 35	
	p. 96	Integración	

Teacher Activity 1
Presentational Speaking

For each of the Presentational Speaking Student Activities, there is a recommended reading and listening selection. Students should:

1. Listen to the indicated audio selection, taking notes as they listen.

2. Complete the reading selection silently.

3. Prepare an oral presentation citing information from the audio and reading sources.

4. After the audio selection, allow students no more than 10 minutes to complete the reading selection and prepare the oral presentation. Students should not try to script every word of the presentation, but rather make notes about ideas they wish to express, noting key vocabulary expressions, conjugations, etc.

5. Students are then allowed two minutes to record their presentations, or they may make their presentations to a group of three or four students, and occasionally to the whole class.

6. Recordings are the preferred method of presentation, as this will allow students, in groups of three or four, to listen to each recording (or hear each presentation) and discuss the content and quality using the scoring guidelines on p. 49 of this book. Teachers may also consider using the "Speaking and Writing Rubrics for the *Examen del capítulo* available in the *Realidades* Assessment Program front matter. Near the end of *Realidades* 3, teachers might wish to begin using adapted versions of the official AP* Spanish Language and Culture Scoring Guidelines for the presentational speaking task found at: apcentral.collegeboard.com/spanlang.

Teacher Activity 2
Evaluating with Rubrics

After students have completed the Interpersonal Writing task, make three photocopies of each student's written work. Place students in groups of four. Distribute copies of the scoring guidelines found on p. 49 of this book. (Since this is a writing task, the *Fluency* category on the bottom row can be ignored at this time.) Distribute the copies of the students' work within each group. Have each student read his or her writing aloud to the group, one piece at a time, and discuss the content and quality of each writing piece using the scoring guidelines. Each group may select one sample to share with the whole class. Near the end of *Realidades* 3, teachers might wish to begin using adapted versions of the official AP* Spanish Language and Culture Scoring Guidelines for the interpersonal writing task found at: apcentral.collegeboard.com/spanlang.

Teacher Activity 3
Interpretive Communicative, Audiovisual Texts

1. Have the students read the questions for *El arte en el mundo hispano* (Video Program, Chapter 2, *Realidades* TRB, p.100) before viewing the video.

2. The students should answer the questions during and/or after viewing the video, whichever they choose.

3. It is a good idea to do Student Activity 1 before Student Activity 2 so that students are very familiar with the content of the video.

Student Activity 1
Interpretive Communication, Audiovisual Texts

Directions: Before viewing *El arte en el mundo hispano*, read the questions below. Select the correct answer to each question during or after viewing the video.

1. En sus obras, Diego Rivera pintó _____.

   a. la historia de México

   b. la naturaleza de México

   c. el paisaje de México

   d. la familia real de México

2. La forma de arte que se asocia con un grupo minoritario de España es _____.

   a. la pintura

   b. la danza

   c. la literatura

   d. la cerámica

3. El tango se identifica con _____.

   a. Colombia

   b. México

   c. España

   d. Argentina

Student Activity 2
Presentational Speaking

Imagine that you must give an oral presentation on the topic of art and inspiration. Tell the class what sort of art you would like to express (music, dance, painting, sculpture, etc.) and why. Be sure to explain what you would use for your inspiration. To prepare for your presentation:

1. Listen to the Video Script, *El arte en el mundo hispano*, Capítulo 2. (*Realidades* TRB p. 100)

2. Read *Entrevista con Dina Bursztyn*. (*Realidades* Student Textbook, p. 70)

3. Prepare an outline of the presentation, noting key vocabulary words and ideas. Be sure to cite information and/or examples from the reading as well as from the audio portion of this activity. (Do not try to write an entire script. You will have 10 minutes to complete steps 2 and 3.)

4. Make a live presentation to your classmates, or record your oral presentation. The maximum presentation length is two minutes.

Student Activity 3
Interpersonal Writing

Write an e-mail to your friend inviting him or her to go with you to visit your favorite art museum on Sunday afternoon. Let your friend know:

- What he or she can expect to see there
- Why you love to visit this particular museum
- What time you would like to go

You have 10 minutes to complete this task.

Pre-AP* Resource Chart

	Teacher's Edition		Ancillaries
	Page #	Activity	
Vocabulary	p. 129	Pre-AP* Support	*realidades.com*
Listening	p. 115	Pre-AP* Support	*Video Program* Chapter 3
	p. 121	Pre-AP* Support	*Video Teacher's Guide* Chapter 3
	p. 148	Pre-AP* Support	*Communication Workbook:* Act. 4, p. 38
			Communication Workbook: Act. 5, p. 39
			Pre-AP Resource Book:* pp. 145–146
Reading	p. 112	Fondo cultural	Communication Workbook: Practice Test, p. 179
	p. 120	Fondo cultural	*Realidades* para hispanohablantes: Act. Z, p. 91
	p. 131	Fondo cultural	*Realidades* para hispanohablantes: Puente a la cultura, pp. 98–100
	pp. 140–145	Puente a la cultura	*realidades.com*
	p. 148	Pre-AP* Support	*Pre-AP* Resource Book:* pp. 145–146
	p. 149	Fondo cultural	
Speaking	p. 115	Pre-AP* Support	*Assessment Program:* Examen del capítulo 3, Hablar, p. 80
	p. 121	Pre-AP* Support	*Teacher's Resource Book:* Communicative Activity 3–4, pp. 159–166
	p. 129	Pre-AP* Support	
	p. 134	Differentiated Instruction: Advanced Learners/Pre-AP*	*Teacher's Resource Book:* Situation cards, p. 167
	p. 137	Supplemental Pre-AP* Activity	*Realidades* para hispanohablantes: Presentación oral, p. 102
	p. 143	(talk!) Presentación oral	*Pre-AP* Resource Book:* pp. 145–146
	p. 148	Pre-AP* Support	
Writing	p. 115	Pre-AP* Support	*Communication Workbook:* Act. 7, p. 41
	p. 122	Differentiated Instruction: Advanced Learners/Pre-AP*	*Communication Workbook:* Act. 8, p. 42
			Communication Workbook: Act. 13, p. 47
	p. 134	Differentiated Instruction: Advanced Learners/Pre-AP*	*Communication Workbook:* Practice Test, p. 179
			Realidades para hispanohablantes: Act. Z, p. 91
	p. 137	Pre-AP* Support	*Realidades* para hispanohablantes: El español en el mundo del trabajo, p. 93
	p. 144	Presentación escrita	*Realidades* para hispanohablantes: Presentación escrita, p. 103
	p. 148	Pre-AP* Support	*realidades.com*
			ExamView: Pre-AP* Question Bank
			Assessment Program: Examen del capítulo 3, Escribir, p. 80
			Assessment Program: Examen del capítulo 3, Cultura, p. 80
			Pre-AP Resource Book:* pp. 145–146
Integrated Skills	p. 120	Act. 10	*Communication Workbook:* Integrated Performance Assessment, p. 178
	p. 124	Act. 17	
	p. 139	Act. 40	
	p. 142	Integración	

Teacher Activity 1
Interpersonal Speaking, Conversation

1. Allow students one minute to prepare to record the conversation. Allowing too much preparation time will lead to students' writing the script of what they want to say, and subsequently reading it. The purpose of the preparation time is to get a sense of the conversation and to generally gather thoughts.

2. Students should record their conversations. (See Recording and Evaluating on p. 44.) (See also "Administering the *Examen del capítulo* Speaking Proficiency Test" on p. T66 of the *Realidades* Assessment Program.) The teacher can be the voice of the other person in the conversation, allowing no more than 20 seconds for each response from the students.

3. In groups of three or four, students should listen to each recording and discuss the content and quality using the scoring guidelines on p. 49 of this book. Teachers may also consider using the "Speaking and Writing Rubrics for the *Examen del capítulo*" available in the *Realidades* Assessment Program front matter. Near the end of *Realidades* 3, teachers might wish to begin using adapted versions of the official AP* Spanish Language and Culture Scoring Guidelines for the interpersonal speaking task found at: apcentral.collegeboard.com/spanlang.

Teacher Activity 2
Presentational Writing

For Student Activity 2 follow the instructions for Presentational Writing in Teacher Activity 2, Chapter 1, of this book.

Building Speaking and Writing Skills

As students continue the development of their language skills, there are a number of strategies that teachers should use to help students make their speaking and writing more effective. For example:

1. Remind students to use transition words they have learned to link ideas and improve the flow of information. In Spanish 1 and 2, students work with basic expressions. In Spanish 3, students should be encouraged to use a variety of transition words, including recently learned expressions.

2. Students should continue to use a variety of adverbs to enrich the content of their speaking and writing samples.

3. Students typically express themselves using short, simple sentences early in Spanish 1. However, they should gradually raise their level of discourse by using a variety of conjunctions to form multi-clause sentences.

4. To continue the development of their interpersonal speaking skills, students should participate in increasingly complex conversations, always remembering to listen to each other and respond to each other's comments in a natural and authentic way.

5. Students should learn to use a rich variety of vocabulary, including idiomatic expressions, appropriate to a given context.

Student Activity 1
Interpersonal Speaking, Conversation

Directions: You will now participate in a simulated telephone conversation and will have one minute to read the outline of the conversation. During that time, plan how you will respond by making brief notes to yourself. Do not try to write out your answers, as there will not be sufficient time, and the purpose of this exercise is to strengthen your ability to engage in sustained conversations in Spanish. After the preparation time ends, the phone conversation will begin. When it is your turn to speak, you will have 20 seconds to respond. Use your 20 seconds to give an appropriate and thorough response, using up the allocated time as fully as possible.

Scenario: You and your classmate, Lisa, are assigned to give a talk to a group of elementary students next week about health and fitness. Lisa calls you to begin to plan your presentation.

LISA: Hola, amigo(a). Quisiera hablarte sobre nuestra presentación a los estudiantes de la escuela elemental. ¿Tienes ideas?

TÚ: _____

LISA: ¿Qué tipos de ejercicios y actividades debemos recomendarles?

TÚ: _____

LISA: ¿Cuáles aspectos de la dieta quieres presentar?

TÚ: _____

LISA: Bien. ¿Y qué te parece si les mostramos algunos ejercicios físicos?

TÚ: _____

LISA: Pues, ¿qué más debemos incluir en la presentatión?

TÚ: _____

LISA: Perfecto. Me gusta este plan. Nos vemos mañana.

TÚ: _____

Student Activity 2
Presentational Writing

Directions: First, you will hear an audio recording. You should take notes as you listen. Next, you will read the print articles. You will have a maximum of 15 minutes to accomplish these steps. Then, you will have 45 minutes to write a well-organized, formal essay on the topic below. Be sure to state your viewpoint clearly and explain it thoroughly, using information from all three sources to support your ideas. You should also cite the sources appropriately as they are used. Remember that this essay is not intended to be a summary of the three sources, but rather, an opportunity for you to synthesize these sources into your own ideas. Save a few minutes before the end of the writing time to proofread your work.

Topic: Explique la importancia de una dieta nutritiva y equilibrada.

Audio Source: Audio Activity 1 (*Realidades* TRB, p. 111)

Reading Source 1: *Conexiones: Las ciencias* (*Realidades* Student Textbook, p. 124)

Reading Source 2: *¡Cambia tus hábitos!* (*Realidades* Student Textbook, pp. 146–148)

	Teacher's Edition		Ancillaries
	Page #	Activity	
Vocabulary	p. 162	Pre-AP* Support	*realidades.com*
	p. 177	Pre-AP* Support	
Listening	p. 162	Pre-AP* Support	*Communication Workbook:* Act. 4, p. 52
	p. 164	Differentiated Instruction: Advanced Learners/Pre-AP*	*Communication Workbook:* Act. 5, p. 53
			Video Program Chapter 4
	p. 177	Pre-AP* Support	*Video Teacher's Guide* Chapter 4
	p. 193	Pre-AP* Support	*Pre-AP* Resource Book:* pp. 148–149
Reading	p. 158	Fondo cultural	*Communication Workbook:* Practice Test, p. 186
	p. 167	Fondo cultural	*Realidades* para hispanohablantes: Fondo cultural, p. 114
	p. 178	Fondo cultural	
	pp. 186–187	Puente a la cultura	*Realidades* para hispanohablantes: Puente a la cultura, pp. 130–132
	p. 195	Fondo cultural	*realidades.com*
			Pre-AP Resource Book:* pp. 148–149
Speaking	p. 162	Pre-AP* Support	*Assessment Program:* Examen del capítulo 4, Hablar, p. 102
	p. 164	Differentiated Instruction: Advanced Learners/Pre-AP*	*Teacher's Resource Book:* Communicative Activities, pp. 221–227
	p. 171	Pre-AP* Support	
	p. 177	Pre-AP* Support	*Teacher's Resource Book:* Situation cards, p. 228
	p. 189	(talk!) Presentación oral	*Realidades* para hispanohablantes: Presentación oral, p. 134
	p. 193	Pre-AP* Support	*Pre-AP* Resource Book:* pp. 148–149
Writing	p. 162	Pre-AP* Support	*Assessment Program:* Examen del capítulo 4, Escribir, p. 102
	p. 164	Differentiated Instruction: Advanced Learners/Pre-AP*	*Assessment Program:* Examen del capítulo 4, Cultura, p. 102
	p. 171	Pre-AP* Support	*Communication Workbook:* Act. 9, p. 57
	p. 178	Differentiated Instruction: Advanced Learners/Pre-AP*	*Communication Workbook:* Act. 13, p. 61
			Communication Workbook: Practice Test, p. 186
	p. 183	Pre-AP* Support	*Realidades* para hispanohablantes: Act. A, p. 108
	p. 190	Presentación escrita	*Realidades* para hispanohablantes: Fondo cultural, p. 123
	p. 193	Supplemental Pre-AP* Activity Pre-AP* Support	*Realidades* para hispanohablantes: Presentación escrita, p. 135
			realidades.com
			ExamView: Pre-AP* Question Bank
			Pre-AP Resource Book:* pp. 148–149
Integrated Skills	p. 173	Act. 21	*Communication Workbook:* Integrated Performance Assessment, p. 185
	p. 181	Act. 32	
	p. 184	Act. 38	
	p. 188	Integración	

Teacher Activity 1
Presentational Speaking

For each of the Presentational Speaking Student Activities, there is a recommend reading as well as a recommended listening selection. Students should:

1. Listen to the indicated audio selection, taking notes as they listen.

2. Complete the reading selection silently.

3. Prepare an oral presentation citing information from the audio and reading sources.

4. After the audio selection, allow students no more than 10 minutes to complete the reading selection and prepare the oral presentation. Students should not try to script every word of the presentation, but rather make notes about ideas they wish to express, noting key vocabulary expressions, conjugations, etc.

5. Students are then allowed two minutes to record their presentations, or they may make their presentations to a group of three or four students, and occasionally to the whole class.

6. Recordings are the preferred method of presentation, as this will allow students, in groups of three or four, to listen to each recording (or hear each presentation) and discuss the content and quality using the scoring guidelines on p. 49 of this book. Teachers may also consider using the "Speaking and Writing Rubrics for the *Examen del capítulo* available in the *Realidades* Assessment Program front matter. Near the end of *Realidades* 3, teachers might wish to begin using adapted versions of the official AP* Spanish Language and Culture Scoring Guidelines for the presentational speaking task found at: apcentral.collegeboard.com/spanlang.

Teacher Activity 2
Evaluating with Rubrics

After students have completed the Interpersonal Writing task on p. 149, follow the instructions for Evaluating with Rubrics in Teacher Activity 2 in Chapter 2 of this book.

Using the *Fondo cultural*

The *Fondo cultural* activities of each chapter offer additional insight into the cultures of the Spanish-speaking world. Because the information is in Spanish and the questions typically involve a comparison to the students' own culture, these activities can be a very effective tool for partner, small group, and whole class discussions. Teachers might want to have students read the information and write an answer to the question. Students can then read and discuss their answers with a partner or in a small group. Or teachers might have small groups read the information and use the question to prompt a group discussion. Each group should prepare a short answer to present to the class. The teacher can then guide a class discussion, comparing and commenting on each group's answer.

Student Activity 1
Interpretive Communication, Audiovisual Texts

Directions: Before viewing *Una amistad entre hermanos*, read the questions below. Select the correct answer to each question during or after viewing the video.

1. Cuando Lina tiene problemas, prefiere hablar con _____.
   a. su papá
   b. su mamá
   c. su hermano
   d. su abuela

2. Según Andrés, su papá es más _____ que su mamá.
   a. bonito
   b. sincero
   c. chistoso
   d. serio

3. Después de ver el video, se puede decir que Lina y Andrés _____.
   a. tienen muchos conflictos
   b. se llevan muy bien
   c. prefieren escuchar la misma clase de música
   d. tienen una relación mala con sus padres

Student Activity 2
Presentational Speaking

Imagine that you must give an oral presentation for your Spanish class on the topic of friendship. You must tell the class why you believe that lasting friendships are important. To prepare for your presentation:

1. Listen to the Video Script, *Una amistad entre hermanos*, Capítulo 4. (*Realidades* TRB. p. 220)

2. Read *La amistad*. (*Realidades* Student Textbook, p. 70)

3. Prepare an outline of the presentation, noting key vocabulary words and ideas. (Do not try to write an entire script. You will have 10 minutes to complete steps 2 and 3.)

4. Make a live presentation to your classmates, or record your oral presentation. The maximum presentation length is two minutes.

Student Activity 3
Interpersonal Writing

You and your best friend just had a big disagreement. Write an e-mail message to Carolina la Consejera's web site asking her advice. In your message:

- Explain both sides of the disagreement.
- Tell why you think you are right.
- Ask what you should do to resolve this conflict.

You have 10 minutes to complete this task. Write as complete a message as possible, using rich details and appropriate language.

	Teacher's Edition		Ancillaries
	Page #	Activity	
Vocabulary	p. 209	Pre-AP* Support	*realidades.com*
	p. 223	Pre-AP* Support	
Listening	p. 209	Pre-AP* Support	*Video Program* Chapter 5
	p. 219	Pre-AP* Support	*Video Teacher's Guide* Chapter 5
			Communication Workbook: Act. 3, p. 65
			Communication Workbook: Act. 5, p. 67
			Pre-AP* Resource Book: pp. 151–152
Reading	p. 204	Fondo cultural	*Communication Workbook:* Practice Test, p. 192
	p. 212	Fondo cultural	*Realidades* para hispanohablantes: Fondo cultural, p. 156
	p. 216	Fondo cultural	*Realidades* para hispanohablantes: Puente a la cultura, pp. 162-164
	p. 226	Fondo cultural	
	p. 231	Fondo cultural	*realidades.com*
	pp. 232–233	Puente a la cultura	*Pre-AP* Resource Book:* pp. 151–152
	p. 240	Pre-AP* Support	
	p. 241	Fondo cultural	
Speaking	p. 209	Pre-AP* Support	*Assessment Program:* Examen del capítulo 5, Hablar, p. 124
	p. 228	Differentiated Instruction: Advanced Learners/ Pre-AP*	*Teacher's Resource Book:* Communicative Activities: pp. 18–25
			Teacher's Resource Book: Situation cards, p. 26
	p. 235	Presentación oral	*Realidades* para hispanohablantes: Presentación oral, p. 166
	p. 240	Supplemental Pre-AP* Activity	*Pre-AP* Resource Book:* pp. 151–152
Writing	p. 209	Pre-AP* Support	*Assessment Program:* Examen del capítulo 5, Escribir, p. 124
	p. 210	Differentiated Instruction: Advanced Learners/Pre-AP*	*Assessment Program:* Examen del capítulo 5, Cultura, p.124
			Communication Workbook: Act. 9, p. 71
			Communication Workbook: Act. 13, p. 75
	p. 219	Pre-AP* Support	*Communication Workbook:* Practice Test, p. 192
	p. 223	Pre-AP* Support	*Realidades* para hispanohablantes: Fondo cultural, p. 148
	p. 227	Pre-AP* Support	*Realidades* para hispanohablantes: Act. Ñ, p. 150
	p. 236	Presentación escrita	*Realidades* para hispanohablantes: Act. O, p. 151
			Realidades para hispanohablantes: El español en la comunidad, p. 161
			Realidades para hispanohablantes: Presentación escrita, p. 167
			realidades.com
			ExamView: Pre-AP* Question Bank
			Pre-AP* Resource Book: pp. 151–152
Integrated Skills	p. 216	Act. 17	*Communication Workbook:* Integrated Performance Assessment, p. 191
	p. 218	Act. 20	
	p. 231	Act. 39	
	p. 234	Integración	

Teacher Activity 1
Interpersonal Speaking, Conversation

1. Allow students one minute to prepare to record the conversation. Allowing too much preparation time will lead to students' writing the script of what they want to say, and subsequently reading it. The purpose of the preparation time is to get a sense of the conversation and to generally gather thoughts.

2. Students should record their conversations. (See Recording and Evaluating on p. 44.) (See also "Administering the *Examen del capítulo* Speaking Proficiency Test" on p. T66 of the *Realidades* Assessment Program.) The teacher can be the voice of the other person in the conversation, allowing no more than 20 seconds for each response from the students.

3. In groups of three or four, students should listen to each recording and discuss the content and quality using the scoring guidelines on p. 49 of this book. Teachers may also consider using the "Speaking and Writing Rubrics for the *Examen del capítulo*" available in the *Realidades* Assessment Program front matter. Near the end of *Realidades* 3, teachers might wish to begin using adapted versions of the official AP* Spanish Language and Culture Scoring Guidelines for the interpersonal speaking task found at: apcentral.collegeboard.com/spanlang.

Teacher Activity 2
Presentational Writing

For each of the Presentational Writing Student Activities, there is a prompt with recommended readings as well as a recommended listening selection that present different aspects of the prompt. Students should:

1. Listen to the indicated audio selection, taking notes as they listen.

2. Complete the 2 reading selections silently.

3. Prepare a written essay in response to the prompt citing information from the audio and reading sources. Students should state their own point of view and explain it thoroughly. By the end of the academic year, students should be given 40 minutes to prepare and to write approximately 200 words. In addition, students should learn to save a few minutes before the end of the writing time to proofread their work.

Once students have finished writing, make three photocopies of each student's written work. Place students in groups of four. Distribute copies of the scoring guidelines found on p. 49 of this book. (Since this is a writing task, the *Fluency* category on the bottom row can be ignored at this time.) Distribute the copies of the students' work within each group. Have each student read his or her writing aloud to the group, one piece at a time, and discuss the content and quality of each writing piece using the scoring guidelines. Each group may select one sample to share with the whole class, as time permits. Near the end of *Realidades* 3, teachers might wish to begin using adapted versions of the official AP* Spanish Language and Culture Scoring Guidelines for the formal writing task found at: apcentral.collegeboard.com/spanlang.

Note: Continue to consider and to bring to students' attention the many writing tips offered in the *Realidades* Student Textbook as well as in the "Preparing to Write an Essay" section of this Pre-AP* Resource Book.

Student Activity 1
Interpersonal Speaking, Conversation

Directions: You will now participate in a simulated face-to-face conversation. You will have one minute seconds to read the outline of the conversation. During that time, plan how you will respond by making brief notes to yourself. Do not try to write out your answers, as there will not be sufficient time, and the purpose of this exercise is to strengthen your ability to engage in sustained conversations in Spanish. After the preparation time ends, the conversation will begin. When it is your turn to speak, you will have 20 seconds to respond. Use your 20 seconds to give an appropriate and thorough response, using up the allocated time as fully as possible.

Scenario: You have been invited to interview as a sales associate in a large department store by the store manager, Señora Robles.

SEÑORA ROBLES: Bienvenido(a), Señor(ita). ¿Quiere sentarse? Me llamo Señora Robles y soy gerente del almacén.

TÚ: _____

SEÑORA ROBLES: ¿Por qué quiere Ud. trabajar de dependiente(a) aquí?

TÚ: _____

SEÑORA ROBLES: En su opinión, ¿qué cualidades son necesarias para tener éxito en este trabajo?

TÚ: _____

SEÑORA ROBLES: Y, ¿qué experiencias previas ha tenido Ud. ?

TÚ: _____

SEÑORA ROBLES: A propósito, ¿busca Ud. un trabajo a tiempo parcial o a tiempo completo? ¿Por qué?

TÚ: _____

SEÑORA ROBLES: Bueno. Gracias por su tiempo. Tomaremos nuestra decisión dentro de una semana.

TÚ: _____

Student Activity 2
Presentational Writing

Directions: First, you will hear an audio recording. You should take notes as you listen. Next, you will read the print articles. You will have a maximum of 15 minutes to accomplish these steps. Next, you will have 45 minutes to write a well-organized, formal essay on the topic below. Be sure to state your viewpoint clearly and explain it thoroughly, using information from all three sources to support your ideas. You should also cite the sources appropriately as they are used. Remember that this essay is not intended to be a summary of the three sources, but rather, an opportunity for you to synthesize these sources into your own ideas. Save a few minutes before the end of the writing time to proofread your work.

Topic: Explique los beneficios del trabajo voluntario para la sociedad y también para el individuo que lo hace.

Audio Source: Video Script: *Un voluntario en la comunidad*, Capítulo 5 (*Realidades* TRB, p. 17)

Reading Source 1: *Profesores voluntarios por la paz, los derechos humanos y el medio ambiente* (*Realidades* Student Textbook, p. 230)

Reading Source 2: *Vuelta de hoja* (*Realidades* Student Textbook, p. 241)

	Teacher's Edition		Ancillaries
	Page #	**Activity**	
Vocabulary	p. 254	Pre-AP* Support	*realidades.com*
	p. 268	Pre-AP* Support	
Listening	p. 254	Pre-AP* Support	*Video Program* Chapter 6
	p. 268	Pre-AP* Support	*Video Teacher's Guide* Chapter 6
			Communication Workbook: Act. 4,5, p. 81
			Pre-AP Resource Book:* pp. 154–155
Reading	p. 250	Fondo cultural	*Communication Workbook:* Practice Test, p. 198
	p. 257	Fondo cultural	*Realidades* para hispanohablantes: Fuente cultural, p. 180
	p. 262	Fondo cultural	
	p. 271	Fondo cultural	*Realidades* para hispanohablantes: Puente a la cultura, pp. 194–196
	pp. 278–279	Puente a la cultura	*realidades.com*
	p. 287	Fondo cultural	*Pre-AP* Resource Book:* pp. 154–155
Speaking	p. 260	Differentiated Instruction, Advanced Learners/Pre-AP*	*Teacher's Resource Book:* Communicative Activities, pp. 77–82
	p. 263	Pre-AP* Support	*Teacher's Resource Book:* Situation cards, p. 83
	p. 270	Differentiated Instruction: Learners/Pre-AP*	*Realidades* para hispanohablantes: Presentación oral, p. 198
	p. 276	Pre-AP* Support	*Assessment Program:* Examen del capítulo 6, Hablar, p. 146
	p. 281	Presentación oral	
	p. 286	Pre-AP* Support	*Pre-AP* Resource Book:* pp. 154–155
Writing	p. 254	Pre-AP* Support	*Communication Workbook:* Act. 9, p. 85
	p. 283	Presentación escrita	*Communication Workbook:* Act. 13, p. 89
	p. 286	Pre-AP* Support	*Communication Workbook:* Practice Test, p. 198
			Realidades para hispanohablantes: Presentación escrita, p. 199
			realidades.com
			ExamView: Pre-AP* Question Bank
			Assessment Program: Examen del capítulo 6, Escribir, p. 146
			Assessment Program: Examen del capítulo 6, Cultura, p. 146
			Pre-AP Resource Book:* pp. 154–155
Integrated Skills	p. 262	Act. 15	*Communication Workbook:* Integrated Performance Assessment, p. 197
	p. 265	Act. 19	
	p. 277	Act. 36	
	p. 280	Integración	

Teacher Activity 1
Presentational Speaking

For each of the Presentational Speaking Student Activities, there is a recommend reading as well as a recommended listening selection. Students should:

1. Listen to the indicated audio selection, taking notes as they listen.

2. Complete the reading selection silently.

3. Prepare an oral presentation citing information from the audio and reading sources.

4. After the audio selection, allow students no more than 10 minutes to complete the reading selection and prepare the oral presentation. Students should not try to script every word of the presentation, but rather make notes about ideas they wish to express, noting key vocabulary expressions, conjugations, etc.

5. Students are then allowed two minutes to record their presentations, or they may make their presentations to a group of three or four students, and occasionally to the whole class.

6. Recordings are the preferred method of presentation, as this will allow students, in groups of three or four, to listen to each recording (or hear each presentation) and discuss the content and quality using the scoring guidelines on p. 49 of this book. Teachers may also consider using the "Speaking and Writing Rubrics for the *Examen del capítulo* available in the *Realidades* Assessment Program front matter. Near the end of *Realidades* 3, teachers might wish to begin using adapted versions of the official AP* Spanish Language and Culture Scoring Guidelines for the presentational speaking task found at: apcentral.collegeboard.com/spanlang.

Teacher Activity 2
Evaluating with Rubrics

After students have completed the Interpersonal Writing task on p. 151, make three photocopies of each student's written work. Place students in groups of four. Distribute copies of the scoring guidelines found on p. 49 of this book. (Since this is a writing task, the *Fluency* category on the bottom row can be ignored at this time.) Distribute the copies of the students' work within each group. Have each student read his or her writing aloud to the group, one piece at a time, and discuss the content and quality of each writing piece using the scoring guidelines. Each group may select one sample to share with the whole class. Near the end of *Realidades* 3, teachers might wish to begin using adapted versions of the official AP* Spanish Language and Culture Scoring Guidelines for the interpersonal writing task found at: apcentral.collegeboard.com/spanlang.

Student Activity 1
Interpretive Communication, Print Texts

Directions: Read Rosa on pp. 284–286 of the *Realidades* Student Textbook and answer the questions below.

1. Hace mucho tiempo que Rosa _____.
   a. conoce a Betty y a Carmen
   b. tiene problemas en su trabajo
   c. quiere ir a la Cámara de Aniquilación
   d. trabaja en su lugar de empleo

2. Rosa está muy orgullosa _____.
   a. de recibir una merecida recompensa
   b. de sus amigas Betty y Carmen
   c. del trabajo que ha hecho
   d. de siempre obedecer a su jefe

3. ¿Para qué llegaron los jóvenes?
   a. Para animar a Rosa.
   b. Para sacar a Rosa.
   c. Para reemplazar a Rosa.
   d. Para limpiar a Rosa.

Student Activity 2
Presentational Speaking

Imagine that you must give an oral presentation to the hiring committee at a company where you would like to work. You must tell the committee why you believe you are the ideal candidate for the company and what interests you about working there. To prepare:

1. Listen to the Video Script, *La tecnología en la carrera de un profesional, Capítulo 6.* (*Realidades* TRB, p. 76)

2. Read *A primera vista 2.* (*Realidades* Student Textbook, pp. 266–67)

3. Prepare an outline of the presentation, noting key vocabulary words and ideas. You will have 10 minutes to complete steps 2 and 3.)

4. Make a live presentation to your classmates, or record your oral presentation. The maximum presentation length is two minutes.

Student Activity 3
Interpersonal Writing

You were just accepted to your first college choice. In 10 minutes, write an e-mail to your grandparents telling them:
- Where you were accepted
- Why you want to attend this college or university
- What you will study there
- What you hope to do after you graduate.

You have 10 minutes to complete this task. Be sure to include a greeting, a closing, and at least two questions for your grandparents to answer.

Pre-AP* Resource Chart

	Teacher's Edition		Ancillaries
	Page #	Activity	
Vocabulary	p. 301	Pre-AP* Support	*realidades*.com
Listening	p. 304	Pre-AP* Support	*Video Program* Chapter 7
	p. 320	Pre-AP* Support	*Video Teacher's Guide* Chapter 7
			Communication Workbook: Act. 5, p. 95
			Pre-AP Resource Book:* pp. 157–158
Reading	p. 296	Fondo cultural	*Communication Workbook:* Practice Test, p. 204
	p. 304	Pre-AP* Support	*Realidades* para hispanohablantes: Puente a la cultura, pp. 226–228
	p. 310	Fondo cultural	
	p. 312	Pre-AP* Support	*realidades*.com
	pp. 324–325	Puente a la cultura	*Pre-AP* Resource Book:* pp. 157–158
	p. 333	Fondo cultural	
	p. 331	Pre-AP* Support	
Speaking	p. 301	Pre-AP* Support	*Teacher's Resource Book:* Communicative Activities, pp. 137–143
	p. 304	Pre-AP* Support	*Realidades* para hispanohablantes: Presentación oral, p. 230
	p. 306	Differentiated Instruction: Learners/Pre-AP*	*Teacher's Resource Book:* Situation cards, p. 144
	p. 312	Pre-AP* Support	*Assessment Program:* Examen del capítulo 7, Hablar, p. 167
	p. 320	Pre-AP* Support	*Pre-AP* Resource Book:* pp. 157–158
	p. 320	Differentiated Instruction: Advanced Learners/Pre-AP*	
	p. 327	(talk!) Presentación oral	
	p. 331	Pre-AP* Support	
Writing	p. 306	Differentiated Instruction: Advanced Learners/Pre-AP*	*Communication Workbook:* Act. 9, p. 99
			Communication Workbook: Act. 13, p. 103
	p. 312	Pre-AP* Support	*Communication Workbook:* Practice Test, p. 204
	p. 320	Differentiated Instruction: Learners/Pre-AP*	*Realidades* para hispanohablantes: Act. G, p. 209
	p. 328	Presentación escrita	*Realidades* para hispanohablantes: Presentación escrita, p. 231
			realidades.com
			ExamView: Pre-AP* Question Bank
			Assessment Program: Examen del capítulo 7, Escribir, p. 167
			Assessment Program: Examen del capítulo 7, Cultura, p. 167
			Pre-AP Resource Book:* pp. 157–158
Integrated Skills	p. 309	Act. 16	*Communication Workbook:* Integrated Performance Assessment, p. 203
	p. 311	Act. 18	
	p. 323	Act. 34	
	p. 326	Integración	

Realidades 3

Capítulo 7

Teacher Activity Sheet

Teacher Activity 1
Interpersonal Writing, E-mail Reply

Another type of Interpersonal Writing activity is the e-mail reply. Students read an e-mail message sent to them and write a reply to it. The message may be slightly more formal than a casual communication. Students should:

1. Have 15 minutes to read the message and write their reply.

2. Begin their reply with an appropriate greeting and end with a closing.

3. Respond to all questions and requests posed in the message and ask for details of something in the original message.

4. Use a formal form of address.

5. Remember to use transitions words to enhance the flow of information in their presentations and multi-clause sentences to raise the level of discourse.

Once students have finished writing, make three photocopies of each student's written work. Place students in groups of four. Distribute copies of the scoring guidelines found on p. 49 of this book.

(Since this is a writing task, the *Fluency* category on the bottom row can be ignored at this time.) Distribute the copies of the students' work within each group. Have each student read his or her writing aloud to the group, one piece at a time, and discuss the content and quality of each writing piece using the scoring guidelines. Each group may select one sample to share with the whole class, as time permits. Near the end of *Realidades* 3, teachers might wish to begin using adapted versions of the official AP* Spanish Language and Culture Scoring Guidelines for the interpersonal writing task found at: apcentral.collegeboard.com/spanlang.

Student Activity 1
Interpersonal Writing: E-Mail Reply

Directions: Read the e-mail message below and write a reply to it. You should include a greeting and a closing in your reply. You should also respond to all the questions and requests in the message as well as ask for more information about something mentioned in the message. Be sure to use a formal form of address. You have 15 minutes to read the message and write your reply.

Introduction

Este mensaje electronico es de la señora Daniela López del Instituto Nacional de Arqueología en México. Has recibido este mensaje porque vas a pasar el verano en México trabajando de voluntario para el Instituto.

DE: Daniela López

ASUNTO: Trabajo Voluntario en el Instituto Nacional de Arqueología de México

Estimado(a) Voluntario(a),

Muchas gracias por haber aceptado participar en el Programa Voluntario del Instituto Nacional de Arqueología este verano. El Instituto depende mucho de voluntarios como usted para seguir descubriendo e investigando nuestros recursos arqueológicos.

Al Instituto le importa que su experiencia en México sea muy buena. Por eso, le pido que me mande alguna información para que yo pueda finalizar los planes para su visita:

• Primero, este verano el Instituto estará excavando un sitio en las montañas y otro sitio cerca de la playa. ¿En cuál de los dos sitios le gustaría trabajar? ¿Por qué?

• Segundo, usted vivirá con una familia muy cerca del sitio de excavación. ¿Qué datos personales debo saber para escoger una familia apropiada para usted?

• Finalmente, necesito saber un poco de sus intereses arqueológicos. ¿Qué actividades prefiere hacer durante su trabajo aquí?

Por favor, mándeme esta información lo más pronto posible. Estoy a sus órdenes.

Atentamente,

Daniela López

Instituto Nacional de Arqueología

	Teacher's Edition		Ancillaries
	Page #	**Activity**	
Vocabulary	p. 346	Pre-AP* Support	*realidades.com*
	p. 356	Pre-AP* Support	
Listening	p. 356	Pre-AP* Support	*Video Program* Chapter 8
			Video Teacher's Guide Chapter 8
			Communication Workbook: Act. 3, p. 108
			Communication Workbook: Act. 5, p. 109
			Pre-AP* Resource Book: pp. 160–161
Reading	p. 342	Fondo cultural	*Communication Workbook:* Practice Test, p. 210
	p. 355	Fondo cultural	*Realidades* para hispanohablantes: Puente a la
	p. 362	Fondo cultural	cultura, pp. 258–260
	p. 362	Pre-AP* Support	*realidades.com*
	p. 370	Puente a la cultura	*Pre-AP* Resource Book:* pp. 160–161
	p. 379	Fondo cultural	
Speaking	p. 348	Differentiated Instruction: Advanced Learners/Pre-AP*	*Teacher's Resource Book:* Communicative Activities, pp. 194–200
	p. 356	Pre-AP* Support	*Teacher's Resource Book:* Situation cards, p. 201
	p. 373	Presentación oral	*Realidades* para hispanohablantes: Act. AA, p. 261
	p. 378	Pre-AP* Support	*Realidades* para hispanohablantes: Presentación oral, p. 262
			Assessment Program: Examen del capítulo 8, Hablar, p. 189
			Pre-AP* Resource Book: pp. 160–161
Writing	p. 346	Pre-AP* Support	*Communication Workbook:* Act. 8, p. 112
	p. 348	Differentiated Instruction, Advanced Learners/Pre-AP*	*Communication Workbook:* Act. 13, p. 117
	p. 353	Pre-AP* Support	*Communication Workbook:* Practice Test, p. 210
	p. 362	Pre-AP* Support	*Realidades* para hispanohablantes: Fondo cultural, p. 252
	p. 364	Differentiated Instruction: Advanced Learners/Pre-AP*	*Realidades* para hispanohablantes: Presentación escrita, p. 263
	p. 374	Presentación escrita	*realidades.com*
			ExamView: Pre-AP* Question Bank
			Assessment Program: Examen del capítulo 8, Escribir, p. 189
			Assessment Program: Examen del capítulo 8, Cultura, p. 189
			Pre-AP* Resource Book: pp. 160–161
Integrated Skills	p. 354	Act. 15	*Communication Workbook:* Integrated Performance Assessment, p. 209
	p. 362	Act. 24	
	p. 369	Act. 35	
	p. 372	Integración	

Teacher Activity 1
Presentational Speaking, Cultural Comparison

Some presentational speaking activities ask students to make cultural comparisons in response to a prompt on a cultural topic. In this activity, students compare cultural features of their own community to those found in an area of the Spanish–speaking world. Students are encouraged to cite examples from materials they have studied as well as from personal experiences. For these activities students should:

1. Use a graphic organizer to plan their presentations. Since they are preparing a cultural comparison, a Venn diagram is often very useful.

2. Respond to the prompt, comparing their own community to an area of the Spanish-speaking world with which they are familiar.

3. Organize their presentation clearly.

4. Remember to use transitions words to enhance the flow of information in their presentations and multi-clause sentences to raise the level of discourse.

5. Have 4–8 minutes to prepare. If the activity includes reading material, give the students four minutes to read the material and take notes; then give them four minutes to organize their presentations. For this activity students will read Activity 8, p. 350 of *Realidades* 3 and use a Venn diagram to organize their thoughts. If there is no material provided, give the students four minutes to prepare. Under all circumstances, the maximum length of time for the presentation is two minutes.

Recordings are the preferred method of presentation, as this will allow students, in groups of three or four, to listen to each recording (or hear each presentation) and discuss the content and quality using the scoring guidelines on p. 49 of this book. Teachers may also consider using the "Speaking and Writing Rubrics for the *Examen del capítulo* available in the *Realidades* Assessment Program front matter. Near the end of *Realidades* 3, teachers might wish to begin using adapted versions of the official AP* Spanish Language and Culture Scoring Guidelines for the presentational speaking task found at: apcentral.collegeboard.com/spanlang.

Teacher Activity 2
Interpretive Communication, Audiovisual Texts

Give students a copy of the questions in Student Activity 2. Have them read the questions before viewing *Unas herencias ricas* (Video Program, Chapter 8, *Realidades* TRB, p. 193). Students may select their answers during or after the video.

Student Activity 1
Presentational Speaking, Cultural Comparison

Directions: Your teacher will give you a Venn diagram or ask you to draw one. Label the first section: *Buenos Aires*, the middle section *Las dos comunidades*, and the last section *Mi comunidad*. As you read about Buenos Aires (REALIDADES 3, Act. 8, p. 350), make a list of its special features in the first section of the Venn diagram. Be sure to write key words only. Then think about your community and write key words to represent its features in the last section. In the middle section write key words that represent features of both communities. Using your Venn diagram, give an oral presentation in Spanish that responds to the prompt below. You will have four minutes to read Activity 8 and complete the first section of the Venn diagram. Then you will have four minutes to complete your Venn diagram and organize your thoughts. Afterwards, you will have two minutes to speak. Be sure to include appropriate transition words to facilitate the flow of information in your presentation and some multi-clause sentences to raise the level of discourse.

Topic: En tu libro de texto leíste sobre la historia y la gente de Buenos Aires. Compara tu comunidad a la ciudad de Buenos Aires. ¿En qué se parecen? ¿En qué se diferencian?

Student Activity 2
Interpretive Communication, Audiovisual Texts

Directions: Before viewing *Unas herencias ricas*, read the questions below. Select the correct answer to each question during or after viewing the video.

1. La idea principal de este videodocumentario es describir cómo _____.
    a. varias poblaciones han influido en la cultura de Norteamérica
    b. varios grupos étnicos han influido en la cultura de Latinoamérica
    c. el maíz llegó a ser la base de muchos platos latinoamericanos
    d. los españoles crearon las misiones durante la época colonial

2. ¿Qué se puede decir con respecto al idioma de los países latinoamericanos?
    a. Las palabras indígenas han desaparecido de la lengua.
    b. La palabra "huracán" es una palabra derivada de una lengua indígena de México.
    c. Hay varias palabras para la misma cosa debido a la variedad de lenguas indígenas.
    d. Hay muchas palabras derivadas de lenguas africanas.

3. Los indígenas de México dejaron sus huellas en el diseño de _____.
    a. las pirámides
    b. las misiones
    c. los balcones de hierro
    d. los azulejos

4. _____ son un ejemplo de la influencia africana en la comida de Latinoamérica.
    a. Los frijoles
    b. Las tortillas
    c. Los tacos
    d. Los tostones

Pre-AP* Resource Chart

	Teacher's Edition		Ancillaries
	Page #	**Activity**	
Vocabulary	p. 392	Pre-AP* Support	*realidades.com*
	p. 407	Pre-AP* Support	
Listening	p. 400	Pre-AP* Support	*Video Program* Chapter 9
			Video Teacher's Guide: Chapter 9
			Communication Workbook: Act. 4, p. 122
			Communication Workbook: Act. 5, p. 123
			Pre-AP Resource Book:* pp. 163–164
Reading	p. 388	Fondo cultural	*Communication Workbook:* Practice Test, p. 216
	p. 396	Fondo cultural	*Realidades* para hispanohablantes: Act. X, p. 288
	p. 400	Pre-AP* Support	*Realidades* para hispanohablantes: Puente a la
	p. 407	Pre-AP* Support	cultura, pp. 290–292
	p. 409	Fondo cultural	*Pre-AP* Resource Book:* pp. 163–164
	p. 425	Fondo cultural	
	p. 416	Puente a la cultura	
	p. 423	Pre-AP* Support	
Speaking	p. 392	Pre-AP* Support	*Teacher's Resource Book:*
	p. 400	Pre-AP* Support	*Teacher's Resource Book:* Situation cards, p. 256
	p. 402	Differentiated Instruction: Advanced Learners/Pre-AP*	*Realidades* para hispanohablantes: Presentación oral, p. 294
	p. 407	Pre-AP* Support	*Assessment Program:* Examen del capítulo 9,
	p. 412	Differentiated Instruction: Advanced Learners/Pre-AP*	Hablar, p. 211
			Pre-AP Resource Book:* p. 163
	p. 419	🗨 Presentación oral	
	p. 423	Pre-AP* Support	
Writing	p. 402	Differentiated Instruction: Advanced Learners/Pre-AP*	*Communication Workbook:* Act. 9, p. 127
			Communication Workbook: Act. 10, p. 128
	p. 407	Pre-AP* Support	*Communication Workbook:* Act. 13, p. 131
	p. 412	Differentiated Instruction: Advanced Learners/Pre-AP*	*Communication Workbook:* Practice Test, p. 216
			Realidades para hispanohablantes: Fondo
	p. 414	Pre-AP* Support	cultural, p. 274
	p. 420	Presentación escrita	*Realidades* para hispanohablantes: Presentación
	p. 423	Pre-AP* Support	escrita, p. 295
			realidades.com
			ExamView: Pre-AP* Question Bank
			Assessment Program: Examen del capítulo 9, Escribir, p. 211
			Assessment Program: Examen del capítulo 9, Cultura, p. 211
			Pre-AP Resource Book:* pp. 163–164
Integrated Skills	p. 403	Act. 19	*Communication Workbook:* Integrated Performance Assessment, p. 215
	p. 410	Act. 28	
	p. 418	Integración	

Teacher Activity 1
Interpersonal Writing, E-mail Reply

Another type of Interpersonal Writing activity is the e-mail reply. Students read an e-mail message sent to them and write a reply to it. The message may be slightly more formal than a casual communication. Students should:

1. Have 15 minutes to read the message and write their reply.

2. Begin their reply with an appropriate greeting and end with a closing.

3. Respond to all questions and requests posed in the message and ask for details of something in the original message.

4. Use a formal form of address.

Once students have finished writing, make three photocopies of each student's written work. Place students in groups of four. Distribute copies of the scoring guidelines found on p. 49 of this book. Distribute the copies of the students' work within each group. Have each student read his or her writing aloud to the group, one piece at a time, and discuss the content and quality of each writing piece using the scoring guidelines. Each group may select one sample to share with the whole class, as time permits. Near the end of *Realidades* 3, teachers might wish to begin using adapted versions of the official AP* Spanish Language and Culture Scoring Guidelines for the interpersonal writing task found at: apcentral.collegeboard.com/spanlang.

Student Activity 1
Interpersonal Writing, E-Mail Reply

Directions: Read the e-mail message below and write a reply to it. You should include a greeting and a closing in your reply. You should also respond to all the questions and requests in the message as well as ask for more information about something mentioned in the message. Be sure to use a formal form of address. You have 15 minutes to read the message and write your reply.

Introducción
Este mensaje electrónico es del señor Alejandro García, el Director de Fotografía de la revista *¡Mejoremos el mundo!* Has recibido este mensaje porque has ganado un concurso patrocinado por la revista.

DE: Alejandro García

ASUNTO: Su foto

Estimado(a) Fotógrafo(a),

Muchas gracias por haber participado en nuestro concurso de fotografía. El propósito de este mensaje es anunciarle que ¡usted ha ganado! Recibimos miles de fotos, pero su foto del pelícano que no podía volar porque estaba cubierto de petróleo del derrame reciente fue la mejor de la categoría de Tragedias Ambientales. ¡Ay, qué pena! Al ver la foto, podíamos sentir el miedo y la angustia del pobre pájaro. Sabemos que los lectores de *¡Mejoremos el mundo!* sentirán las mismas emociones tan pronto como vean su foto. Puesto que usted ha ganado una de la categorías, lo invitamos a hacer un viaje a una reserva natural en Centroamérica o Suramérica con un grupo de naturalistas y fotógrafos profesionales. Para planear su viaje, necesitamos la siguiente información:

- Primero, ¿cuáles son dos países a los que le gustaría viajar? ¿Cuál prefiere? ¿Por qué? ¿Cuando prefiere hacer el viaje?

Después de recibir su información, haremos los planes y le enviaremos otro mensaje con los detalles. Mientras tanto, contáctenos si tiene preguntas o necesita más información.

Lo felicito por su foto ganadora,

Alejandro García

Director de Fotografía

	Teacher's Edition		Ancillaries
	Page #	**Activity**	
Vocabulary	p. 439	Pre-AP* Support	*realidades.com*
Listening	p. 450	Pre-AP* Support	*Video Program* Chapter 10
	p. 461	Pre-AP* Support	*Video Teacher's Guide* Chapter 10
	p. 471	Pre-AP* Support	*Communication Workbook:* Act. 3, p. 136
			Communication Workbook: Act. 4, 5, p. 137
			Pre-AP* Resource Book: pp. 166–167
Reading	p. 434	Fondo cultural	*Communication Workbook:* Practice Test, p. 222
	p. 443	Fondo cultural	*Realidades* para hispanohablantes: Fondo
	p. 450	Pre-AP* Support	cultural, p. 316
	p. 453	Fondo cultural	*Realidades* para hispanohablantes: Puente a la
	p. 461	Pre-AP* Support	cultura, pp. 322–344
	p. 462	Puente a la cultura	*realidades.com*
	p. 471	Fondo cultural	*Pre-AP* Resource Book:* pp. 166–167
	p. 471	Pre-AP* Support	
Speaking	p. 446	Pre-AP* Support	*Teacher's Resource Book:* Communicative
	p. 450	Pre-AP* Support	Activities: pp. 307–314
	p. 465	Presentación oral	*Teacher's Resource Book:* Situation cards, p. 315
	p. 460	Differentiated Instruction: Advanced Learners/Pre-AP*	*Realidades* para hispanohablantes: Presentación oral, p. 326
	p. 461	Pre-AP* Support	*Assessment Program:* Examen del capítulo 10, Hablar, p. 234
	p. 471	Pre-AP* Support	*Pre-AP* Resource Book:* pp. 166–167
Writing	p. 439	Pre-AP* Support	*Communication Workbook:* Act.13, p. 145
	p. 444	Differentiated Instruction: Advanced Learners/Pre-AP*	*Communication Workbook:* Practice Test, p. 222
	p. 446	Pre-AP* Support	*Realidades* para hispanohablantes: Act. S, p. 315
	p. 466	Presentación escrita	*Realidades* para hispanohablantes: Presentación escrita, p. 327
			realidades.com
			ExamView: Pre-AP* Question Bank
			Assessment Program: Examen del capítulo 10, Escribir, p. 234
			Assessment Program: Examen del capítulo 10, Cultura, p. 234
			Pre-AP* Resource Book: pp. 166–167
Integrated Skills	p. 455	Act. 29	*Communication Workbook:* Integrated Performance Assessment, p. 221
	p. 455	Act. 30	
	p. 461	Act. 39	
	p. 464	Integración	

Teacher Activity 1
Presentational Speaking, Cultural Comparison

Some presentational speaking activities ask students to make cultural comparisons in response to a prompt on a cultural topic. In this activity, students compare cultural features of their own community to those found in an area of the Spanish–speaking world. Students are encouraged to cite examples from materials they have studied as well as from personal experiences. For these activities students should:

1. Use a graphic organizer to plan their presentations. Since they are preparing a cultural comparison, a Venn diagram is often very useful.

2. Respond to the prompt, comparing their own community to an area of the Spanish-speaking world with which they are familiar.

3. Organize their presentation clearly.

4. Remember to use transitions words to enhance the flow of information in their presentations and multi-clause sentences to raise the level of discourse.

5. Have 4–8 minutes to prepare. If the activity includes reading material, give the students four minutes to read the material and take notes; then give them four minutes to organize their presentations. For this activity, students will read Activity 8, p.350 of *Realidades* 3. Use a Venn diagram to organize their thoughts. If there is no material provided, give the students four minutes to prepare. Under all circumstances, the maximum length of time for the presentation is two minutes.

Recordings are the preferred method of presentation, as this will allow students, in groups of three or four, to listen to each recording (or hear each presentation) and discuss the content and quality using the scoring guidelines on p. 49 of this book. Teachers may also consider using the "Speaking and Writing Rubrics for the *Examen del capítulo* available in the *Realidades* Assessment Program front matter. Near the end of Realidades 3, teachers might wish to begin using adapted versions of the official AP* Spanish Language and Culture Scoring Guidelines for the presentational speaking task found at: apcentral.collegeboard.com/spanlang.

Student Activity 1
Presentational Speaking, Cultural Comparison

Directions: Your teacher will give you a Venn diagram or ask you to draw one. Label the first section: *El héroe de América Latina*, the middle section *Los dos héroes*, and the last section *Mi héroe*. As you read *Héroes de América Latina* (**Realidades** 3, pp. 462–463), select one of the heroes described and take notes on him in the first section of the Venn diagram. Then select one national or local hero that you admire in your community and write key words to describe him/her in the last section. In the middle section write key words that represent features of both groups of heroes. Using your Venn diagram, give an oral presentation in Spanish that responds to the prompt below. You will have five minutes to read *Héroes de América Latina* and complete the first section of the Venn diagram. Then you will have four minutes to complete your Venn diagram and organize your thoughts. Afterwards, you will have two minutes to speak. Be sure to include appropriate transition words to facilitate the flow of information in your presentation and some multi-clause sentences to raise the level of discourse.

Topic: En tu libro de texto leíste sobre algunos héroes de América Latina. ¿Cómo afectan los héroes la vida de una comunidad? Compara al héroe de tu comunidad al héroe de América Latina. ¿En qué se parecen? ¿En qué se diferencian?

Level 4
Resource Support

Learning Objectives	Student Edition		Ancillaries
	Page #	**Activity**	
Spoken Interpersonal	p. 12 p. 13 p. 14 p. 29 p. 35	Act. 1-12 Act. 1-14 Act. 1-15 Act. 1-43 Act. 1-57	
Written Interpersonal			Pre-AP* Resource Book: p. 171
Audio, Visual, and Audiovisual Interpretive	p. 17 p. 18 p. 22	Act. 1-22 VideoRed: Act. 1-24, 1-25 Act. 1-31	Workbook: 1-10
Written and Print Interpretive	p. 8, 16, 26 p. 32–33 p. 33–35	Aplicación: Act. 1-6, 1-7; 1-17, 1-18; 1-35, 1-36 Ritmos: Act. 1-51, 1-52, 1-53 Páginas: Act. 1-54, 1-55, 1-56	Workbook: 1-34, 1-35, 1-36
Spoken Presentational	p. 17, p. 29 p. 19 p. 29 pp. 30–31 p. 33	Debate: Act. 1-23, 1-46 Comparaciones: Act. 1-28, 1-29 A explorar: Act. 1-44 Imágenes: Act. 1-47, 1-48, 1-49 A explorar: Act. 1-53	**realidades.com**: Práctica oral
Written Presentational	p. 17 p. 23 p. 36	A explorar: Act. 1-21 A explorar: Act. 1-33 Taller	Workbook: 1-19, 1-22, 1-32, 1-37, 1-38

Student Activity
Interpersonal Writing, E-mail Reply

Directions for the student:
You will write a reply to an e-mail message. First, you should read the message and then write your reply. Your reply should include a greeting and a closing and should respond to all the questions and requests in the message. In your reply, you should also ask for more details about something mentioned in the message. Also, you should use a formal form of address.

Tema curricular: La vida contemporánea

Introducción
Este mensaje electrónico es del señor José Fernández, miembro de la Junta Escolar del distrito donde vives. Has recibido este mensaje porque asistes a una escuela secundaria en su distrito.

De: José Fernández

Asunto: Nuevas Reglas

Estimado Estudiante,

Como miembro de la Junta Escolar de su distrito, me preocupan algunos aspectos de nuestras escuelas. Hace dos o tres años vemos que hay más problemas debido al comportamiento de los estudiantes durante el día escolar y aún más durante las actividades de los programas extracurriculares. Después de leer varios artículos profesionales, mis colegas y yo nos hemos dado cuenta de que el modo de vestir puede influir en el comportamiento de los estudiantes. Por eso estamos pensando en establecer reglas para controlar el modo de vestir en nuestras escuelas.

Antes de tomar una decisión final, me gustaría recibir las opiniones de nuestros estudiantes. Por lo tanto, le pido que conteste algunas preguntas sobre la situación en su escuela. Primero, ¿cómo se visten los estudiantes durante el día escolar? ¿Cree usted que hay una relación entre el modo de vestir y el comportamiento de los estudiantes? Por favor, explique su opinión. Finalmente, por favor mándeme algunas sugerencias para nuevas restricciones. Estoy aquí para servir a nuestra comunidad y para lograr lo mejor en nuestras escuelas. Si usted quiere saber más de este asunto, le recomiendo comunicarse conmigo por medio del correo electrónico. Agradezco mucho su ayuda y su interés en mejorar las escuelas de nuestra comunidad.

Lo saluda atentamente,

José Fernández

Representante, Junta Escolar.

Pre-AP* Resource Chart

Learning Objectives	Student Edition		Ancillaries
	Page #	Activity	
Spoken Interpersonal	p. 58	Act. 2-29	
	p. 66	Act. 2-46	
	p. 71	Act. 2-54	
Written Interpersonal	p. 65	Act. 2-42	
Audio, Visual, and Audiovisual Interpretive	p. 53	Act. 217	Workbook; 2-9, 2-17
	p. 54	*VideoRed*: Act. 2-20, 2-21	
	p. 63	Act. 2-36	
Written and Print Interpretive	p. 40, 42	*¡Así es la vida!*: Act. 2-1, 2-2, 2-3	Workbook: 2-40
	p. 48, 51–52, 63	*Aplicación*: Act. 2-8; 2-13, 2-14; 2-33, 2-34,	*Pre-AP* Resource Book*: p. 173
	p. 56, 58	*¡Así es la vida!*: Act. 2-28, 2-29	
	p. 67	*Ritmos*: Act. 2-47, 2-48, 2-49	
	pp. 68–71	*Páginas*: Act. 2-50, 2-51, 2-52, 2-53	
Spoken Presentational	p. 44	Act. 2-6	**realidades.com**:
	p. 52	Act. 2-15, 2-16	*Práctica oral*
	p. 53, 65	*Debate*: Act. 2-19, 2-43	Workbook: 2-37
	p. 55	*Conexiones*: Act. 2-23	
	p. 55	*Comparaciones*; Act. 2-24, 2-25, 2-26	
	p. 66	*Imágenes*: Act. 2-44, 2-45, 2-46	
Written Presentational	p. 63	*A explorar;* Act. 2-35	Workbook: 2-22, 2-41, 2-42
	p. 66	*A explorar:* Act. 2-45	
	p. 72	*Taller*	

Student Activity
Interpretive Communication, Print Texts

Tema curricular: Los desafíos mundiales
Lee el artículo "Protectores del medio ambiente colombiano" (WKBK 2-40) y contesta las preguntas a continuación:

1. ¿Cómo es el tono de esta selección?
   a. Agresivo
   b. Irónico
   c. Controversial
   d. Optimista

2. ¿Cuál es una consecuencia de la deforestación en Colombia?
   a. Todas las tortugas y muchos caimanes han desaparecido.
   b. Colombia ha llegado a ser un país rico.
   c. Es posible que el país pierda algunos tipos de animales para siempre.
   d. La biodiversidad en Colombia es notable.

3. En Colombia el gobierno _____.
   a. apoya la protección del medio ambiente
   b. permite la destrucción del bosque amazónico
   c. creó la organización APROFAC
   d. lucha con los que promueven la defensa del medio ambiente

4. ¿Cuál es la idea principal de esta selección?
   a. Colombia tiene una variedad de plantas y animales.
   b. El gobierno y varios grupos están trabajando para proteger el medio ambiente.
   c. El gobierno de Colombia ha establecido programas educativos en su sistema escolar.
   d. APROFAC ha establecido leyes para proteger dos especies de cocodrilos.

Learning Objectives	Student Edition		Ancillaries
	Page #	**Activity**	
Spoken Interpersonal	p. 83 p. 87 p. 95 p. 103	Act. 3-19 Act. 3-25 Act. 3-36 Act. 3-54	*Pre-AP* Resource Book:* p. 175
Written Interpersonal	p. 95 p. 98	Act. 3-37 Act. 3-40	Workbook: 3-41, 3-42, 3-43
Audio, Visual, and Audiovisual Interpretive	p. 81 p. 82 p. 98	Act. 3-12 *VideoRed*: Act. 3-14, 3-15 Act. 3-42	Workbook: 3-36
Written and Print Interpretive	p. 76, 78 p. 91 p. 83 pp. 100–101 pp. 102–103	*¡Así es la vida!* Act. 3-1, 3-2, 3-3 *Aplicación:* 3-28, 3-29, 3-30 *Comparaciones:* Act. 3-18, 3-19 *Ritmos:* Act. 3-46, 3-47, 3-48, 3-49 *Páginas:* Act. 3-51, 3-52, 3-53	Workbook: 3-40
Spoken Presentational	p. 78 p. 79 p. 81, 98 p. 82 p. 99 p. 101 p. 103	Act. 3-3 *A explorar:* Act. 3-6 *Debate:* Act.3-13, 3-43 *VideoRed:* Act. 3-15 *Imágenes:* Act. 3-44, 3-45 *A explorar:* Act. 3-50 *A explorar,* Act. 3-55	**realidades.com**: *Práctica oral*
Written Presentational	p. 78 p. 79 p. 83 p. 104	*A explorar:* Act. 3-4 *A explorar:* Act. 3-6 *A explorar:* Act. 3-20 *Taller*	Workbook: 3-16, 3-37, 3-38, 3-41, 3-42

Student Activity

Interpersonal Speaking, Conversation

Directions for the student:
You will participate in a conversation. First, you will read a preview of the conversation, including an outline of each turn in the conversation. Afterward, the conversation will begin, following the outline. Each time it is your turn to speak, give a thorough and appropriate response.

Tema curricular: Los desafíos mundiales

Introducción

Esta es una conversación con Daniela, una compañera de clase. Vas a participar en esta conversación porque ella tiene preguntas sobre las vacaciones de verano.

DANIELA	• Te saluda y te hace una pregunta.
TÚ	• Salúdala y dale una respuesta.
DANIELA	• Te hace dos preguntas
TÚ	• Responde con detalles.
DANIELA	• Continúa la conversación y te hace dos preguntas.
TÚ	• Contéstale con detalles.
DANIELA	• Continúa la conversación y te hace otra pregunta.
TÚ	• Responde y explica por qué.
DANIELA	• Continúa la conversación y te hace otra pregunta.
TÚ	• Contéstale con detalles y despídete.

Script for the activity: The following script is for the student playing the role of Daniela.

DANIELA: Hola. Me alegra que empiecen las vacaciones de verano en un mes. ¿Qué vas a hacer este verano?
(Espera una respuesta.)

DANIELA : Cuéntame un poco más de tus planes. ¿Tienes muchas ganas de hacer eso? ¿Por qué?
(Espera una respuesta.)

DANIELA : Bueno, todavía estoy haciendo mis planes. Creo que me interesa el servicio comunitario. ¿Dónde puedo trabajar de voluntaria en nuestra comunidad? ¿Qué puedo hacer?
(Espera una respuesta.)

DANIELA : La verdad es que estoy un poco confundida. Otra posibilidad es que puedo solicitar una pasantía con una organización como Amnistía Internacional porque me importan los derechos humanos. ¿A ti también te interesan los derechos humanos?
(Espera una respuesta.)

DANIELA : Pues, por un lado la pasantía sería una experiencia beneficiosa. Por otro, tendría que pasar el verano en otra ciudad. En tu opinión, ¿cuál es la mejor opción para mí: el servicio comunitario o la pasantía?
(Espera una respuesta.)

Learning Objectives	Student Edition		Ancillaries
	Page #	Activity	
Spoken Interpersonal	p. 118	VideoRed: Act. 4-16	
Written Interpersonal			
Audio, Visual, and Audiovisual Interpretive	p. 117 p. 118 p. 132	Act. 4-12 *VideoRed*; Act. 4-15, 4-16 Act. 4-36	Workbook: 4-9, 4-30
Written and Print Interpretive	p. 112 p. 116, 127 p. 120, 122 p. 123 pp. 134–135 pp. 135–137	Act. 4-7 *Aplicación*: Act. 4-9, 4-10; 4-27, 4-28 *Así es la vida!* Act.4-21 Act. 4-24 *Ritmos*: Act. 4-40, 4-41, 4-42, 4-43, 4-44 *Páginas*: Act. 4-45, 4-46, 4-47, 4-48, 4-49, 4-50	Workbook: 4-38 *Pre-AP* Resource Book*: p. 177
Spoken Presentational	p. 111 p. 117, 132 p. 119 p. 119 p. 128 p. 133 p. 133	Act. 4-6 *Debate*: Act. 4-14, 4-37 *Conexiones;* Act. 4-18 *Comparaciones*: Act. 4-19, 4-20 Act. 4-30 *Imágenes*: Act. 4-38 *A explorar*: Act. 4-39	**realidades.com**: *Práctica oral* *Pre-AP* Resource Book*: p. 177
Written Presentational	p. 111 p. 138	*A explorar*: Act. 4-4 *Taller*	Workbook: Act. 4-15, 4-35, 4-36, 4-39, 4-40

Student Activity 1
Presentational Speaking, Cultural Comparison

Directions for the student:
You will make an oral presentation on a specific topic to your class. In your presentation, compare your own community to an area of the Spanish-speaking world with which you are familiar. You should demonstrate your understanding of cultural features of the Spanish-speaking world. You should also organize your presentation clearly.

Tema curricular: Las identidades personales y públicas

Tema de la presentación:
En tu libro de texto, leíste sobre la vida personal y las acciones de personas famosas como Carlos Santana y Cristina Fernández, y de personas que trabajan en instituciones públicas, como Hombro a Hombro ¿En qué forma la vida personal y las acciones de estas personas o grupos que generalmente tienen gran acceso a los medios de comunicación afectan la cultura hoy?

Compara tus observaciones sobre personajes en tu cultura con tus observaciones de personajes de alguna región del mundo hispanohablante que te sea familiar. En tu presentación, puedes referirte a los que has estudiado, vivido, observado, etc.

Student Activity 2
Interpretive Communication, Print Texts

Tema curricular: Las identidades personales y públicas
Lee el artículo "¡Ejercita tu mente!" (Capítulo 4, ¡Así es la vida! Segunda Parte) y contesta las siguientes preguntas:

1. Muchas personas tienen mala memoria porque están _____.
   a. aburridas
   b. ocupadas
   c. enfermas
   d. avergonzadas

2. ¿Cuál es una actividad para encontrar algo que uno ha perdido?
   a. Organizar su oficina
   b. Leer más
   c. Hacer ejercicio
   d. Relajarse

3. ¿Para qué sirven las reglas mnemotécnicas?
   a. Para ejercitar el cuerpo
   b. Para estudiar sin distraerse
   c. Para aprender algo de memoria
   d. Para dormir mejor

4. Con respecto a la memoria, se puede decir que _____.
   a. es casi imposible mejorar la memoria
   b. la imaginación bloquea la memoria
   c. el estrés desarrolla la memoria
   d. la música tiene un impacto positivo en la memoria

Learning Objectives	Student Edition		Ancillaries
	Page #	**Activity**	
Spoken Interpersonal	p. 148 p. 161 p. 162	Act. 5-12 Act. 5-30 Act. 5-33	*Pre-AP* Resource Book:* p. 179
Written Interpersonal	p. 170	Taller	Workbook: 5-39, 5-40, 5-41
Audio, Visual, and Audiovisual Interpretive	p. 145 p. 150 p. 163	Act. 5-5 VideoRed; Act. 5-15, 5-16 Act. 5-35	Workbook: 5-10, 5-11, 5-22
Written and Print Interpretive	p. 142, 144 p. 151 p. 152, 154 pp. 165–166 pp. 167–169	*¡Así es la vida;* Act. 5-1 *Comparaciones:* Act. 5-19, 5-20 *¡Así es la vida:* Act. 5-21 *Ritmos:* Act. 5-39, 5-40, 5-41 *Páginas:* Act. 5-42, 5-43, 5-44, 5-45, 5-46, 5-47	Workbook: 5-13, 5-35, 5-36, 5-38
Spoken Presentational	p. 149, 163 p. 151 p. 154 p. 164	*Debate:* Act. 5-14, 5-37 *Conexiones:* Act. 5-18 Act. 5-23 *Imágenes:* Act. 5-38	**realidades.com**: *Práctica oral*
Written Presentational	p. 149 p. 163 p. 169	*A explorar:* Act. 5-13 *A explorar:* Act. 5-36 *A explorar:* Act. 5-48	Workbook: 5-36

Student Activity

Interpersonal Speaking, Conversation

Directions for the student:
You will participate in a conversation. First, you will read a preview of the conversation, including an outline of each turn in the conversation. Afterward, the conversation will begin, following the outline. Each time it is your turn to speak, give a thorough and appropriate response.

Tema curricular: La vida contemporánea

Introducción
Esta es una conversación con Mariana, una compañera de clase. Vas a participar en esta conversación porque Mariana tiene un problema y necesita tu ayuda.

MARIANA	• Te saluda y te hace una pregunta.
TÚ	• Salúdala y dale una respuesta.
MARIANA	• Te hace otra pregunta.
TÚ	• Responde con detalles.
MARIANA	• Continúa la conversación y te hace otra pregunta.
TÚ	• Responde y explica por qué.
MARIANA	• Continúa la conversación y te hace otra pregunta.
TÚ	• Contéstale con detalles.
MARIANA	• Continúa la conversación y te hace otra pregunta.
TÚ	• Contéstale con detalles y despídete.

Script for the activity: The following script is for the student playing the role of Mariana.

MARIANA: Hola, ¿qué tal? Hoy estoy un poco aburrida y quisiera conocer nuevos amigos. Creo que voy a buscarlos usando uno de esos servicios de la Internet que son tan populares. ¿Qué te parece la idea?
(Espera una respuesta.)

MARIANA : ¿Has oído hablar de alguien que haya tenido una experiencia buena o que haya tenido problemas con esos servicios?
(Espera una respuesta.)

MARIANA : Si decido usar uno de esos servicios, sé que podré mencionar los atributos que considero importantes en un amigo. Pienso que es importante que mis amigos sean honrados y que no sean malcriados. ¿Me puedes sugerir otros atributos y explicarme por qué son importantes?
(Espera una respuesta.)

MARIANA : Ay, no sé qué hacer. Y si no uso la Internet para conocer nuevos amigos, ¿qué otras opciones recomiendas?
(Espera una respuesta.)

MARIANA : Gracias por las sugerencias. De veras, quisiera conocer nuevos amigos, pero me preocupa cómo hacerlo. En fin, ¿qué me aconsejas?
(Espera una respuesta.)

Learning Objectives	Student Edition		Ancillaries
	Page #	**Activity**	
Spoken Interpersonal	p. 176	Act. 6-2	
	p. 177	Act. 6-4	
	p. 183	Act. 6-14	
Written Interpersonal	p. 177	Act. 6-5	*Pre-AP* Resource Book:* p. 181
	p. 195	Act. 6-37	
Audio, Visual, and Audiovisual Interpretive	p. 177	Act. 6-7	Workbook: 6-6, 6-14
	p. 184	*VideoRed:* Act. 6-16, 6-17	
	p. 190	Act. 6-31	
Written and Print Interpretive	p. 174, 176	*¡Así es la vida!:* Act. 6-1	Workbook: 6-39, 6-40, 6-42
	p. 181	*Aplicación:* Act. 6-9, 6-10	
	p. 189	Act. 6-30	
	pp. 199–200	*Ritmos:* Act. 6-49, 6-50, 6-51, 6-52	
	pp. 201–203	*Páginas:* Act. 6-54, 6-55, 6-56, 6-57, 6-58, 6-59	
Spoken Presentational	p. 177	Act. 6-6	**realidades.com:** *Práctica oral*
	p. 182	*A explorar:* Act. 6-11	
	p. 183, 197	*Debate:* Act. 6-15, 6-46	
	p. 185	*Comparaciones:* Act. 6-21, 6-22	
	p. 185	*A explorar:* Act. 6-23	
	p. 188	*A explorar:* Act. 6-26	
	p. 195	*A explorar:* Act. 6-40	
	p. 198	*Imágenes:* Act. 6-47, 6-48	
	p. 200	*A explorar:* Act. 6-53	
Written Presentational	p. 178	Act. 6-8	Workbook: 6-7, 6-16
	p. 184	*A explorar:* Act. 6-18	
	p. 188	*A explorar:* Act. 6-28	
	p. 204	*Taller*	

Student Activity
Interpersonal Writing, E-mail Reply

Directions to the student:
You will write a reply to an e-mail message. First, you should read the message and then write your reply. Your reply should include a greeting and a closing and should respond to all the questions and requests in the message. In your reply, you should also ask for more details about something mentioned in the message. Also, you should use a formal form of address.

Tema curricular: La vida contemporánea

Introducción
Este mensaje es del señor Fabián Romero, Director de Mercadeo de ¡Mejor Talento Mundial! Has recibido este mensaje porque has ganado un concurso patrocinado por ¡Mejor Talento Mundial!

De: Fabián Romero
Asunto: Nuestro Concurso

Estimado participante:

Muchas gracias por haber participado en nuestro concurso. El propósito de este mensaje es informarle que ¡usted ha ganado! Miles de jóvenes nos han mandado ensayos contestando la pregunta "¿Cómo influye el mundo del espectáculo en la vida contemporánea?" y el comité ha seleccionado el ensayo suyo como el mejor.

Como usted sabe, ¡Mejor Talento Mundial! representa a los mejores artistas del mundo, sean actores, bailarines, o músicos. Actualmente nuestra compañía, que se especializa en espectáculos populares y clásicos, arregla y presenta programas por todo el mundo.

Puesto que usted ha ganado nuestro concurso, lo invitamos a asistir a cualquier espectáculo nuestro que le interese. Como ganador, organizaremos y pagaremos los costos de viaje y alojamiento. Además, tendrá la oportunidad de conocer y pasar tiempo con el artista que escoja. Para planear una experiencia formidable, necesitamos la siguiente información:

- Primero, ¿qué tipo de espectáculo desea ver? Es importante que usted nos dé algunos detalles. También, le pido que incluya los nombres de sus artistas favoritos y que explique por qué le gustan.
- Segundo, ¿en qué país le gustaría asistir al espectáculo y durante qué mes?
  Mándeme dos opciones en caso de que su primera preferencia no sea posible.

Después de recibir su información, haremos los planes y le mandaremos otro mensaje con los detalles. Mientras tanto, contáctenos si necesita más información.

Lo felicita por su ensayo ganador,

Fabián Romero
Director de Mercadeo
¡Mejor Talento Mundial!

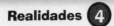
Learning Objectives	Student Edition		Ancillaries
	Page #	Activity	
Spoken Interpersonal	p. 210	Act. 7-3	
	p. 211	Act. 7-4	
	p. 219	*Conexiones:* Act. 7-25	
	p. 223	Act. 7-31	
	p. 232	Act. 7-43	
Written Interpersonal	p. 233	Act. 7-45	
Audio, Visual, and Audiovisual Interpretive	p. 214	Act. 7-13	Workbook: 7-18
	p. 218	*VideoRed:* Act. 7-22, 7-23	
	p. 233	Act. 7-47	
Written and Print Interpretive	p. 220, 222	*¡Así es la vida!:* Act. 7-28	Workbook: 7-37
	p. 223	Act. 7-30	
	p. 227	*Aplicación:* Act. 7-34, 7-35	
	pp. 236–237	*Ritmos:* Act. 7-51, 7-52, 7-53, 7-54	
	pp. 238–239	*Páginas:* Act. 7-55, 7-56, 7-57, 7-58, 7-59	
Spoken Presentational	p. 210	Act. 7-2	**realidades.com**: *Práctica oral*
	p. 211	*A explorar:* Act. 7-6	*Pre-AP* Resource Book:* p. 183
	p. 217, 234	*Debate:* Act. 7-21, 7-48	
	p. 219	*Comparaciones:* Act. 7-26, 7-27	
	p. 223	*A explorar:* Act. 7-32	
	p. 234	*Imágenes:* Act. 7-49	
	p. 235	*A explorar:* Act. 7-50	
	p. 239	*A explorar:* Act. 7-60	
Written Presentational	p. 223	*A explorar:* Act. 7-32	Workbook: 7-16, 7-34, 7-35, 7-38, 7-39, 7-40
	p. 228	*A explorar:* Act. 7-39	*Pre-AP* Resource Book:* p. 183
	p. 240	*Taller*	

Realidades 4

Capítulo 7

Student Activity 1
Presentational Writing, Persuasive Essay

Directions for the student:
You will write an essay to submit to a Spanish writing contest. The essay topic is based on three sources, which present different viewpoints on the topic and include both print and audio material. First, you should read the essay topic and the printed material. Afterward, you will hear the audio material twice; you should take notes while you listen. Then you will write your essay. In your essay, you should present the sources' different viewpoints on the topic and also clearly indicate your own viewpoint and defend it thoroughly. Use information from all the sources to support your essay. As you refer to the sources, identify them appropriately. Also, organize your essay into clear paragraphs.

Tema curricular: Los desafíos mundiales

Tema del ensayo:
¿Estás a favor de la acción afirmativa?

Fuente número 1
"Discriminación positiva: ¿Qué tan positiva?" (*Realidades* 4, Actividad 7-32)

Fuente número 2
"Demógrafa" (*Realidades* 4, p. 208)

Fuente número 3
"El reto educativo" (*Realidades* 4, Actividad 7-47)

Student Activity 2
Presentational Speaking, Cultural Comparison

Directions for the student:
You will make an oral presentation on a specific topic to your class. In your presentation, compare your own community to an area of the Spanish-speaking world with which you are familiar. You should demonstrate your understanding of cultural features of the Spanish-speaking world. You should also organize your presentation clearly.

Tema curricular: Las familias y las comunidades

Tema de la presentación:
El artículo sobre flamenco en tu libro de texto presenta el problema de la inclusión social de minorías étnicas: en algunas comunidades, los grupos minoritarios sienten que no tienen voz y que su opinión no es respetada. ¿Crees que esta situación se presenta en la comunidad donde vives?

Compara tus observaciones sobre personajes en tu cultura con tus observaciones de personajes de alguna región del mundo hispanohablante que te sea familiar. En tu presentación, puedes referirte a los que has estudiado, vivido, observado, etc.

Learning Objectives	Student Edition		Ancillaries
	Page #	**Activity**	
Spoken Interpersonal	p. 247	Act. 8-5	
	p. 253	Act. 8-18	
	p. 268	Act. 8-44	
	p. 271	Act. 8-48	
Written Interpersonal			Pre-AP* Resource Book: p. 185
Audio, Visual, and Audiovisual Interpretive	p. 247	Act. 8-7	Workbook: 8-5
	p. 253	VideoRed: Act. 8-15, 8-16	
	p. 258	Act. 8-27	
Written and Print Interpretive	p. 254,	¡Así es la vida!: Act. 8-21	Workbook: 8-36
	p. 257	Act. 8-25	
	pp. 267–268	Ritmos: Act. 8-41, 8-42, 8-43	
	pp. 269–271	Páginas: Act. 8-45, 8-46, 8-47	
Spoken Presentational	p. 247	A explorar: Act. 8-6	**realidades.com**: Práctica oral
	p. 251, 265	Debate: Act. 8-14, 8-39	
	p. 252	VideoRed: Act. 8-16	
	p. 253	Comparaciones: Act. 8-19, 8-20	
	p. 265	A explorar: Act. 8-38	
	p. 266	Imágenes: Act. 8-40	
Written Presentational	p. 256	A explorar: Act. 8-22	Workbook: 8-13, 8-33, 8-37, 8-38, 8-39
	p. 271	A explorar: Act. 8-50	
	p. 273	Taller	

Student Activity
Interpersonal Writing, E-mail Reply

Directions to the student:
You will write a reply to an e-mail message. First, you should read the message and then write your reply. Your reply should include a greeting and a closing and should respond to all the questions and requests in the message. In your reply, you should also ask for more details about something mentioned in the message. Also, you should use a formal form of address.

Tema curricular: La ciencia y la tecnología

Introducción
Este mensaje electrónico es del señor Pablo Sánchez, el dueño de un restaurante de primera clase en tu comunidad. Has recibido este mensaje porque tú lo llamaste al restaurante para hablarle de un problema que tuviste después de cenar allí.

De: Pablo Sánchez

Asunto: Su problema

Estimado cliente,

Para empezar, déjeme expresar mis más sentidas disculpas por el problema que tuvo usted después de cenar en mi restaurante anoche. Para nosotros, lo más importante es que nuestros clientes tengan la mejor experiencia y que regresen a cenar con nosotros frecuentemente. A fin de cuentas, si no tuviéramos clientes, ¡no tendríamos restaurante!

Estamos orgullosos de mantener un nivel de excelencia inmejorable por la calidad de nuestra comida y servicio. Por eso, haremos todo lo posible para resolver el problema que usted sufrió. Para ello, necesito un poco más de información. Primero, necesito saber todo lo que comió y bebió anoche. Perdóneme por preguntárselo, pero ¿me puede describir los síntomas del malestar que sintió después de la cena?

Finalmente, para compensarlo por esta desagradable experiencia, quisiera invitarlo a regresar al restaurante para una cena especial. Le pido que escoja la fecha de su preferencia y que me la mande con la información solicitada. Estoy a sus órdenes para servirlo mejor en el futuro.

Lo saluda atentamente,

Pablo Sánchez

Dueño

Restaurante de la Plaza

Learning Objectives	Student Edition		Ancillaries
	Page #	**Activity**	
Spoken Interpersonal	p. 278	Act. 9-4	
	p. 285	*Conexiones*: Act. 9-19	
	p. 288	Act. 9-25	
	p. 289	Act. 9-26, 9-27	
	p. 292	Act. 9-32	
	p. 295	Act. 9-37	
	p. 296	Act. 9-39	
	p. 299	Act. 9-48	
	'p. 303	Act. 9-53	
Written Interpersonal			
Audio, Visual, and Audiovisual Interpretive	p. 283	Act. 9-13	Workbook: 9-8
	p. 284	*VideoRed*: Act. 9-16, 9-17	*Pre-AP* Resource Book:*
	p. 295	Act. 9-38	p. 187
Written and Print Interpretive	p. 267, 268	*¡Así es la vida!*: Act. 9-2	Workbook: 9-36
	p. 279	Act. 9-7	
	p. 286, 288	*¡Así es la vida!*: Act. 9-22, 9-23	
	p. 296	*A explorar*: Act. 9-40	
	pp. 298–299	*Ritmos*: Act. 9-45, 9-46, 9-47	
	pp. 300–303	*Páginas*: Act. 9-49, 9-50, 9-51, 9-52	
Spoken Presentational	p. 283, 296	*Debate*: Act. 9-15, 9-41	**realidades.com:**
	p. 285	*Comparaciones*: Act. 9-20, 9-21	*Práctica oral*
	p. 297	*Imágenes*: Act. 9-42, 9-43	*Pre-AP* Resource Book:* p. 187
Written Presentational	p. 278	*A explorar*: Act. 9-3	Workbook: 9-14, 9-33, 9-37, 9-38, 9-39
	p. 283	*A explorar*: Act. 9-14	
	p. 289	*A explorar*: Act. 9-28	
	p. 297	*A explorar*: Act. 9-44	
	p. 304	*Taller*	

Student Activity 1
Presentational Speaking, Cultural Comparison

Directions for the student:
You will make an oral presentation on a specific topic to your class. In your presentation, compare your own community to an area of the Spanish-speaking world with which you are familiar. You should demonstrate your understanding of cultural features of the Spanish-speaking world. You should also organize your presentation clearly.

Tema curricular: La vida contemporánea

Tema de la presentación:
¿Cómo afectan las adicciones personales el bienestar del individuo y de la comunidad?

Compara tus observaciones acerca de las comunidades en las que has vivido con tus observaciones de una región del mundo hispanohablante que te sea familiar. En tu presentación, puedes referirte a las que has estudiado, vivido, observado, etc.

Student Activity 2
Interpretive Communication, Audio Text

Tema curricular: La vida contemporánea
Escucha la canción "Esto fue lo que vi" (Capítulo 9, Ritmos) y contesta las preguntas a continuación:

1. ¿Qué hicieron los que vieron que un hombre iba a atacar a otro?
   a. Llamaron a la policía
   b. Dispararon una pistola
   c. Miraron sin hacer nada
   d. Gritaron para avisar a la víctima

2. ¿Por qué lucharon los dos choferes?
   a. Tuvieron un accidente
   b. El chofer del autobús sobrepasaba la velocidad máxima
   c. El chofer del camión atropelló a una mujer gorda
   d. Tenían palos en sus vehículos

3. ¿Por qué critica a los políticos Ramón Orlando?
   a. Dan muchos discursos
   b. No limpian las calles
   c. Gastan demasiado dinero
   d. No cumplen con sus promesas

4. Ramón Orlando quiere que sepamos que _____.
   a. llueve muy poco en su ciudad
   b. hay mucha indiferencia en su ciudad
   c. su ciudad no tiene un problema de drogas
   d. está muy orgulloso de su ciudad

Learning Objectives	Student Edition		Ancillaries
	Page #	**Activity**	
Spoken Interpersonal	p. 301	Act. 10-3	
	p. 311	Act. 10-6, 10-8	
	p. 317	*Conexiones:* Act. 10-19	
	p. 321	10-26	
	p. 322	10-28, 10-29	
	p. 336	Act. 10-53	
Written Interpersonal			
Audio, Visual, and Audiovisual Interpretive	p. 311	Act. 10-7	Workbook: 10-7
	p. 316	*VideoRed:* Act. 10-16, 10-17	
	p. 331	Act. 10-42	
Written and Print Interpretive	p. 318, 320	*¡Así es la vida!* Act. 10-22	Workbook: 10-35
	p. 321	Act. 10-27	
	p. 322	Act. 10-30	
	p. 329	*Aplicación:* Act. 10-37, 10–38	
	p. 333	*Ritmos:* Act. 10-46, 10-47, 10-48	
	pp. 334–336	*Páginas:* Act. 10-49, 10-50, 10-51, 10-52	
Spoken Presentational	p. 310	*A explorar:* Act. 10-4	**realidades.com**
	p. 315, 331	*Debate:* Act. 10-15, 10-43	*Práctica oral*
	p. 317	*Comparaciones:* Act. 10-20, 10-21	
	p. 332	*Imágenes:* Act. 10-44	
	p. 332	*A explorar:* Act. 10-45	
Written Presentational	p. 310	*A explorar:* Act. 10-5	Workbook: 10-13, 10-32, 10-33, 10-36, 10-37, 10-38
	p. 317	*A explorar;* Act. 10-18	
	p. 320	*A explorar:* Act. 10-25	*Pre-AP* Resource Book:* p. 189
	p. 330	*A explorar:* Act. 10-40	
	p. 336	*Taller*	

Student Activity
Presentational Writing, Persuasive Essay

Directions for the student:

You will write an essay to submit to a Spanish writing contest. The essay topic is based on three sources, which present different viewpoints on the topic and include both print and audio material. First, you should read the essay topic and the printed material. Afterward, you will hear the audio material twice; you should take notes while you listen. Then you will write your essay. In your essay, you should present the sourcesí different viewpoints on the topic and also clearly indicate your own viewpoint and defend it thoroughly. Use information from all the sources to support your essay. As you refer to the sources, identify them appropriately. Also, organize your essay into clear paragraphs.

Tema curricular: Los desafíos mundiales

Tema del ensayo:

¿Qué deben hacer los jóvenes para asegurar su futuro financiero?

Fuente número 1

"Mitos y verdades sobre su informe de crédito" (*Realidades* 4, p. 318)

Fuente número 2

"El préstamo Federal de Consolidación" (*Realidades* 4, p. 322)

Fuente número 3

"¡Fraude!" (*Realidades* 4, Actividad 10-42)

Learning Objectives	Student Edition		Ancillaries
	Page #	**Activity**	
Spoken Interpersonal	p. 342 p. 343 p. 348 p. 351 p. 355 p. 367	Act. 11-2 Act. 11-3 Act. 11-13 *Conexiones:* Act. 11-19 Act. 11-25, 11-26, 11-27 Act. 11-50	*Pre-AP* Resource Book:* p. 191
Written Interpersonal			
Audio, Visual, and Audiovisual Interpretive	p. 349 p. 350 p. 362	Act. 11-14 *VideoRed:* Act. 11-16, 11-17 Act. 11-38	Workbook: 11-22

Written and Print Interpretive	p. 340, 342
	p. 345
	p. 364
	
	p. 365
		¡Así es la vida!: Act. 11-1
		Aplicación: Act. 11-7, 11-8
		Ritmos: Act. 11-42, 11-43, 11-44,
		  11-45
		Páginas: Act. 11-46, 11-47, 11-48,
		  11-49, 11-50
			Workbook; 11-36

Spoken Presentational	p. 343 p. 349, 362 p. 350 p. 351 p. 359 p. 363 p. 363	*A explorar:* Act. 11-4 *Debate:* Act. 11-15, 11-39 *VideoRed:* Act. 11-17 *Comparaciones;* Act. 11-20, 11-21 *A explorar:* Act. 11-31 *Imágenes:* Act. 11-40 *A explorar:* Act. 11-41	**realidades.com** *Práctica oral*
Written Presentational	p. 352 p. 363 p. 368	*Comunidades:* Act. 11-18 *A explorar:* Act. 11-41 *Taller*	Workbook: 11-14, 11-33, 11-34, 11-37, 11-38, 11-39

Realidades 4

Capítulo 11

Student Activity Sheet

Student Activity
Interpersonal Speaking, Conversation

Directions for the student:
You will participate in a conversation. First, you will read a preview of the conversation, including an outline of each turn in the conversation. Afterward, the conversation will begin, following the outline. Each time it is your turn to speak, you should give a thorough and appropriate response.

Tema curricular: La vida contemporánea

Introducción
Esta es una conversación con Vicente Díaz, un agente de viajes. Vas a participar en esta conversación porque quieres hacer planes para un viaje especial.

VICENTE	• Te Saluda y te hace una pregunta.
TÚ	• Salúdalo y dale una respuesta con detalles.
VICENTE	• Continúa la conversación y te hace una pregunta.
TÚ	• Responde con detalles.
VICENTE	• Continúa la conversación y te hace dos preguntas.
TÚ	• Contesta y explica por qué.
VICENTE	• Continúa la conversación y te hace otra pregunta.
TÚ	• Responde con detalles.
VICENTE	• Continúa la conversación y te hace otra pregunta.
TÚ	• Contéstale con detalles y despídete.

Script for the activity: The following script is for the student playing the role of Vicente.

VICENTE: Buenos días. Gracias por visitar nuestra agencia de viajes. Me llamo Vicente Díaz. Aquí te ofrecemos viajes de aventuras y experiencias inolvidables. Para servirte mejor, quisiera hacerte algunas preguntas. Primero, ¿cuáles son las actividades que más te interesan?
(Espera una respuesta.)

VICENTE: Bien. Con algunas actividades existe el riesgo de correr peligro. ¿Cómo reaccionas ante esta posibilidad?
(Espera una respuesta.)

VICENTE: Ahora podemos empezar a planear tu viaje. Ya sabes que ofrecemos excursiones en todos los países hispanos. ¿A qué país te gustaría viajar y por qué? ¿Durante qué mes del año?
(Espera una respuesta.)

VICENTE: Viajarás en un grupo pequeño, acompañado de un coordinador de nuestra agencia. Es importante que los miembros del grupo lo respeten. Entonces, si pudieras escoger al coordinador de tu grupo, ¿qué tipo de persona escogerías?
(Espera una respuesta.)

VICENTE: Bueno, tengo mucha información. Antes de recomendarte un itinerario, ¿qué más debo saber para planear el viaje perfecto para ti?
(Espera una respuesta.)

Learning Objectives	Student Edition		Ancillaries
	Page #	**Activity**	
Spoken Interpersonal	p. 374 p. 381 p. 384	Act. 12-3, 12-4 *Conexiones*: Act. 12-19 Act. 12-23, 12-24	
Written Interpersonal			*Pre-AP* Resource Book:* p. 193
Audio, Visual, and Audiovisual Interpretive	p. 379 p. 380 p. 384	Act. 12-14 *VideoRed*: Act. 12-16, 12-17 Act. 12-25	Workbook: 12-7
Written and Print Interpretive	p. 372, 374 p. 375 p. 381 p. 382, 384 p. 394 pp. 395–397	*¡Así es la vida!* Act. 1-1 Act. 12-5 *Comparaciones*: Act. 12-20, 12-21 *¡Así es la vida!*: Act. 12-22 *Ritmos*: Act. 12-41, 12-42, 12-43 *Páginas*: Act. 12-44, 12-45, 12-46, 12-47, 12-48	Workbook: 12-33
Spoken Presentational	p. 379, 392 p. 388 p. 393 p. 397	*Debate*: Act. 12-15, 12-38 *A explorar*: Act. 12-31 *Imágenes*: Act. 12-39, 12-40 *A explorar*: Act. 12-49	**realidades.com** *Práctica oral*
Written Presentational	p. 375 p. 380 p. 391 p. 398	*A explorar*: Act. 12-6 *A explorar*: Act. 12-18 *A explorar*: Act. 12-37 *Taller*	Workbook: 12-13, 12-30, 12-34, 12-35, 12-36

Student Activity
Interpersonal Writing, E-mail Reply
Directions to the student:
You will write a reply to an e-mail message. First, you should read the message and then write your reply. Your reply should include a greeting and a closing and should respond to all the questions and requests in the message. In your reply, you should also ask for more details about something mentioned in the message. Also, you should use a formal form of address.

Tema curricular: La ciencia y la tecnología

Introducción
Este mensaje electrónico es de la señora Antonia López, editora de la revista *Tecnología y tú*. Has recibido este mensaje porque la revista ha decidido publicar un artículo que escribiste.

De: Antonia López

Asunto: Su artículo

Estimado autor:

Tengo el placer de anunciarle que la revista *Tecnología y tú* ha decidido publicar su artículo "La tecnología, el futuro y yo" en el próximo número, cuyo propósito es predecir y explicar la tecnología del futuro. Durante el año recibimos más de tres mil ensayos de estudiantes de todas partes del mundo. Algunos describieron varios avances posibles en el campo de la medicina y otros se enfocaron en la exploración intergaláctica. Muchos predijeron un aumento en la manipulación genética de las plantas y animales, con sus consecuencias positivas y negativas. Otros señalaron más posibilidades en cuanto a los usos personales de la tecnología.

En fin, recibimos muy pocos ensayos tan profundos y completos como el suyo. Por eso, será uno de los cinco artículos publicados. ¡Felicitaciones! Con su artículo incluiremos una breve biografía para la cual le pido que me mande alguna información. Por ejemplo, ¿cuándo empezó usted a usar la tecnología y cuáles fueron sus primeros usos? Para un joven, ¿cómo llegó a saber y entender la gran variedad de información sobre la tecnología que describió en su ensayo? También quisiera saber si planea una carrera relacionada con tecnología. Explique su respuesta, por favor. A propósito, no se olvide de mandarme una foto para su biografía.

Atentamente,

Antonia López

Editora de *Tecnología y tú*

Pre-AP* Resources

Professional Organizations and Resources

There are a number of professional organizations and resources available to support Pre-AP* teachers. Their Web sites offer a variety of helpful resources to foreign language educators and can easily be found by searching the Web.

- The American Council on the Teaching of Foreign Languages has information about the National Standards for Foreign Language Learning and the Performance Guidelines for K-12 Learners. It also provides teacher resources, publications, opportunities for professional development, and information about ACTFL's national conference.

- The American Association of Teachers of Spanish and Portuguese offers classroom resources, publications, and other important information for teachers of Spanish and Portuguese. In addition, AATSP sponsors the National Spanish Examination. This examination, a competitive measure of students' abilities in Spanish, provides multiple-choice testing practice for beginning through advanced students in the areas of listening and reading.

- The CollegeBoard offers up-to-date information about the AP Spanish Language and Culture Exam and the AP Spanish Literature and Culture Exam. Its Web site, AP Central, includes a special section dedicated to Pre-AP* World Languages and Cultures and an extensive link to Web sites dedicated to Spanish instruction.

- Discovery Education provides Puzzlemaker, a free service that is useful for quickly creating printable crossword puzzles.

Bibliography*

National Standards in Foreign Language Education Project. *Standards for Foreign Language Learning in the 21st Century*. Lawrence, KS, 2006.

- This book introduces the standards common to all second-language learning. Each standard is clearly described and fully developed with progress indicators and learning scenarios.

American Council on the Teaching of Foreign Languages. *ACTFL Performance Guidelines for K-12 Learners*, Yonkers, New York, ACTFL 1999.

- These guidelines describe the language proficiency of K-12 language learners at different levels of their language development. They are organized around the 3 Modes of Communication, as defined in the *Standards for Foreign Language Learning in the 21st Century*, and focus on learners at the Novice, Intermediate, and pre-Advanced levels.

College Board. *AP Vertical Teams Guide for World Languages and Cultures*, College Board, 2009.

- This book provides guidelines for developing department-wide vertical teams for teachers of World Languages. It also presents instructional strategies and suggested activities related to the AP Curriculum Framework for teachers at all levels.

Pearson also offers a number of additional books that teachers might want to use in their pre-AP* classes. They can be found at: PearsonSchool.com/World Languages.

*For ordering information on any of the Pearson Prentice Hall products, visit our online catalog at www.PHSchool.com.

Preguntas rápidas:
Additional Activities

Here are some additional activities incorporating the bank of *preguntas rápidas* to be found on pp. 196–199.

Daily Practice

Use the questions as warm-up or end-of-class activities, for team competitions, or simply as a break in the middle of class. Take a question from the bank of *preguntas rápidas* on pp. 196–199 and ask the class to respond. Ask for volunteers or call on students randomly. Award participation points on students' ability to answer questions. On any particular day you will not have all students participate, but by doing this activity on a regular basis, you can involve many students and give credit for their participation. As the semester or year progresses and you continue to add questions to the bank, you will keep recycling information from earlier chapters. As students begin Spanish 2, 3, or 4, bring out the banks of questions from the previous level(s) and use these to recycle questions from year to year.

La silla caliente

Periodically have students sit on the "hot seat" to answer questions. This activity can be done as a small group activity or in front of the entire class. If the activity is done in small groups, the teacher will divide the bank of questions among the different groups and then rotate the sets of questions from group to group throughout the time allotted. The student who is on the hot seat is asked several questions by other students or the teacher. By using the bank of *preguntas rápidas* on pp. 196–199, the student may answer questions taken from several chapters. Students can be evaluated on how well they are able to respond. After one student has sat on the "hot seat" to answer several questions, another student takes the spot and begins to answer questions. This activity can be also used as a competition in which students attempt to be the student who is able to answer most questions correctly before being "eliminated."

Preguntas rápidas—*Realidades* 1

1. ¿Qué tiempo hace en el invierno?
2. ¿Qué te gusta hacer en junio?
3. Según tu familia, ¿cómo eres?
4. ¿Qué estudias en la primera hora?
5. En tu escuela, ¿quién enseña la clase de arte?
6. ¿Cuál es tu almuerzo favorito?
7. ¿Qué frutas te gustan más?
8. ¿Crees que la pizza es buena o mala para la salud? ¿Por qué?
9. ¿Qué haces para mantener la salud?
10. Cuando vas de compras, ¿adónde vas?
11. ¿Adónde vas los fines de semana?
12. ¿Qué deportes te gustan más?
13. ¿Qué vas a hacer mañana a las ocho de la noche?
14. Describe a una persona de tu familia o de otra familia.
15. ¿Qué te gusta hacer durante una fiesta de cumpleaños?
16. ¿Quiénes vienen más a tu casa? ¿Qué traen ellos?
17. ¿Qué te gusta pedir en un restaurante?
18. ¿De qué colores son los libros y las carpetas que tienes?
19. ¿Qué posesiones tienes en tu dormitorio? ¿De qué colores son?
20. ¿Ayudas mucho o poco en casa? ¿Cuáles son tus quehaceres?
21. Para ti, ¿cuáles son los tres peores quehaceres?
22. ¿Qué ropa llevas en el verano?
23. ¿Cuáles son tres artículos de ropa que te gustaría comprar?
24. ¿Para quiénes compras regalos? ¿Qué tipo de regalos compras?
25. ¿Qué deportes practicaste el año pasado?
26. Para el cumpleaños de tu mejor amigo(a), ¿qué compraste?
27. ¿Adónde te gustaría ir de vacaciones? ¿Qué te gustaría hacer?
28. ¿Cuándo fuiste a ver una obra de teatro en tu comunidad o en tu escuela? ¿Te gustó?
29. ¿Qué lugares puedes visitar en tu comunidad?
30. ¿Qué cosas reciclan Uds. en casa?
31. ¿Qué podemos hacer para tener un barrio más limpio?
32. ¿Qué hiciste el verano pasado?
33. ¿Qué hizo la gente de tu comunidad el año pasado para ayudar a las víctimas de un desastre?
34. ¿Qué clase de programas de televisión ves más?
35. ¿Qué sabes crear en la computadora?
36. Si necesitas ayuda con la computadora, ¿a quién pides ayuda?

Preguntas rápidas—*Realidades* 2

1. ¿Qué actividades te gusta hacer en tus clases?
2. ¿Qué reglas de la escuela te gustan (o no te gustan)?
3. ¿Qué te gusta más, ser miembro de un club o participar en un deporte? ¿Por qué?
4. ¿Cuáles son las actividades más populares en tu escuela? ¿Por qué son populares?
5. ¿Cómo te preparas para un evento especial? ¿Qué haces primero?
6. ¿Qué ropa y accesorios te pones para ir a una fiesta o un baile?
7. Describe la ropa que está de moda ahora.
8. ¿En qué tienda o almacén puedes encontrar gangas? ¿Cómo son los precios allí?
9. ¿Cuándo compraste un regalo recientemente? ¿Dónde lo compraste?
10. ¿Qué tipo de tiendas y servicios hay en el centro de tu comunidad?
11. ¿Qué haces para ganar dinero? ¿Te gusta el trabajo?
12. ¿Cuál fue tu día más divertido del mes pasado? ¿Por qué?
13. ¿Qué debe hacer un joven para aprender las reglas y señales de tráfico?
14. Explica cómo se va de tu casa a la escuela.
15. ¿Con qué juguetes te gustaba jugar de pequeño(a)?
16. De niño(a), ¿cómo eras?
17. En tu comunidad, ¿en qué días festivos hay fuegos artificiales?
18. ¿Cuándo te reúnes con tus parientes? ¿Dónde se reúnen Uds.?
19. ¿Cuántos años tenías cuando aprendiste a caminar?
20. Para ti, ¿quién es un héroe o una heroína? ¿Por qué?
21. ¿Qué tipo de desastres naturales afectan a tu comunidad o región?
22. ¿Qué hora era cuando te levantaste hoy?
23. ¿Cómo te sientes cuando un(a) enfermero(a) te pone una inyección?
24. Cuando tienes dolor de cabeza o estómago, ¿qué haces para sentirte mejor?
25. ¿Te lastimaste alguna vez cuando estabas practicando un deporte o haciendo otra actividad?
26. ¿Qué clase de programa te interesa ver más en la televisión?
27. ¿Quién es tu jugador(a) profesional favorito(a)? ¿En qué deporte compite?
28. ¿Qué es más importante en una película, mucha acción o personajes interesantes? ¿Por qué?
29. ¿Qué película en el cine va a tener mucho éxito este año?
30. ¿Cómo se prepara tu comida favorita?
31. ¿Qué comida picante te gusta más (o menos)?
32. ¿Adónde has viajado? ¿Qué hiciste para planear el viaje?
33. ¿Qué recomiendas que haga un turista cuando acaba de llegar a un país extranjero?
34. ¿Qué serás algún día? ¿Cómo sería un día típico para ti?
35. ¿Qué clases estudiarás en la universidad?
36. ¿Cuáles son algunos de los problemas ecológicos de tu región?

Preguntas rápidas—*Realidades* 3

1. ¿Qué aspectos de la naturaleza de tu región te impresionan más?

2. ¿Qué parque nacional te gustaría visitar? ¿Qué actividades al aire libre puedes hacer allí?

3. Describe el lugar más bello adónde fuiste.

4. ¿Qué atletas de habla hispana conoces? ¿Qué hacen ellos?

5. ¿Qué juegos y actividades hacías de niño(a)? ¿Con quién los hacías?

6. Describe una obra de arte que está en la escuela o en tu casa.

7. ¿Qué o quién te inspiró a pintar o dibujar algo? Cuenta la experiencia.

8. Describe tu disco compacto o canción favorita.

9. Piensa en un momento en que quisiste hacer algo pero no pudiste. Cuenta la experiencia.

10. ¿Qué artista influyó más en el arte o la música de los jóvenes de hoy? ¿Cómo?

11. Explícale a un amigo cómo preparar una receta favorita tuya.

12. Diles a unos jóvenes lo que deben hacer para mantener la salud.

13. ¿Qué debe hacer una persona para reducir el estrés?

14. ¿Cuáles son los beneficios de hacer ejercicio?

15. Para ti, ¿cuáles son las cualidades más importantes que debe tener un(a) profesor(a)?

16. Piensa en una amistad o relación familiar tuya. Descríbela.

17. ¿Qué debe hacer una familia para evitar o resolver conflictos?

18. Tú y tu amigo(a) se pelearon. ¿Qué pueden hacer para reconciliarse?

19. ¿Qué requisitos se solicitan generalmente en un anuncio clasificado?

20. ¿Qué consejos puedes dar a un(a) estudiante que busca un trabajo de tiempo parcial?

21. En tu opinión, ¿cuáles son las responsabilidades de los ciudadanos?

22. ¿Qué habilidades o conocimientos tienes que puedes usar para mejorar tu comunidad?

23. ¿Piensas seguir la misma carrera que tiene una persona de tu familia? ¿Por qué?

24. ¿Cuál es un sueño que quieres realizar?

25. En tu opinión, ¿cuáles serán los mejores avances tecnológicos que verás en el futuro?

26. Describe un monumento, estatua o lugar arqueológico que conoces.

27. Describe un fenómeno o misterio inexplicable que te interesa.

28. ¿Qué culturas han contribuido a la cultura de tu región? Explica qué contribuciones han hecho.

29. Explícale a un(a) nuevo(a) estudiante de otro país lo que puede hacer para integrarse a la cultura de tu región.

30. Piensa en un problema del medio ambiente. Describe el problema y lo que se puede hacer para resolverlo.

31. ¿Cuáles serán los problemas más graves si la población del mundo sigue creciendo?

32. ¿Qué situación del mundo te preocupa más? ¿Por qué?

33. ¿Qué derechos debe garantizar el gobierno para los ciudadanos?

34. ¿Crees que existe la igualdad entre los hombres y las mujeres? Explica.

35. ¿Qué tipos de discriminación existían en tu comunidad hace 50 años? Explica.

36. Describe una manifestación en que tú u otra persona hayan participado.

Preguntas rápidas—*Realidades* 4

1. Describe la ropa que está de moda entre los jóvenes de hoy.

2. En tu opinión, ¿cuál fue el invento más importante del siglo XX? ¿Por qué?

3. ¿Cómo han cambiado los automóviles durante la última década?

4. ¿Es importante que la gente use fuentes renovables de energía? ¿Por qué?

5. ¿Cuál será el avance médico más benéfico del futuro?

6. ¿Qué te parece el uso de la ingeniería genética para manipular los comestibles?

7. Describe las oportunidades que existen en tu comunidad para trabajar de voluntario.

8. ¿A quién admiras tú por haber defendido los derechos humanos? ¿Qué hizo esa persona?

9. ¿Cómo era el mejor profesor o la mejor profesora de tu carrera estudiantil?

10. ¿Cómo se puede resolver el problema de los estudiantes que abusan de otros estudiantes en la escuela?

11. ¿Qué cualidades son importantes en un novio o una novia?

12. ¿Quién ha influido más en tu vida? ¿Por qué?

13. Una decisión controvertida de muchas escuelas es eliminar las clases de arte y música debido a la falta de fondos. Explica por qué apoyas o te opones a este cambio.

14. Si pudieras conocer a un cantante o actor hispano, ¿quién sería? ¿Por qué?

15. ¿Qué impacto ha tenido la población hispana en tu comunidad?

16. ¿Qué se puede hacer para erradicar la discriminación en el futuro?

17. Si pudieras ser el (la) director(a) de tu escuela, ¿qué cambios harías en la cafetería?

18. Si hubieras vivido hace 100 años, ¿cómo habría sido diferente tu dieta?

19. Describe un crimen que ocurrió recientemente en tu comunidad.

20. En tu opinión, ¿por qué hay tanto cibervandalismo hoy en día?

21. Recomiendas tú que tus amigos tengan sus propias tarjetas de crédito? ¿Por qué?

22. ¿Cuáles son las ventajas y desventajas de aceptar préstamos estudiantiles para asistir a la universidad?

23. ¿Cómo ha influido la televisión en la vida de los jóvenes?

24. Describe un viaje que hiciste y que te gustó mucho.

25. ¿Harán un papel importante los autómatas en la vida del futuro? Explica tu respuesta.

26. Si pudieras ayudar a resolver un problema mundial en tu vida, ¿cuál sería y por qué?

Tema 2
Student Activity 1
(1) b; (2) c; (3) b

Tema 3

Tema 6
Student Activity 1
(1) c; (2) c; (3) a

Tema 8
Student Activity 2
(1) c; (2) a; (3) b

Tema 4
Teacher Activity 3
(1) a; (2) c; (3) b

Capítulo 2
Student Activity 1
(1) a (2) b (3) d

Capítulo 4
Student Activity 1
(1) b (2) c (3) b

Capítulo 6
Student Activity 1
(1) d (2) c (3) b

Capítulo 2
Student Activity 2
(1) d (2) c (3) a (4) b

Capítulo 4
Student Activity 2
(1) b (2) d (3) c (4) d

Capítulo 9
Student Activity 2
(1) c (2) a (3) d (4) b

Capítulo 8
Student Activity 2
(1) b (2) c (3) a (4) d

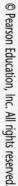